FIRST CONVERTS

Nostalgia Jewishness is a lullaby for old men

gumming soaked white bread.

J. GLADSTEIN, *modernist Yiddish poet*

CONTRAVERSIONS

JEWS AND OTHER DIFFERENCES

DANIEL BOYARIN,

CHANA KRONFELD, AND

NAOMI SEIDMAN, EDITORS

The task of "The Science of Judaism"

is to give Judaism a decent burial.

MORITZ STEINSCHNEIDER,

founder of nineteenth-century

philological Jewish Studies

FIRST CONVERTS

RICH PAGAN WOMEN AND THE RHETORIC OF MISSION IN EARLY JUDAISM AND CHRISTIANITY

SHELLY MATTHEWS

Stanford University Press · Stanford, California

Stanford University Press

Stanford, California

© 2001 by the Board of Trustees of the Leland Stanford Junior University

Printed in the United States of America on acid-free, archival-quality paper.

Library of Congress Cataloging-in-Publication Data

Matthews, Shelly.

First converts : rich pagan women and the rhetoric of mission in early Judaism and
Christianity / Shelly Matthews.

    p. cm. — (Contraversions)

Includes bibliographical references and index.

ISBN 0-8047-3592-1 (alk. paper)

Proselytizing—Judaism. 2. Evangelistic work. 3. Josephus, Flavius. Antiquitates Judaicae.
4. Bible. N.T. Acts—Criticism, interpretation, etc. 5. Women in Judaism—Historiography.
6. Women in Christianity—Historiography. I. Title. II. Contraversions (Stanford, Calif.)

BM729.P7 .M34   2001

296.6'9'09015—dc21   2001031196

Original printing 2001

Last figure below indicates year of this printing:

10   09   08   07   06   05   04   03   02   01

Designed by Sandy Drooker

Typeset by Keystone Typesetting, Inc. in 10/14.5 Minion

For George, Nathan, and Alice

ACKNOWLEDGMENTS

I WOULD LIKE TO THANK first the erudite and generous scholars who assisted me in putting this work into its initial form as a Harvard Divinity School dissertation in 1997: my thesis advisor, Elisabeth Schüssler Fiorenza, and committee members Helmut Koester and Lawrence Wills. Bernadette Brooten also played an important role in the initial stages of my writing. I am thankful to colleagues from the Harvard New Testament Dissertation Seminar—Ellen Aitken, Denise Kimber Buell, and Cynthia Briggs Kittredge—who read and commented on portions of the manuscript.

In transforming the dissertation into its present form, thanks goes first to Melanie Johnson-DeBaufre for her initial editorial work. Readers Elizabeth Castelli and Richard Pervo offered helpful and constructive feedback. Furman University generously supported the final stages of the completion of the manuscript. A special nod goes to Edgar McKnight for his encouragement and counsel. I thank the editors at Stanford University Press, especially Kate Warne, who has overseen the final editorial process with graciousness and skill.

I thank Daniel Boyarin for including this work in his series, Contraversions: Jews and Other Differences. Finally, I would like to acknowledge a wider circle of mentors, friends, and family both inside and outside of the academy: for inspiration and support I am indebted to Elizabeth Bettenhausen, Elizabeth Davis, Catherine Lord Kelsey, Mary Ann Thompson, and

Christine Wagner-Hecht. My two small children, Nathan Louis and Alice Grace, have tolerated my absence while I have tended to this project, in spite of their inability to fathom why anybody would want to make a book without any pictures in it. George Frein has been there from start to finish, and for that I thank him most of all.

CONTENTS

ABBREVIATIONS OF CLASSICAL WORKS

Ann.	Tacitus *Annales* (Annals)
Ant.	Josephus *Antiquitates judaicae* (Jewish Antiquities)
Anton.	Plutarch *Antonius* (Life of Anthony)
Aug.	Suetonius *Divus Augustus* (The Deified Augustus)
Cels.	Origen *Contra Celsum* (Against Celsus)
Claud.	Suetonius *Divus Claudius* (The Deified Claudius)
Conj. praec.	Plutarch *Conjugalia Praecepta* (Advice to Bride and Groom)
Contempl. Life	Philo *De vita contemplativa* (On the Contemplative Life)
Dom.	Suetonius *Domitianus* (Domitian)
Eccl. Hist.	Eusebius *Historia ecclesiastica* (Ecclesiastical History)
Eleg.	Propertius *Elegeiae* (Elegies)
Ep.	Pliny the Younger *Epistulae* (Letters)
Epigr.	Martial *Epigrammata* (Epigrams)
Fact. et dict.	Valerius Maximus *Factorum et dictorum memorabilium libri novem* (Memorable Deeds and Sayings)
Hist.	*Historiae* (author will be indicated in textual citation)

J.W.	Josephus *Bellum judaicum* (*Jewish War*)
Leg.	Cicero *De legibus* (On the Laws)
Quaest. conv.	Plutarch *Quaestionum convivialum libri IX* (Table Talk)
Sat.	Juvenal *Satirae* (Satires)
Spec. Laws	Philo *De specialibus legibus* (On the Special Laws)
Tib.	Suetonius *Tiberius*
Tit.	Suetonius *Divus Titus* (The Deified Titus)
Vesp.	Suetonius *Vespasianus* (Vespasian)

FIRST CONVERTS

INTRODUCTION

*No sooner has that fellow departed than a trembling Jewess, leaving her
basket and her hay, comes begging to her secret ear; she is an interpreter of
the laws of Jerusalem, a high priestess of the tree, a faithful messenger of
highest heaven [interpres legum Solymarum et magna sacerdos arboris ac
summi fida internuntia caeli]. She, too, fills her palm, but more sparingly,
for a Jew will tell you dreams of any kind you please for the smallest of coins.*

—JUVENAL *Sat.* 6.542–47

The Jewish Missionary

THIS PORTRAIT OF A female Jewish "beggar" interpreting the law for an
inquiring Roman matron is part of Juvenal's vitriolic sixth satire, which
ridicules women both for their promiscuity and for their gullibility in matters of religion.[1] The satire exploits the stereotypical claim that women in
particular were attracted to "foreign" religions such as the cults of Dionysos,
Isis, and Cybele, as well as Judaism. In the excerpt above, in which Judaism is
the focus, Juvenal depicts not only the seeker but also the distributor of
wisdom as a woman.

By privileging the ascription "interpreter of the law of Jerusalem" (*interpres legum Solymarum*), Dieter Georgi has argued persuasively that the basis
for Juvenal's portrait of the Jewish woman is not a mendicant, but a profes-

sional Jewish missionary. The woman shares her prophetic gift and then asks for payment. Although for Juvenal this is yet another instance of the beggarly nature of Jews in Rome (cf. *Sat.* 3.13–14, 3.292–301), it is possible to understand the solicitation of payment more sympathetically: the interpreter requires economic support if she is to continue sharing her prophetic gift.[2] This argument is part of Georgi's larger thesis that the mission impulse in early Christianity was derived from the widespread missionary practice of its parent religion. Georgi situates Jewish missionary activity within the broader complex of Hellenistic religious propaganda and apologetics. He conceptualizes Judaism as self-confidently offering up its monotheism and its ancient laws as contributions to the Hellenistic quest for truth and desire for univocity.[3] The contours of this thesis have been elaborated in various forms by several Jewish and Christian scholars since the turn of the century.[4]

Within the last fifteen years, however, a number of scholars have called into question the view of Georgi and others that Judaism in antiquity was a missionary religion. Scot McKnight, Edouard Will and Claude Orrieux, and Martin Goodman have all written monographs in support of this position.[5] A. Thomas Kraabel and Shaye Cohen have addressed the issue in several articles.[6] This convergence has led Cohen to characterize the view of diaspora Judaism as nonmissionary as the "new consensus."[7] By revisiting a question once thought settled, these scholars have done much to enrich the conversation about the nature of Judaism in antiquity and the relationship of early Christianity to its parent religion. Cohen's several studies relating to Jewish conversion in antiquity are exemplary in this regard.[8] Moreover, their studies linking derisive depictions of Hellenistic Jewish mission to the anti-Jewish biases of nineteenth-century Christian biblical scholars serve as a reminder that scholarly conceptualizations of Jews as missionary or nonmissionary in antiquity are inevitably bound up with valuations of the terms Jew, Christian, and missionary.[9]

However, proponents of this new consensus have framed the terms of the debate over Hellenistic Judaism's stance toward outsiders problematically. Disregarding Georgi's argument for Hellenistic religious propaganda and apologetics as the appropriate framework within which to interpret Jewish communicative practices, and refusing to account for early Christian texts within the framework of Hellenistic Judaism, these studies have focused on a minimal collection of sources deemed relevant solely to the question of Jewish mission.[10] They neither look for analogies between Jewish and pagan communicative practices, nor give serious attention to sources deriding Judaism along with other "foreign" cults as holding sway over gullible Romans. For example, scholars holding to the new consensus do not discuss Juvenal's sixth satire, which views Judaism as one of many propagandizing cults. Discussion of Josephus's *Antiquities* 18.65–84, a story suggesting *both* Jewish and Isis proselytizing in Rome, is dissected so that only the lines dealing with Judaism receive mention. The work of scholars of Hellenistic religious propaganda and aretalogy, such as Otto Weinreich, Moses Hadas, and Morton Smith is passed over.[11] Only Martin Goodman has considered the question of Jewish mission in relation to other religious cults and philosophical schools in the pagan Roman Empire. Because his understanding of what constitutes missionary activity is predicated so narrowly on its Christian expression, however, he can see no analogy between Christian mission and anything that preceded it in Jewish or pagan practice. For him, the phenomenon of early Christian mission activity is sui generis.[12]

This new consensus is built not only from a minimal collection of sources but also from a minimal definition of what constitutes missionary activity. None of these scholars will argue that Hellenistic Jews did not speak with their neighbors, accept converts, argue for the truth value of their religious customs, or adopt Hellenistic rhetorical practices in communicating. But Cohen and Will and Orrieux argue that Jews were passive, not active in these communicative processes, and hence not truly missionary.[13] Goodman and McKnight, who concede that Jews actively communicated with Gentiles, still distinguish this active communication from true proselytizing. Jews were involved in "missions to inform," "missions to educate," and "missions in defense of cult," argues Goodman, but these kinds of missions are qualitatively different from proselytizing activity.[14] Scot McKnight proposes the hairsplitting distinction between "encouraging Gentiles to convert" (something, he concedes, that Jews did) and "aggressively drawing Gentiles into their religion" (something, he argues, that Jews did not do) in order to conclude that Jews were not engaged in missionary activity.[15]

This book seeks, in part, to challenge the narrow bounds with which the question of Jewish mission has been framed by those holding to the new consensus. With Georgi, I presume that Hellenistic Jews engaged in religious apologetics and propaganda, that the study of these communicative processes is enhanced by considering pagan analogies, and that early Christian missionary activity should be considered as an extension of something already occurring in Hellenistic Judaism. I will not pursue the question of whether Jews were active or passive in communicating with their neighbors—whether they "eagerly accepted" those interested in things Jewish, without "eagerly seeking" them. Juvenal's satire, in which the laws of Jerusalem are interpreted by a Jew for a Roman matron, suggests that such a communicative practice was common enough in early-second-century Rome. If not, his lampoonery could not have been effective.[16] Whether the "begging" Jewish woman or the gullible Roman matron initiated such interaction seems a moot point.

Unlike recent studies on Hellenistic mission and conversion, I privilege a set of texts that has until now been on the margins of the debate. These are the texts suggesting that women, particularly those of high standing, were attracted to Judaism and Christianity and actively propagated these religions. Although Adolf Harnack catalogued passages that indicate a link between Christian mission and women's leadership already at the turn of the century,[17] and the notion that more highborn Gentile women than men were attracted to early Judaism is widespread,[18] the issue of women among missionaries, converts, and adherents has been eclipsed in the current debate. For those who work in the discipline of women's history, this eclipse is dishearteningly familiar. In the last thirty years scholarship on women in antiquity, including Jewish and Christian women, has increased in quantum leaps.[19] Yet this knowledge production seems of little consequence to those who focus on mainstream/"malestream" questions. Again, Juvenal's sixth satire illustrates both the problem I am addressing and the corrective I propose. Scholars on the antimissionary side of the debate dismiss Georgi's thesis, yet none of them have proposed an alternative interpretation of Juvenal's specific attack on the female Jewish interpreter of the law, or of his general attack on the detrimental effect of missionary practices on women from all classes in Rome. I ask here: What historical situation inspires a misogynist satirist writing in Rome around the turn of the first century CE to devote a large portion of a catalogue of women's vices to ridiculing their participation in religions foreign to Rome, including Judaism? Do conceptualizations of religious propaganda and apologetics in antiquity change if this source, along with other sources depicting women adherents, converts, and missionaries are brought into focus? Can the history of women in religions of antiquity be integrated into mainstream historical narratives?

The *Antiquities*, written by the Jewish historian Josephus, and the New

Testament Book of Acts, whose author is conventionally referred to as Luke, are the two texts at the center of this study, since many of the claims that highborn women were attracted to Judaism and Christianity are clustered there. Because both Josephus and Luke are apologists for their respective faith communities and are near contemporaries of Juvenal, they grapple with the problem illustrated by the Roman satirist.[20] Both are cognizant that all "foreign" religions are susceptible to the charge that they prey on gullible and promiscuous women. The configuration of women in their narratives serves as an attempt to counter and/or deflect those charges.

I begin with a story of two duped Roman matrons that employs the same topos as Juvenal's sixth satire. In *Antiquities* 18 these two matrons are prominent in scandals leading to the expulsion of both Jews and Isis worshippers from Rome. Here Josephus confirms that the Isis cult is indeed one of those "foreign" religions corrupting noble Roman matrons; thus, he utilizes the topos to demarcate Isis worship from Jewish cultic practice. I will then argue that in spite of this tendency to denigrate "foreign" cults as corrupting influences on high-standing women, a competing topos utilized the association of such women with a religious community for positive rhetorical effect. An examination of the repeated turn to high-standing Gentile women in the narratives of the *Antiquities* and Acts shows that Josephus and Luke told stories of such women as a means of achieving cultural acceptability. Understanding the many references to Gentile noblewomen converts, adherents, and benefactors in these two works provides a new angle on questions of Hellenistic Jewish and Christian missionary propaganda and apologetics.

Rhetoric and Reality

In each of the following chapters I employ a two-step method: first I subject the texts in question to rhetorical analysis, and then I engage in historical reconstruction of women's involvement in missionary religions of antiquity. I use the phrase "rhetorical analysis," not as a technical term for dissecting ancient writings according to the categories employed in the handbooks of classical rhetoricians, but to signal my understanding of these texts as public, political discourses that attempt to persuade their audiences to accept their narratives as authoritative.[21] To speak of rhetoric in terms of power and persuasion is to adopt the basic premise that historical narratives do not reflect a given reality, but rather attempt to create it. In the works of the apologetic historians Josephus and Luke, who frequently depict Roman-Jewish and Roman-Christian relations as more cordial than they actually were, such attempts at creating reality are readily recognized.[22]

In my rhetorical analysis, I am especially concerned with identifying in the narratives of Josephus and Acts the uses to which women are put; or, to adopt a phrase common among feminist and gender scholars, the ways women are used "to think with."[23] Here I am indebted to scholars who have analyzed how representations of women in texts serve elite male discourse on sexuality, politics, morality, and religious allegiance, even in texts that generally fall under the genre of history rather than fiction. The classicist Sandra Joshel, for example, in her brilliant exposition of Tacitus's narrative of the third wife of the Roman princeps Claudius, demonstrates how Tacitus distinguishes between the bad (former) and good (present) empire through his image of a savage, obsessively desiring Messalina. Because the sexual Messalina functions metonymically to represent empire, Joshel notes the futility of attempts to disentangle a "core of political fact" from a narrative "encrusted with sexual disinformation," or of recovering the lived reality of Messalina. She writes, "In Messalina's case, woman's vision, action, and voice function as a discursive screen that displaces female agency. . . . Ironically, Messalina may be more absent than if she was not in the narrative at all. In her place, a figure of desire becomes woman's desire whose most powerful representation is sexual."[24]

In a similar mode of interpretation, Kate Cooper proposes that women in Greek and Latin prose frequently function as rhetorical markers of the character of the men under whose control they stand. As signs of men's character, she argues, women protagonists in fiction were particularly well-suited rhetorical vehicles for supporting or undermining the sacrosanct Greco-Roman institutions of marriage, family, and city. Turning to two related genres in which women protagonists figure prominently, the Hellenistic romance and the early Christian Apocryphal Acts, Cooper marks out the following rhetorical contrast: in the former, focus on the consummation of the nubile hero and heroine's desire serves to celebrate the replenishment of the social order; in the latter, focus on the ascetic heroine and the denigration of sexuality subvert the social order. In opposition to those who have read the Apocryphal Acts as an indication of historical women's primacy in early Christianity, Cooper insists that the centrality of the heroine in these texts has nothing to do with women per se:

> The challenge by the apostle to the householder is the urgent message of these narratives, and it is essentially a conflict *between men*. The challenge posed here by Christianity is not really about women . . . but about authority and the social order. In this way, tales of continence use the narrative momentum of romance, and the enticement of the romantic heroine, to mask a contest for authority, encoded in the contest between two pretenders to the heroine's allegiance.[25]

Attention to the representation of woman as a rhetorical strategy in my own consideration of Josephus's and Luke's narratives of mission and conversion is especially useful, since—as anyone who recognizes the joke in the phrase "missionary position" knows—the language of mission and conversion is frequently gendered and sexualized.

As the work of Joshel and Cooper suggests, analyzing the rhetorical uses to which women protagonists are put requires suspension of questions concerning possible mimetic relations between them and actual historical women. Indeed in some instances, as with Tacitus's Messalina, it is perhaps necessary to concede that no aspect of the lived reality of this woman can be retrieved from behind this elite male author's "discursive screen." Nevertheless, recognizing the rhetorical nature of texts should not lead automatically to their relinquishment as sources from which the history of women and subjugated men may be reconstructed. Here I take issue with Cooper's formulation of the relation of rhetoric to reality as an either/or question. After arguing that the "choice of a female protagonist for a given narrative was often governed by rhetorical rather than mimetic necessity," she asks, "Can these stories serve as evidence for the historical role of women, *or* are they not more properly evidence for the history of apologetics?"[26] In my own work on Josephus and Acts, after identifying how women characters function rhetorically, I ask what use these admittedly stylized and distorted images of women can serve in a project to reconstruct ancient women's history.

My efforts to move from text to reality are motivated by an expressly political interest. They are prompted by the insight of feminist historians that contemporary movements of liberation require historical memory of the agency of subjugated people. They attempt to acknowledge the concern that a focus solely on discourse about those marginalized in history potentially displaces study of these persons' experience.[27] That such persons *were* historical agents serves as a basic premise for feminist biblical scholar Elisabeth Schüssler Fiorenza, who argues compellingly that women in the past produced, shaped, and sustained social life in general, and that the marginality of women and subjugated men in historical narratives owes to "kyriocentric"[28] processes of composition. Because this is so, Schüssler Fiorenza proposes that the validity and adequacy of contemporary historical reconstructions be judged on "whether [they] can make centrally present as historical agents and speaking subjects those whom the kyriocentric text marginalizes or excludes."[29]

Since the few, mostly elite, women who make their appearance in ancient texts are "scripted" by elite men with no concern to communicate actual women's histories to readers, such reconstructions are difficult. Yet they are possible because, even if the sources have not adequately articulated the historical agency of marginalized persons, they do presume it. Therefore, traces of their existence remain in the text. Or, as Barbara Gold argues, in spite of the androcentric and patriarchal nature of classical texts:

> We can see a "space" in the fabric, where there is an uneasiness in the representation of gender for both the author and reader, where the language seems to have more potentiality to be interpreted from many different perspectives, where the marginalized characters seem to be trying to "speak," and where there are border challengings (voices speaking against the text). . . . The female characters of Euripides; the freed slaves of Petronius's *Satyricon*; Vergil's Dido and Statius's Hypsipyle; the native leader Calgacus who speaks against Rome in Tacitus's *Agricola*—all these have been seen, or could be seen, as places where the mute are pushing through the fabric of the text.[30]

Enabling the mute to "push through the fabric of the text" requires resisting the reading position engineered by a given text in order to read it against the grain and against other texts, paying close attention not only to what the text says about women, but also to how it constructs what it says and does not say. Dieter Georgi's reconstruction of Juvenal's contemptible "begging Jewess" as a female missionary of a self-confident Judaism, participating in one of the powerful religious and propagandistic movements in the Greco-Roman world is such a reading. This turning of the text on its head, this embrace of the "Strange Woman" at the margins of the historical record, is integral to my work in the following pages.[31]

1 CRIMES OF PASSION

RELIGION, SEX, AND STATE SUBVERSION
IN *ANTIQUITIES* 18:65–84

JOSEPHUS PACKS A LOT into *Antiquities* 18:65–84: a spurned lover, a cunning henchwoman who rescues him from suicide by hatching a devious plot, an exposé of the sordid nature of Egyptian animal-worship, an admission that some Jewish "scoundrels" have caused trouble in Rome, and a carefully crafted attempt to dissociate these scoundrels from authentic practitioners of the Jewish cult. Because this text features a convert to Judaism, it has received much attention in the discussion of the Jewish missionary question. However, scholars have not yet subjected this passage to gender analysis, even though key protagonists are women. Moreover, in the current debate about missionary activity in antiquity only a narrow part of the passage has been analyzed—that dealing with Jewish mission—in spite of the fact that Josephus tells a story of *two* missionary disasters: one for Jewish devotees, and one for Isis worshippers in Rome. Below, I set the story within the historical context of Domitian's contempt for the Jews of Rome and his use of the Isis cult in his imperial propaganda. I devote special attention to how the narrative plays off a common Roman topos that linked religious and sexual misconduct as twin perils to the state. After this discussion of the rhetoric of gender and class in *Antiquities* 18, I close with a historical reconstruction of women's participation in missionary religions in Rome.

∾

Josephus's *Antiquities* is a twenty-volume work on Jewish history from creation to the time of the war with Rome. According to Josephus, the work was completed in Rome during the thirteenth year of Domitian, 93–94 CE (*Ant.* 20.267). It was written under the patronage of Epaphroditus, who is usually identified with the grammarian of that name active in Roman literary circles at the end of the first century.[1] Josephus portrays Judaism in the best possible light in this work, and therefore the *Antiquities* has commonly been classified as apologetic literature.[2] Without denying an apologetic motive, Steve Mason has recently put forth a compelling argument for a more specific aim and audience of the *Antiquities*: it serves to answer the questions of a sympathetic Roman audience that seeks a full account of Judean *politeia* and that may be contemplating the adoption of this way of life.[3] The *Antiquities*, therefore, should be understood as a work that is more promotional than defensive in tone.

Books 18–20 of the *Antiquities* have commonly been understood as "filler," an eclectic collection of stories that Josephus gathered together so that his history could be twenty books in length, equal to the length of the antiquarian history of Dionysius of Halicarnassus, his model historiographer. Mason's work also calls this view into question, arguing that these books are an integral part of the compositional structure of the *Antiquities* that serve to demonstrate the "world-wide effectiveness of the Judean constitution."[4] These latter books figure prominently in the following two chapters, since they contain several stories highlighting the interest of elite Roman women in the Jewish community.

Fulvia and the Missionary Problem in Rome

According to Josephus, one of the most high-ranking converts to Judaism is Fulvia, a Roman matron whose husband is a Roman consular. The following passage introduces Fulvia and is frequently cited as proof that high-standing women were prominent among converts to Judaism:[5]

> There was a certain Jew, a complete scoundrel, who had fled his own country because he was accused of transgressing certain laws and feared punishment on this account. Just at this time he was resident in

Rome and played the part of an interpreter of the Mosaic law and its wisdom. He enlisted three confederates not a whit better in character than himself; and when Fulvia, a woman of high rank who had become a Jewish proselyte [*tōn en axiōmati gynaikōn kai nomimois proselēluthuian tois Ioudaikois*] began to meet with them regularly, they urged her to send purple and gold to the temple in Jerusalem. They, however, took the gifts and used them for their own personal expenses, for it was this that had been their intention in asking for gifts from the start. Saturninus, the husband of Fulvia, at the instigation of his wife, duly reported this to Tiberius, whose friend he was, whereupon the latter ordered the whole Jewish community to leave Rome. The consuls drafted four thousand of these Jews for military service and sent them to the island of Sardinia; but they penalized a good many of them, who refused to serve for fear of breaking the Jewish law. And so because of the wickedness of four men the Jews were banished from the city. (*Ant.* 18.81–84 [Feldman, LCL])

Fulvia's story is embedded in a larger story about the censure of participants in both the Isis and Jewish religions in Rome (*Ant.* 18.65–84). According to Josephus, trouble for the Isis cult comes through the duping of a highstanding matron and Isis devotee named Paulina. The matron first refuses the advances of a pining equestrian admirer named Mundus. When Mundus's despair brings him to the brink of suicide, his freedwoman Ida devises a plot enabling him to have sexual relations with Paulina. After Ida has secured the complicity of the local Isis priests, Mundus disguises himself as the Egyptian god Anubis and invites Paulina to have intercourse with him in the Isis temple. She consents, flattered at having received this divine favor. Josephus says, "She served him all night long, thinking that he was a god" (*Ant.* 18.74). When Mundus later reveals to her "Anubis's" true identity, all those having taken part in the scandal are punished, including the Isis priests and Mundus's plotting freedwoman, Ida. As highborn Fulvia's crossing over to Jewish laws is the source of trouble for the Jews, so highborn Paulina's foray into Isis worship brings trouble on the Isis community.

This passage is one of four texts concerning an expulsion of Jews from Rome that many scholars have linked to Jewish proselytizing. It is interpreted as an elaboration of a decree expelling all Jews and Isis worshippers from Rome during the reign of Tiberius in 19 CE; an expulsion with similar consequences is documented under Tiberius by the Roman historians Tacitus, Suetonius, and Dio Cassius.[6] Writing in the first decades of the second century for an elite Roman audience, Tacitus records the incident as follows:

> Another debate dealt with the proscription of the Egyptian and Jewish rites, and a senatorial edict directed that four thousand descendents of enfranchised slaves [*libertini generis*],[7] tainted with that superstition and suitable in point of age, were to be shipped to Sardinia and there employed in suppressing brigandage: "If they succumbed to the pestilential climate, it was a cheap loss." The rest had orders to leave Italy, unless they had renounced their impious ceremonial by a given date. (*Ann.* 2.85.5 [Jackson, LCL])

The contemporaneous account of Suetonius reads:

> He [sc. Tiberius] abolished foreign cults, especially the Egyptian and the Jewish rites, compelling all who were addicted to such superstitions to burn their religious vestments and all their paraphernalia. Those of the Jews who were of military age he assigned to provinces of less healthy climate, ostensibly to serve in the army; the others of that same race or of similar beliefs he banished from the city, on pain of slavery for life if they did not obey. He banished the astrologers as well, but pardoned such as begged for indulgence and promised to give up their art. (*Tib.* 36 [Rolfe, LCL])

The account of Dio Cassius was written early in the third century CE. It makes no mention of Isis worshippers and is the only account that explicitly states that Jewish proselytizing activity was the cause of the Jewish expulsion: "As the Jews flocked to Rome in great numbers and were converting many of the natives to their ways, he [sc. Tiberius] banished most of them" (Dio *Hist.* 57.18.5a [Cary, LCL]).

A number of scholars have accepted Dio's explanation for the expulsion and have read Tacitus, Suetonius, and *Antiquities* 18 as supporting evidence for Jewish missionary activity in Rome, which was violently, if only temporarily, repressed by Roman authorities in 19 CE.[8] Although Dio Cassius alone makes the explicit link between proselytizing activity and expulsion, the other recorders of the event also suggest that Roman participation in foreign cultic practices is of great concern. The trouble is not just the practice of foreign rites by foreigners, but the appeal of these practices among the Roman population. In Josephus's account, for example, the trickery of a missionary imposter before a high-standing Roman proselyte is at the heart of the scandal. In Tacitus, two phrases imply that converts and adherents are addressed by the edict. He qualifies those subject to the expulsion as "infected with that superstition" [*ea superstitione infecta*]. This phrase more aptly applies to Jewish converts and adherents than to those who are Jewish by birth, because the verb *inficere* implies contamination, not a congenital condition. Further, Tacitus provides the qualification that the banishment does not apply to those who renounce the religious practices (*profanos ritus exuissent*). This qualification suggests that Tacitus has proselytes in mind, for the right of ethnic Jews to practice their ancestral religion was never disputed by Roman authorities.[9] Suetonius also suggests that a larger circle of persons was subject to punishment than those who were Jewish by birth by noting that the ban applies both to ethnic Jews and to those of similar beliefs (*reliquos gentis eiusdem vel similia sectantes*).

These texts suggest elite Roman anxiety about the influence of foreign religions in the capital city, which in broad terms may be categorized as "missionary activity."[10] The texts may even indicate something of the anti-missionary sentiment of Tiberius himself in the second decade of the common era.[11] On the methodological principle that the records of ancient historians are best read for clues about their own sociopolitical situations, I argue that the accounts of Josephus, Suetonius, and Tacitus indicate foremost a hostile sentiment toward foreign religious influence in Rome at the time they were penned—the turn of the first century CE.[12] Multiple attestation for historical incidents is rare in the ancient sources. That three near-contemporary writers chose to elaborate on this incident from Tiberius's reign should not be dismissed as a coincidental convergence of historiographers. Suetonius's knowledge about converts and adherents, Tacitus's contempt for them, and Josephus's carefully crafted apology about a missionary exchange all point to a heightened concern about missionary activity beginning during the reign of Domitian and continuing into the reigns of Trajan and Hadrian.

Concern about turn-of-the-century missionary activity is expressed in other Roman texts as well. Juvenal's portrait of missionary hawkers from the East plying their wares before gullible matrons in the capital provides a general backdrop for the expulsion accounts, suggesting both the commonplace character of missionary exchange and the contempt for the practice in conservative Roman circles. In the sixth satire, he casts aspersions on the hysteric entourage of the Syrian goddess Cybele led by a grotesque eunuch priest; the white Io (Isis) who sends devotees plunging into the icy Tiber or off on wacky Egyptian pilgrimages; Anubis, who freely pardons sexual transgressions in exchange for bribes; the Jewish dream interpreter who also requires payment; the Persian and Syrian soothsayers, the Chaldean astrologers, and the Phrygian and Indian augurs (*Sat.* 6.511–91). In all instances, it is not just the foreignness of these religious practitioners that is parodied but also their impact on elite Roman women over whom they hold sway.

Anti-Jewish rhetoric reaches a new high-water mark in Latin literature under Domitian and the Antonines, and this hostility has been read as a response to successful missionary activity of Jews among Romans.[13] Writing under Domitian, Quintillian denounces Moses as the founder of the Jewish superstition and of a nation "pernicious to others" (*Institutio oratoria* 3.7.21). John Gager identifies this slander as marking a new disdain for Moses, absent from earlier non-Jewish sources that exhibited respect for him as wise lawgiver.[14] Martial spews venom on Jewish women, Jewish boys, and especially on circumcised Jews, whom he characterizes as hypersexed.[15] In his famous account of the Jews in *Histories*, Tacitus also argues that Jews are "prone to lust" and that their customs are base and abominable (Tacitus *Hist.* 5.5.2). Especially noteworthy is Tacitus's understanding that conversion to Judaism subverts Roman order: "Those who are converted to [Jewish] ways follow the same practice, and the earliest lesson they receive is to despise the gods, to disown their country, and to regard their parents, children, and brothers as of little account" (Tacitus *Hist.* 5.5.2 [Moore, LCL]). In his fourteenth satire, Juvenal echoes this understanding of the political ramifications of conversion to Judaism, noting that while converts "disregard the laws of Rome, they learn and practice and revere the Jewish law" [*Romanas autem soliti contemnere leges; Iudaicum ediscunt et servant ac metuunt ius*] (*Sat.* 14.100–1). In viewing conversion to Judaism as the flouting of Roman laws and the abandonment of Roman gods and family ties, these two authors equate conversion with sedition, a sentiment not expressed in the anti-Jewish polemic of previous generations.

Domitian, Jews, and the Isis Cult

It is within this general climate of hostility toward missionary religions among conservative Romans at the turn of the first century, and in light of the new understanding of the political implications of conversion to Judaism in the writings of Tacitus and Juvenal that I read Josephus's expulsion narrative in *Antiquities* 18:65–84. Compared with the Latin recorders of the event, Josephus's rhetorical use of gender is most elaborate, for he alone casts a high-standing Roman matron at the heart of the scandal, both for Isis worshippers and the Jewish community. Josephus's account is the earliest and the only one written during Domitian's reign. It must be considered, therefore, in view of Domitian's stance toward the Jewish and Egyptian cults in Rome.

Precisely how to characterize Domitian's relations with Jews in Rome is a matter of some debate. The conventional view holds that Domitian was hostile toward Jews and those engaged in Jewish practices, particularly among the upper classes in Rome.[16] It is also widely held that, like Juvenal and Tacitus, Domitian believed that interest in "Jewish ways" among the Roman aristocracy was politically subversive. This conceptualization of Domitian is supported by Dio Cassius, who reports that in 95 CE—not long after Josephus's completion of the *Antiquities*—Domitian executed his own relatives, Flavius Clemens and Flavia Domitilla, on the charge of atheism for having drifted into Jewish ways (Dio *Hist.* 67.14.1–2). Suetonius writes that Domitian enforced the *fiscus Judaicus*, a tax levied on Jews from the time of their defeat under Vespasian, with utmost rigor (*Dom.* 12.2). That Nerva issued coins announcing an end to the abuses of this tax collecting within weeks of Domitian's assassination indicates that the abuses were widespread and widely resented.[17] Talmudic, Midrashic, and late Christian sources remember the Domitianic years as years of persecution.[18] The work of Leonard L. Thompson is representative of an opposing school of interpretation that attributes the depictions of Domitian as a "mad tyrant" to a later propaganda campaign encouraged by his successors Nerva, Trajan, and Hadrian. He argues that the assessments of Suetonius and Dio concerning

Domitian's relations with Jews are part and parcel of the smear tactics of post-Flavian authors and that "if it can be shown that Domitian oppressed Jews . . . it must be established by means other than the points of view expressed in Suetonius, Dio, and Nerva's propaganda."[19]

Thompson's appraisal of Domitian's Jewish policy, at least in regard to Jews in the city of Rome,[20] is unjustifiably benign and can be challenged precisely on the grounds he suggests, through the writings of authors not involved in the *damnatio memoriae* campaign. This is most apparent in the *Antiquities*, where Josephus betrays his anxiousness concerning the state of Jewish liberty under Domitian's reign. Included within the latter books of the *Antiquities* are the *Acta Pro Judaeis*, legal decrees of previous emperors favorable to Jews.[21] Josephus is explicit about his reason for incorporating these decrees: he hopes they will serve to preserve peace among Jews and their neighbors in his own day:

> Now it was necessary for me to cite these decrees since this account of our history is chiefly meant to reach the Greeks in order to show them that in former times we were treated with all respect and were not prevented by our rulers from practicing any of our ancestral customs but, on the contrary, even had their co-operation in preserving our religion and our ways of honoring God. And if I frequently mention these decrees, it is to reconcile the other nations to us and to remove the causes for hatred which have taken root in thoughtless persons among us as well as among them. (*Ant.* 16.174–75 [Marcus and Wikgren, LCL])

As Shirley Jackson Case has argued, Josephus's care to demonstrate Rome's long-standing practice of tolerating Jewish religious customs suggests that continued Roman tolerance was in question. Case further notes two passages in the *Antiquities* concerning the emperor Gaius Caligula's failed attempt to erect his statue in the Jerusalem temple and his subsequent assassination. Josephus moralizes at length here about the fate of wicked rulers who affront the Jews, a theme not addressed in his concise narration of the incident in the *Jewish War*. This preoccupation with an emperor's handling of Jewish matters is best explained as a means of addressing a potential political crisis for Jews under Domitian.[22] Josephus's defensive writing is contemporaneous with the anti-Jewish barbs of Martial and Quintillian discussed above. Given the sycophancy of writers during Domitian's reign, Margaret Williams argues that the hostility of Martial and Quintillian toward Jews should also be read as indicators of the "sneering animus" that characterized Domitian's dealings with them.[23]

In contrast, Domitian venerated the goddess Isis and made use of Isis symbolism in his own propaganda, a practice in keeping with the Egyptian proclivities of his Flavian predecessors Vespasian and Titus.[24] Domitian restored the temple of Isis on the Campus Martius after it had been destroyed by fire in 80 CE. To commemorate this occasion, he erected an obelisk before the temple, on which he is depicted receiving a crown from Isis. Hieroglyphic inscriptions from the obelisk proclaim Domitian "lover of Isis."[25] Other indications of Domitian's Egypto-philia include his importing sphinxes and cynocephali from the Nile River valley into Rome, along with several obelisks bearing borders of hieroglyphics of great Egyptian pharaohs.[26]

The Flavians linked the goddess Isis with success in military conquest, including the conquest of Judea. It is Josephus himself who reports that Titus and Vespasian spent the night preceding the triumph celebrating the victory over Judea inside the Iseum on the Campus Martius (*J.W.* 7.123). Two coins of Vespasian commemorating this event portray the Iseum on their reverse.[27] This linkage was not forgotten by Domitian, as his erection of an Arch to Isis on the Campus Martius clearly shows. Minerva stands at the center of the Arch flanked by Isis and Anubis. Above the three gods, captives are depicted chained to palm trees, a symbolic representation of Judea's submission after the war with Rome.[28]

Domitian's hostility toward the Jews in Rome and his fascination with Isis, reflected in the way he inscribes the defeat of Judea as an Isean triumph in his imperial propaganda, provide the context for Josephus's detailing of differences between these two religions in his own propagandistic enterprise. Noting these differences is essential to the explication of this dual expulsion account.[29] That Josephus's account is guided by the rhetorical principle of comparison is evident from his introduction to these two stories:

About this same time another outrage threw the Jews into an uproar; and simultaneously certain actions of a scandalous nature occurred in connection with the temple of Isis at Rome. I shall first give an account of the daring deed of the followers of Isis and shall then come back to the fate of the Jews. (*Ant.* 18.65 [Feldman, LCL])

Lest the reader forget that these two accounts are to be a study in comparison and contrast, Josephus reminds them again after he has narrated the Isis incident: "Such were the insolent acts of the priests in the temple of Isis. I shall now return to the story, which I promised to tell, of what happened at the same time to the Jews in Rome" (*Ant.* 18.80 [Feldman, LCL]). In several instances the accounts can be compared point by point: in both trouble is due to the deception of a matron of exemplary moral standing from the senatorial class whose husband is of consular rank;[30] each woman, upon realizing the deception, reports to her husband; each group of religious devotees is punished. A distinction is made, however, between the instigators of the Isis and the Jewish scandal. The mover behind the Isis scandal is Ida, the cunning freedwoman who receives total cooperation in her scheme from the Isis priests, the legitimate representatives of the Isis religion. Josephus withholds from the Jewish swindlers such legitimation (*Ant.* 18.81–82). Their leader is a scoundrel (*poneros eis ta panta*) accused of transgressing certain Jewish laws (*parabaseon nomon tinon*) who has departed from his country for fear of punishment by his compatriots. He is not an authentic interpreter of Mosaic law and wisdom, rather he merely plays the part (*prospoieo*).[31] Josephus concedes that Jews caused trouble in Rome, but he scripts them as outcasts. The central distinction in the narrative concerns the nature of the crime at the heart of each scandal. Trouble for Isis worshippers stems from the sexual violation of a notable Roman matron by a lusting admirer; no comparable crime of passion lies at the heart of the Jewish scandal.

The Rhetoric of Gender and Class in *Antiquities* 18:65–84

Literary Antecedents

As Otto Weinreich demonstrated at the turn of the nineteenth century, the legend concerning the paternity of Alexander the Great contained in the *Greek Alexander Romance* closely parallels Josephus's story of Paulina and

Mundus.[32] In this legend, Alexander is fathered by Nektanebos, the deposed Egyptian Pharaoh-turned-magician, who is able to sleep with Olympias, wife of Philip, after disguising himself as the god Ammon and entering her bed chamber at night (*Greek Alexander Romance* 1.4–7). In both stories, initial interest in a foreign missionary teaching culminates in the woman's unwitting adulterous practice under the guise of religious devotion. As Paulina's seduction is possible because of her zealous devotion to Isis, so the relationship between Olympias and Nektanebos is possible because of Olympias's initial desire to benefit from the prophetic utterances of this miracle-working, immigrant holy man.[33] In both stories the sexual activity of the woman serves propagandistic purposes. The claim that Alexander the Great was the son of Pharaoh Nektanebos was a means for Egyptians to reconcile themselves to the rule of Alexander over Egypt. As I shall argue below, Josephus's demonstration that Isis religion violates the chastity of Roman women is his indictment of Rome's tolerance of this religion and an assertion of Judaism's superiority over the Isis cult.

Propelled by a trickster-as-god motif, the Nektanebos-Olympias and Mundus-Paulina stories are humorous variations of a more sadistic motif preserved in Livy's history of Rome. There, narratives of the rape or attempted rape of chaste women by pining admirers who have no legitimate access to them are the impetus for a new order of relations among Roman men. The violation and subsequent death of Lucretia, a woman whose chastity was exemplary, leads to the fall of the monarchy and birth of the Republic (Livy *Hist.* 1.57–60). The attempted rape of the beautiful Verginia, prevented only by her murder, results in the overthrow of the corrupt decemvirate and the restoration of the tribunate (Livy *Hist.* 3.44–58).[34]

They may also be viewed as prototypes of early Christian conversion stories, because they contain in brief the elements that will dominate the Christian Apocryphal Acts written in the late second and third centuries: a high-standing woman, a missionary encounter, and a conversion experience represented in terms of sexual allegiance. In all of the Apocryphal Acts, the highborn heroine renounces sexual ties with husband or fiancé and assumes a continent lifestyle in service of an ascetic male apostle. As the sexual violation in the Mundus-Paulina tale serves to denigrate the foreign missionary's influence, so the inviolate convert in the Acts functions as an assertion of the moral superiority of Christianity.[35]

The Roman Context: Pollutae caerimoniae, magna adulteria

In the story of how Ida and Mundus plot to violate Paulina in the Isis temple at Rome, Josephus fleshes out in elaborate detail a notion communicated by Roman poets and satirists only through aside and innuendo: devotees of the Egyptian goddess practice fornication and adultery. Ovid's work contains the greatest number of references to Isis temples as sites of sexual abandon;[36] Martial and Juvenal make similar claims. Asides like this one in Juvenal's sixth satire, where he depicts the Isis chapel as a likely spot for a lover's tryst while ridiculing an elite woman's attention to her coiffure, are typical: "If she has an appointment and wishes to be turned out more nicely than usual, and is in a hurry to meet someone waiting for her in the gardens, or more likely near the chapel of the wanton Isis, the unhappy maiden that does her hair will have her own hair torn . . ." (*Sat.* 6.487–89 [Ramsay, LCL]).[37] Josephus's tale exploits a common Roman topos linking chastity of married women with proper practice of religion, on the one hand, and sexual violation with foreign religious practice, on the other. Hanging in the balance is the security of the Roman household and state.[38] The locus classicus for the denigration of foreign cults as sites of uncontrolled sexuality and subversion is Livy's account of the spread of Bacchic rites to Rome in 186 BCE.[39] Livy claims that the participants in Bacchic worship would stop at no wrongdoing, and that their numbers were so large they almost constituted a second state (*alter populus*). In order to highlight female sexual misbehavior as a central part of Bacchic rites, he puts these words into the mouth of the consul Postumius: "First, then, a great part of them are women, and they are the source of this mischief; then there are the men very like the women, debauched and debauchers, fanatical, with senses dulled by wakefulness, wine, noise and shouts at night" (Livy *Hist.* 39.15.9 [Sage, LCL]). Augustus presented himself as a restorer of both proper religious and moral conduct, and these two areas of reform are linked in his legislation, ceremonies, and poetry.[40] The poet Horace, who promotes Augustan ideology in verse form, makes this link most clearly in his *Odes* 3.6. The poem begins with the claim that neglect of the gods is one of the ultimate causes of Roman sufferings: "Thy father's sins, O Roman, thou, though guiltless, shalt expiate, till thou dost restore the crumbling temples and shrines of the gods and their statues soiled with grimy smoke" (*Odes* 3.6.1–4 [Bennett, LCL]. It continues by linking this neglect with a second source of misfortune, adulterous married women: "Teeming with sin, our times have sullied first the marriage-bed, our offspring, and our homes; sprung from this source, disaster's stream has overflowed the folk and fatherland. The maiden early takes delight in learning Grecian dances, and trains herself in coquetry even now, and plans unholy amours, with passion unrestrained" (*Odes* 3.6.17–24 [Bennett, LCL]). The association of religious and sexual misconduct as twin perils to the Roman state is made more than one hundred years later by Tacitus in his remarks evoking the tumultuous experiences of Rome in the late 60s CE. After recalling the eruption of Vesuvius and the great fires in Rome, he pines that "sacred rites were defiled; there were adulteries in high places" [*pollutae caerimoniae, magna adulteria*] (Tacitus *Hist.* 1.2).[41]

Tacitus also understands the expulsion of Jews and Isis worshippers from Rome in 19 CE as part of the senate's response to the twin perils of sexual and religious misconduct. This is clear from the structure of *Annals* 2.85–86, where he has chosen, apparently from the *Acta Senatus*, three actions to memorialize for the year 19 CE.[42] Although Margaret Williams argues that these three actions are not linked and exemplify the heterogeneity of Tacitus's end-of-the-year summaries, I argue that the order here is not random, but rather is a variation on the *pollutae caerimoniae, magna adulteria* theme.[43] The first action that Tacitus records is the account of a senate resolution attempting to restrain female desire (*libido feminarum*) by forbidding elite women to practice prostitution (*quaestum corpore faceret*).[44] The second is the resolution concerning the expulsion of Jews and Isis worshippers from Rome. The third concerns the nomination of a woman to replace the retiring president of the Vestal Virgins. Thus Tacitus sandwiches the repercussions against practitioners of foreign religious rites between the punishment of an elite woman's profligacy and the reaffirmation of the state cult in which virginal purity is sacrosanct.[45]

This general tendency in Roman literature to fuse subversive religious and sexual activity, which serves as the structure for Tacitus's account of the events of 19 CE, elucidates two rhetorical functions of Josephus's own version of the expulsion. First, by elaborating on the sexual misconduct of Isis practitioners, Josephus attempts to deflect accusations of similar misconduct concerning the Jewish religion. Jewish scoundrels may have attempted to deceive a Roman matron, but greed, rather than lust, motivated this deception. Judaism, even when propagated by missionary imposters, does not threaten the chastity of Roman matrons. Second, Josephus's story of how easily a Roman matron devoted to Isis can be tricked into an adulterous encounter is an assertion that this religion is a threat to the Roman state. The implication, which could not have been lost on readers aware of Domitian's flirtation with the cult, is that the man who tolerates the Isis religion positions himself squarely in the role of the cuckolded husband.

Mixing with the Lower Classes

Because elite Roman males sought to maintain a rigidly ordered hierarchical society, the notion that elite Roman matrons willfully disrupted this order by mixing with the lower classes is a preoccupation of the literature. Adulterous relationships between women of high status and men of inferior classes were viewed with horror by moralists, and depraved elite women lusting after slaves and others among the rabble is a common literary topos.[46] The intermingling of the classes is integral to Juvenal's attacks on the religious practices of women.[47] The orgy of the Bona Dea, the "religious" ceremony at the center of the sixth satire, features women of unequal status engaged in athletic contest. The pimp's slave girls (lenonum ancillae) are no match for the ladies (dominae): "Saufeia [an aristocratic name] challenges the pimp's slave-girls to a contest. Her agility wins the prize, but she has herself in turn to bow the knee to Medullina [also an aristocratic name]. And so the palm remains with the mistress, whose exploits match her birth!" (Sat. 6.320–23). Juvenal describes an orgy in which the dominae would willingly copulate with slaves, or water carriers, or at last resort, even donkeys (Sat. 6.329–34).[48] In Juvenal's sixth satire elite women are almost exclusively the targets of his verbal abuse. Within the segment of the satire that ridicules women's obsession with fanatic religions (Sat. 6.511–91), however, he casts his net wide enough to include women of all classes. The superstitions of rich ladies are comparable to those of plebeian women (Sat. 6.582–88).

The expulsion accounts of Suetonius and Tacitus suggest that the involvement of the lower classes of Rome in these non-Roman religions was at issue. Tacitus notes that four thousand "freedpersons" (libertini generis) involved in the rites were conscripted to suppress brigandage in Sardinia. Further, the punishments suggested by both Tacitus and Suetonius—expulsion, perpetual slavery, and conscription—would have been most easily directed against freedpersons, slaves, and foreigners, because Roman citizens could not incur these penalties en masse but only on a case-by-case basis.[49]

The Roman sentiment associating illegitimate religious practices with indiscriminate mixing of social classes, and the suggestion in Tacitus and Suetonius that freedpersons and other noncitizens were targeted by the expulsion decree, illuminate Josephus's own inscriptions of social distinctions in his expulsion story. In the Isis plot, players from a wide range of social classes appear on the stage. Their willingness to "mingle" propels the story to its tragic outcome. Paulina is of noble Roman descent with a husband of senatorial stature. Decius Mundus, the man who pines for her, is of equestrian rank. The true force behind Mundus's deception of Paulina is the freedwoman, Ida, "expert in every kind of mischief" [*pantoiōn idris kakōn*] (*Ant.* 18.69), who plots with the priests at the temple of Isis to arrange Paulina's encounter with Mundus-Anubis.

The character of Ida the freedwoman, like the cunning slave (*servus callidus*, or *servus fallax*) found in new comedy, or the selfless slave of the ideal novel, lives only to satisfy her master's pleasure.[50] After Mundus resolves to starve himself to death because he sees no hope of having intercourse with Paulina, it is Ida who insists that it is possible for his desire to be met. As is typical of slaves in new comedy, she stands to gain nothing—not even financial reward—from the exploit. Although she requests 50,000 drachmas from Mundus to carry out the plot, she pays this sum in full to the Isis priests for their complicity.[51]

The Josephan account closely correlates punishments with class status.[52] Although none of the Latin sources mention such a punishment for Isis devotees, Josephus subjects Ida along with the Isis priests to crucifixion, the cruelest form of Roman torture. In his eyes the punishment is just, "for she was the source of this hellish thing and it was she who contrived the whole plot against the woman's honor" [*olethrou genomenēn aitian kai ta panta eph' hybrei syntheisan*] (*Ant.* 18.79). The equestrian Mundus, more noble than the plotting priests and freedwoman, is exiled rather than killed. Josephus reports that Tiberius spared Mundus from harsher punishment because his crime was born of passion ("*meta erōtos*" [*Ant.* 18.80]).[53] Paulina the matron is the duped but innocent, and hence unpunished, victim.

In contrast, there are only two parties involved in the Jewish scandal, the high-ranking matron and the swindlers of unspecified rank who meet with her, presumably in private. Although Paulina's violation occurs within the

Isis temple, a locus of class boundary transgressions, Josephus offers no indication that Fulvia ventures into a Jewish synagogue to expose herself to similar risk. Although Josephus and Tacitus concur that four thousand Jews were conscripted to suppress brigandage in Sardina as punishment, Josephus is silent about their status. Only Tacitus specifies their rank with his phrase *libertini generis*. Josephus thus deflects any anxiety his Roman readers might have about Judaism as a religion in which the respectable mingle with the rabble. Although Tacitus sees the involvement of freedpersons at the heart of the scandal of both Jewish and Egyptian rites, Josephus includes a culpable freedwoman only in his account of the Isis scandal. Josephus reports that she is crucified summarily and gives no indication that she, or anyone of such low breeding, has tainted Fulvia's encounter with Judaism.

Traces of Women's Existence: Cracks, Fissures, Countertexts

My reading of Josephus's expulsion account as a play on common Roman tropes and stereotypes concerning the prominence of notable women in foreign religions necessarily displaces a reading of the narrative as a transcript of events in the lives of actual historical women, Paulina, Fulvia, and Ida. Yet I conclude this chapter with a discussion of the relationship of this text to historical reality. When read against the grain, against other texts, and for what they do and do not say, the stories of Paulina, Fulvia, and Ida still serve as a springboard into a reconstruction of women as historical agents, actively participating in "foreign" religious cults in Rome.

That women of all classes were prominent among those attracted to religions foreign to Rome is strongly suggested by a convergence of literary sources from several genres on this point. In addition to Josephus's story, Juvenal's sixth satire caricatures women's involvement in "foreign" religious practices, but is only effective as satire if it has some correspondence to reality. Likewise, the proscriptions against women's involvement in nocturnal cults found in both Cicero (*Leg.* 2.35–37) and Plutarch (*Conj. praec.* 140D) only make sense if they are written in response to actual women's religious practices.[54] A literary source that suggests the involvement of women slaves, freedpersons, and possibly even citizens in shaping and sustaining religious practice among minority religions in Rome is the sixteenth chapter of Paul's letter to the Romans, in which he acknowledges several women as leading church functionaries. These include Phoebe, a deacon of the church in Cenchreae and benefactor of Paul; Prisca, whom Paul names as a coworker; and Junia, singled out as "prominent among the apostles."[55]

The prominence of women in the Isis, Jewish, and also Dionysos cults in Rome can be argued from the epigraphical sources.[56] In the Latin inscriptions from the Jewish Via Appia catacomb in Rome, there are more females named than males. Ross Kraemer suggests that this is "possibly due to an influx of non-Jewish women, through conversion, loosely or narrowly construed."[57] Harry Leon identifies only seven inscriptions from Rome that signify Jewish proselytes—an admittedly small number. Yet five out of seven of these epitaphs are for women, including Beturia Paulla, a proselyte who is recognized as the mother of the synagogues of Campus and Volumnius.[58] Although little information on social status can be gleaned from these inscriptions, Leon does suggest that two of them, Felicitas (*CII* #462), and Nicetas (*CII* #256), were freedwomen.[59]

In her study of women's devotion to the Isis cult, Heyob notes that 48.6 percent of the Athenian and 37.1 percent of the Roman inscriptions concern female devotees, and inscriptions identifying women devotees are considerably scarcer in other regions. Because these calculations do not exceed 50 percent, Heyob concludes that women did not make up the majority of Isis devotees.[60] Heyob's conclusions are often cited by scholars as a way to dismiss the significance of women's participation in the Isis cult.[61] However, given the androcentric nature of the sources, including epigraphical ones, women tend to be underrepresented in them. The fact that women figure in nearly 40 percent of extant inscriptions concerning Isis devotees in Rome supports rather than detracts from my argument that women were prominent in the Isis cult at Rome.[62]

Another important inscription indicating the prominence of women in cults foreign to Rome comes from the marble base of a statue dedicated to Pompeia Agrippinilla, wife of a Roman consul and Bacchic priestess, by members of her religious association (*thiasos*) active in the early part of the reign of Marcus Aurelius.[63] This *thiasos*, located in the Roman Campagna, has been characterized by Albert Henrichs as "the most spectacular example of a private Dionysiac cult transplanted from the Greek east to the very heart of Rome."[64] It is significant to note that Pompeia Agrippinilla, member of an illustrious Roman family whose origin can be traced to the Greek island of

Lesbos, is a high-ranking cultic official. Further, approximately one-third of the four hundred members of this *thiasos* are women from various classes.

In the sense that women among the upper classes, along with women of all classes, were prominent among those involved in religions foreign to Rome, Josephus's tale has some correspondence to historical reality. But one does well to resist his gendered representation of missionary-as-active-male and convert-as-passive-female for belying the historical contributions of women as propagators of the faith. The letters of Paul reveal that women were Christian missionaries, and not merely recipients of Christian teaching. Juvenal's critiques of missionary religions also suggest more about women's initiative in Judaism and Isis worship than the stylized conversion stories that position women as receptacles of men's indoctrination. In his sixth satire, the interpreter of the law of Jerusalem, *interpres legum Solymarum*, is a woman (*Sat.* 6.542–47). One of the outrageous aspects of the Isiac's devotion, according to Juvenal, is that her encounter with the divinity is unmediated. She hears and acts, not according to the instructions of a priestly intermediary, but upon the direction of the goddess herself: "If the white Io shall so order, she will journey to the confines of Egypt, and fetch water got from hot Meroe with which to sprinkle the Temple of Isis. . . . For she believes that the command was given by the voice of the Goddess herself—a pretty kind of mind and spirit for the Gods to have converse with by night!" (*Sat.* 6.526–31 [Ramsey, LCL]). The equation of conversion with adultery in the Paulina-Mundus tale, like the depiction of the Isis cult as locus of immorality by the Roman poets, can be read as male anxiety that women involved in missionary religions are not properly under the control of their husbands. Read as anxious responses to women's greater autonomy, these texts support the thesis of feminist scholars that missionary cults held emancipatory possibilities for women.[65] An author can signal that a woman is out of sexual control either through depicting her as involved in improper sexual relations, or as renouncing proper relations. Hence the Roman poets depict seemingly contradictory portraits of Isis devotees as both sexually immoral and prone to ascetic tendencies.[66] But whether depicted as fornicator or ascetic, these textual women who are not bound in proper sexual relations suggest historical situations in which real women held a measure of authority and autonomy.[67]

Finally, more can be said of the importance of freedwomen in foreign cults in Rome when one remembers what Josephus does and does not say

about class in his narrative. In spite of the suggestions of Tacitus and Suetonius that freedpersons are at the heart of the problem with the Jewish cult in
Rome, the only freedwoman in Josephus's narrative is the cunning Ida,
whom he pegs as the source (*aitia*) of the Isis scandal, and then removes
from the narrative through crucifixion. The high-standing Fulvia, in contrast, is presented as receiving Jewish laws without having contact with
religious practitioners outside of her own home. This representation of the
missionary religion as the "parlor religion" of rich women serves as an
apologetic device to deflect attention from persons of less eminent ranks
who participated in Judaism as well as Isis worship.[68]

2 LADIES' AID

GENTILE NOBLEWOMEN AS SAVIORS AND BENEFACTORS IN THE *ANTIQUITIES*

AS I DISCUSSED IN CHAPTER 1, Josephus's account of the expulsion of Isis worshippers and Jews from Rome can be understood as a variation of a topos condemning foreign religions as the locus of sexual immorality and state subversion. Texts that express this negative sentiment concerning women's involvement in foreign rites will surface again in this study, but now the focus of inquiry shifts. It is, perhaps, commonsensical to note that women in apologetic/propagandistic narratives can serve negative rhetorical functions: in patriarchal cultures, then as well as now, what better way to insult a male opponent than to accuse him of catering to the wiles of women? For the remainder of this book, however, I explore a different phenomenon that is not so widely recognized in scholarship on women in antiquity: the use of high-standing Gentile women for positive rhetorical effect. The placement of prominent women in the *Antiquities* and Acts suggests that in particular circumstances the claim that one has the (right kind of) women on one's side is a means of achieving cultural acceptability.

Among the prominent pagan women considered in this chapter are three who are famed for their purported devotion to Jewish cultic practices: (1) Poppaea Sabina, the consort/wife[1] of the emperor Nero, whom Josephus describes as "God-fearing" (*theosebēs*), a term generally understood as denoting reverence for the Jewish deity (*Ant.* 20.195); (2) Fulvia, the Roman convert of consular rank featured above in Chapter 1; and (3) Helena, Queen of Adiabene, also a well-known convert to Judaism (*Ant.* 20.17–53). Until now, scholarly studies of prominent pagan women in Josephus have tended to focus solely on these three women because their interest in Judaism includes a religious component. My purpose here is to show that these three narratives of high-standing women who have some interest in Jewish religious practices are part of a larger narrative pattern in the *Antiquities* that repeatedly characterizes Gentile noblewomen as saviors and benefactors of the Jewish people. In the *Antiquities* imperial women intercede before every Julio-Claudian emperor on behalf of Jewish aristocrats, often with ramifications for the entire Jewish population. Josephus also claims that Domitia, the wife of the emperor Domitian, was one of his own patrons. Patronage on behalf of the Jewish community is integral to both the stories of Fulvia and Queen Helena of Adiabene. Furthermore, the salvific acts of foreign noblewomen feature prominently in Josephus's retelling of the story of Moses early in the *Antiquities*.

In this chapter I proceed first by analyzing incidences of noblewomen's benefaction in the *Antiquities*, drawing attention to literary motifs employed by Josephus, suggesting the rhetorical effects of some of his specific arguments, and providing relevant background information on political, social, and religious issues. I then discuss Josephus's general rhetorical aim in claiming noblewomen benefactors in light of Roman authors who portray noblewomen as political agents. After making these explorations, I set forth a brief historical reconstruction of the nature of Roman imperial women's benefaction on behalf of the Jews. Further discussion of the apologetic effect of this literary motif, and of the historical phenomenon of noblewomen's benefaction, is postponed until Chapter 3, in which I explore the role of prominent Gentile women in Acts.

All the Emperor's Women: Patronage and Intercession by Women of the Imperial House

Livia, Friend of Herod and Salome

The interactions that Josephus records between Livia, the wife of Augustus, and the Herodian family fit a predictable pattern of imperial benefaction.[2] Livia is involved in convincing Salome to accept the marriage partner whom Herod has chosen for her (*Ant.* 17.10; cf. *J.W.* 1.566). Because elite Roman women were often involved in arranging political marriages, Josephus's mention of such political activity on Livia's part is unremarkable.[3] One also reads that Livia, along with Augustus, sends gifts from Rome to Caesarea when Herod completes this city's construction (*Ant*. 16.139). Both Herod and Salome name Livia as a beneficiary in their wills (*J.W*. 2.167; *Ant*. 17.146, 17.190, 18.31). Again, these are pro forma exchanges between imperial house and the family of a client king.[4] Because of their perfunctory nature, I mention these incidents primarily to establish that according to Josephus, imperial women's special relations with Jewish aristocrats are in place from the beginning of the principate of Augustus.

Josephus does, however, suggest that these formal exchanges between Livia and Herod's family were part of a more intimate relationship. In speaking of the consultation between Livia and Salome concerning Salome's prospective marriage, he reminds readers of Livia's high status and claims that she was Salome's constant confidant: "And [Salome] took [Livia's] advice both because she was the wife of Caesar and because on other occasions she would give very useful counsel" (*Ant*. 17.10).

Antonia, Mediator for Agrippa I

Agrippa I, grandson of Herod the Great, was appointed in 37 CE by Gaius Caligula to rule the former tetrarchies of Lysanias (Abilene) and Philip (Trachonitis, Gaulanitis, and Auranitis). He later acquired the territories of Herod Antipas (Galilee and Perea). In 41 CE, the emperor Claudius appointed him to rule over all of the territories that had formerly comprised the kingdom of Herod the Great.

Although there are various indications of King Agrippa's ties to the imperial family in other literary and numismatic sources, Josephus provides the longest continuous narrative of this ruler, including stories of his life in Rome before he became king.[5] In this preaccession narrative, Agrippa's mother Berenice and especially Antonia, who is the daughter of Mark Antony, mother of Germanicus, and grandmother of the emperor Caligula, play prominent roles.[6] Readers learn that Berenice is esteemed by Antonia and arranges the friendship (*philia*) between Antonia and Agrippa with the request that Antonia promote her son's interests (*Ant*. 18.143). When Agrippa's debts threaten to prevent him from entering into imperial circles, Antonia lends him money (*Ant*. 18.164). When he is imprisoned for slandering Tiberius, Antonia makes an unsuccessful attempt to win his pardon from the emperor (*Ant.* 18.184–86) and, after deciding that further appeals to Tiberius would be ineffective, secures favorable treatment for him while he is imprisoned (*Ant.* 18.202–3). At the death of Tiberius, his successor, Gaius Caligula, is eager to release Agrippa on the very day of Tiberius's funeral. Once again Antonia intercedes with an emperor for Agrippa's bene-fit. Sensing the impropriety of such an untimely release, Antonia advises Gaius to handle the affair more discreetly by postponing it for a few days (*Ant.* 18.236). After he is set free, Agrippa becomes a close advisor to the emperor.

Josephus uses the story of Agrippa's decline, imprisonment, release, and eventual kingship to moralize on how God exalts the fallen (*Ant.* 19.292–96). Daniel Schwartz has shown that the story of Joseph's fall and rise before the Egyptian Pharaoh in Genesis serves as Josephus's biblical prototype, both in its theme of the wrongly imprisoned Jew rising to prominence in a foreign court and in its finer details. Agrippa, like Joseph, is treated kindly by his jailers (cf. *Ant.* 18.203–4; Gen. 39:21–23); when Agrippa is released, he re-ceives a haircut and a change of clothes, as does Joseph (cf. *Ant.* 18.237; Gen. 41:14); a fellow prisoner's conversation with Agrippa concerning the flight of a bird as an omen of his impending release has overtones of Joseph's conver-sations with the Pharaoh's butler and baker (cf. *Ant.* 18.195–202; Gen. 40:12–15, 40:17–19).[7] Although the biblical story of Joseph may provide the frame for the story of Agrippa's imprisonment, Antonia is no Potiphar's wife. As Agrippa's patron, intercessor, and wise counselor, Antonia is the antithesis of the biblical femme fatale, the wife of Potiphar, whose lust and deception lead to Joseph's imprisonment.

Agrippina the Younger Pleads a Jewish Cause

Agrippina the Younger appears in *Antiquities* 20 at the conclusion of an account of a conflict between Jews and Samaritans under the procuratorship of Cumanus in 51 CE.[8] In Josephus's telling, several Galilean pilgrims en route to Jerusalem are slaughtered by Samaritans, and Cumanus's unwilling-ness to avenge them provokes the Jewish peasantry to retaliate. The story takes several turns toward further violence and failed attempts to restore order. The incident is finally resolved when leaders of the Jewish aristocracy are sent in chains to Rome, along with Cumanus and Samaritan notables, to render an account before Claudius.

In Rome, because Claudius's freedmen and friends show "the greatest partiality" toward Cumanus and the Samaritans, the Jews are vindicated only through the intervention of Agrippina II, the emperor's wife:

> [The Samaritans] would have got the better of the Jews, had not Agrippa the Younger, who was in Rome and saw that the Jewish leaders were losing the race for influence, urgently entreated Agrippina, the wife of the emperor, to persuade her husband to give the case a thorough hearing in a manner befitting his respect for law and to punish the instigators of the revolt. Claudius was favorably impressed by this petition. He then heard the case through, and on discovering that the Samaritans were the first to move in stirring up trouble, he ordered those of them who had come before him to be put to death. (*Ant.* 20.135–36 [Feldman, LCL])

In this bit of court intrigue capping the Cumanus episode, Josephus makes a distinction that will become the stock assessment of Claudius by later Roman historiographers: Claudius was subject to his wives and freedmen in conducting all affairs of the state.[9] Regardless of whether the power struggle between the freedmen and Claudius's wife is formulaic at the time Josephus writes, it is significant to note the place of the Jews in this struggle: Agrippa II, and through him, the Jewish representatives, are aligned with Agrippina and not with the freedmen.

Moreover, by making Agrippina mediate before Claudius on Agrippa II's behalf, the text decenters the Jewish king. Agrippa II has access to the emperor, but only through the emperor's wife. This is a marked contrast to the account of the hearing in the *Jewish War* where Agrippina is not mentioned and Agrippa II takes center stage, presenting the case before the emperor and thus effecting the Jews' vindication.[10] The minimization of Agrippa II's role in the affair is in line with the general hostility toward him in *Antiquities* 20.[11]

Poppaea Sabina, Defender of the Jewish Temple's Sanctity

Josephus records two instances of Poppaea's benefaction on behalf of the Jews, one during the procuratorship of Festus (60–62 CE, *Ant.* 20.189–96), and one on the eve of the Jewish War (c. 64 CE, *Life* 13–16).[12]

The story in the *Antiquities*, in which Poppaea is said to be "God-fearing," begins with Agrippa II's decision to build an addition to his palace enabling him to "spy" on temple proceedings. Jerusalemites of high standing (τῶν Ἱεροσολυμιτῶν οἱ προὔχοντες) respond defiantly by erecting a wall in the temple to block Agrippa II's view. This construction brings Roman authorities into the dispute since the wall also obstructs the view of Roman guards supervising the temple from the western portico. Festus, the Roman procurator, shares Agrippa's indignation and orders the wall's demolition. The Jerusalemites respond that, since the wall is now an integral part of the temple, its preservation is of utmost importance. When a deputation consisting of ten Jerusalem notables, along with Ishmael the high priest and Helcias the temple treasurer, is sent to plead before the emperor, Josephus records the following resolution:

> Nero, after a full hearing, not only condoned what they had done, but also consented to leave the building as it was, showing favor to his wife Poppaea because she pleaded on behalf of the Jews—for she revered [the Jewish] God. She then gave orders for the ten to depart, but detained Helcias and Ishmael as hostages in her own house.[13] (*Ant.* 20.195)

> Νέρων δὲ διακούσας αὐτῶν οὐ μόνον συνέγνω περὶ τοῦ πραχθέντος, ἀλλὰ καὶ συνεχώρησεν ἐᾶν οὕτως τὴν οἰκοδομίαν, τῇ γυναικὶ Ποππαίᾳ, θεοσεβὴς γὰρ ἦν, ὑπὲρ τῶν Ἰουδαίων δεηθείσῃ χαριζόμενος, ἣ τοῖς μὲν δέκα προσέταξεν ἀπιέναι, τὸν δ᾽ Ἑλκίαν καὶ τὸν Ἰσμάηλον ὁμηρεύσοντας παρ᾽ ἑαυτῇ κατέσχεν.

The narrative explicitly ascribes religious motivation to Poppaea—θεοσεβὴς γὰρ ἦν. Scholars tend to read this ascription as an historically accurate reflection of Poppaea's motive and proceed to debate the degree of Poppaea's attachment to the Jewish religion connoted by the term θεοσεβής. The debate has generated a broad spectrum of interpretations, from the proposal that Poppaea was a full-fledged Jewish proselyte,[14] to the dismissal of her motive as trivial pagan superstition devoid of any specifically Jewish component.[15] Margaret Williams takes a middle course, noting, on the one hand, that it is unlikely that Josephus intends to cast Poppaea as a proselyte, because he uses different and more specific terminology to talk about proselytes elsewhere in his work; and, on the other hand, that when Josephus uses the word *theosebēs* he generally implies that the person was attached to the Jewish religion in some manner. I concur with Williams that it is best to read the text as scripting Poppaea with a pious attachment to Judaism somewhere between the two extremes of a proselyte's devotion and a pagan's nonspecific "superstition."[16]

Yet, the question remains: What is Josephus's rhetorical aim in assigning religious motive to the emperor's wife? Richard Horsley observes that Josephus has the tendency to "[avoid] the social-political aspects of certain figures' words or actions and [reduce] them to personal piety or morals."[17] This tendency is clearly in operation here, and its rhetorical effect is to mask the politically subversive implications of Poppaea's actions.[18] If one shifts attention away from Poppaea's piety and toward her politics, it becomes possible to see a striking political alignment. The Roman empress stands with the Jerusalemites against King Agrippa and the Roman procurator Festus, championing Jewish ancestral tradition in the face of Roman desire to police Jewish religious affairs in Jerusalem. In contrast to Poppaea's positive portrayal, King Agrippa II is cast even more negatively here than in the Cumanus affair as the flagrant violator of Jewish religious sensibilities. Poppaea defends the sovereignty of the Jerusalemites in matters of the temple even when the Jewish client king does not.[19]

Poppaea's Benefaction on Behalf of Imprisoned Priests

The story in *Life* 13–16 recounts Poppaea's benefaction on the eve of the Jewish war (64 CE) and implies that Poppaea was known as a likely supporter of Jewish causes. When Jewish priests are brought in chains to Rome, Josephus is part of the deputation sent to secure their deliverance. He explains that through his friendship with a Jewish actor under Nero's favor, he makes the acquaintance of Poppaea and immediately requests that she work to liberate the priests. He adds that in addition to receiving this favor (*euergesia*), he departs to his native home bearing large gifts from Poppaea.

Josephus again downplays the political—indeed, subversive—nature of this incident by stressing the piety of the priests ("even in affliction, they had not forgotten the pious practices of religion, and supported themselves on figs and nuts" [*Life* 14]), and by characterizing the charges against them as "slight and trifling" [*mikra kai hē tychousa aitia*] (*Life* 13). Shaye Cohen argues that here, as in the only other passage where Josephus uses this phrase (*Ant.* 20.215), it serves as a cover for revolutionary activities: "Priests were not sent to Rome to make their defense before the emperor for petty peculations nor, if they had been, would a young man soon to be in command of the revolutionary forces in Galilee have gone after them to help them."[20] Here, as in the incident concerning the Jerusalem temple wall, Josephus does not direct a spotlight on the subversive nature of Poppaea's actions. Nevertheless the narrative implies that Poppaea acts on behalf of Jewish nationalists and revolutionaries.

Domitia, Josephus's Benefactor

In addition to citing these instances in which imperial women come to the aid of Jews, Josephus includes himself as beneficiary of the empress Domitia. He concludes the *Life* with a statement that he has received protection and remuneration from Vespasian, Titus, and Domitian. He adds, "Moreover, Domitia, Caesar's wife, never ceased bestowing favors upon me" [*kai polla d' hē tou Kaisaros gynē Dometia dietelesen euergetousa me*] (*Life* 429). Her inclusion in this list suggests that the benefactions of the empress as well as the emperor were valued signs of the high standing that Josephus claimed for himself.

Other Noblewomen

Helena, Queen of Adiabene, Savior of the Jerusalemites (Ant. 20.17–53)

Josephus offers an elaborate account of how Helena, Queen of Adiabene and her royal family convert to Judaism in *Ant.* 20.17–39. The conversion itself is of central interest to scholars considering questions of Jewish mission in antiquity.[21] But it is important to note that Josephus heralds Helena as one who will be "famous forever" among the Jews not merely because she is a prestigious convert, but because she is a benefactor of the Jewish people. When Helena arrives in Jerusalem to make her thank-offering, she discovers that the city has been struck by famine and many are perishing. Through the queen's largess, she provides food for Jerusalem's needy citizens, saving them from starvation. Josephus ends this story with the acclamation, "She has thus left a very great name that will be famous forever among our whole people for her benefaction" [*kai megistēn autēs mnēmēn tēs eupoiias tautēs eis to pan hēmōn ethnos kataleloipe*] (*Ant.* 20.49–53, esp. 20.52).

The Duping of Fulvia, a Story of Benefaction Gone Wrong (Ant. 18.81–84)

No such fame is reserved for Fulvia in *Antiquities* 18, whose story I considered in the previous chapter. And yet, benefaction is integral to the plot of the duping of this high-standing matron. The Jewish merchants, whose intent is to swindle Fulvia, request from this convert to Judaism gifts of purple and gold for the temple in Jerusalem (*Ant.* 18.82). Her willingness to comply with this request for benefaction makes it possible for the merchants to carry out their dastardly deed.

The Saviors of Moses

Thermuthis, the Egyptian Pharaoh's Daughter (Ant. 2.224–43)

In his adaptation of the Moses story, Josephus amplifies the role of the Pharaoh's daughter, Thermuthis, beyond that of saving the babe from his papyrus basket in the Nile.[22] This is evident first in a tale of the infant Moses trampling on the Pharaoh's crown, which has parallels in rabbinic tradition.[23] In the midrashic version, the infant Moses takes the crown from the Pharaoh and places it on his head, signifying his future displacement of the Pharaoh. In Josephus's telling, the Pharaoh's daughter takes the initiative, having decided that Moses should be her father's successor:

> Now one day [Thermuthis] brought Moses to her father and showed him to him, and told him how she had been mindful for the succession [*hōs phrontiseie diadochēs*], were it God's will to grant her no child of her own [. . .] and she said, "I thought to make him my child and heir to your kingdom." Saying this, she laid the infant in her

father's arms; and he took and held him affectionately at his breast and, for the sake of his daughter [*charin tēs thugatros*], placed his diadem upon the child's head. (*Ant.* 2.232–33)

Subsequently, a sacred scribe rushes up to kill Moses because he portends Egyptian disaster, but Thermuthis rescues him from death by snatching him away (*Ant.* 2.234–36).[24]

Josephus also assigns the role of protector to Thermuthis in his narrative of Moses conquering Ethiopia on Egypt's behalf. In the version of this story preserved by the Hellenistic Jewish historian Artapanus, Moses is invited to join in the battle against the Ethiopians by a jealous Egyptian Pharaoh who hopes that Moses will be killed in battle. The Pharaoh's daughter plays no part in the episode. In Josephus's telling, before the Egyptian Pharaoh can call Moses to serve as general, he must first ask permission of Thermuthis. She grants it only after extracting a pledge from her father that he will not injure Moses:

The king urged his daughter give up Moses to serve as his general [in the battle with the Ethiopians]. And she, after her father had sworn to do him no injury, surrendered him, judging that great benefit would come of such an alliance, while reproaching the priests who, after having spoken of putting him to death as enemy,[25] were now not ashamed to seek his aid. Moses, summoned both by Thermuthis and by the king, gladly accepted the task. (*Ant.* 2.242–43)

Tharbis, the Ethiopian Princess (Ant. 2.252–53)

When Moses leads the Egyptians into battle against the Ethiopians, he is saved once again by the intercessions of a Gentile noblewoman (*Ant.* 2.252–53). Moses is able to conquer the Ethiopians because Tharbis, the daughter of the Ethiopian king, observes the brave Moses in battle, falls in love with him, and betrays the Ethiopians to Moses' army. As Martin Braun has shown, the motif of a woman betraying her native country to an invading power is a common one in antiquity, beginning with the Greek Scylla legend. It is associated with traditions of various national heroes in Hellenistic times, including Cyrus's involvement with Nanis (Persian), Titus Tatius's with Tarpeia (Roman), and Brennus's with Demonice (Celtic).[26] However, Josephus alters one essential feature of the motif. In all of the instances of this motif identified by Braun, the foreign woman who betrays her city to the commander of the invading force is in turn murdered by him, with the exception of the account in the *Antiquities*. Only in this version is the foreign noblewoman rewarded through marriage to the commander.

This dramatic alteration of a motif that generally ends in the death of the noblewoman can be accounted for in terms of the problem in the biblical text that this midrashic tale attempts to solve. The starting point for all legends of Moses in Ethiopia is the problematic biblical reference in Numbers 12:1, which reports that Moses had either an Ethiopian (LXX), or Cushite (HB) wife.[27] Josephus's story of Moses and the Ethiopian princess, therefore, must end in marriage rather than murder. It is nevertheless remarkable that in order to arrive at this marriage, Josephus chooses this particular apologetic/propagandistic motif and makes this radical adaptation of it.[28]

The Daughters of Reuel/Raguel *(Ant. 2.258–62; cf. LXX, Exod 2:16–21)*

Josephus's tendency to portray the Gentile noblewomen involved with Moses in a good light extends even to the finer details of his portrayal of this hero's encounter with the daughters of Reuel. In this narrative, it is Moses himself who is the initial benefactor. He has come upon the daughters of Reuel, "a priest held in high veneration by the people of his country," as they are watering their flocks. When adversarial shepherds approach the women, Moses beats them off. In these details, Josephus follows the biblical version of the story. But he alters the response of the seven daughters, so that rather than neglecting their benefactor, they meet his favor with proper gratitude and exercise a favor in return. Here is the biblical version, in which Reuel questions his daughters for neglecting to extend hospitality to Moses:

> When they came to Raguel their father he asked them, "Why have you come so quickly today?" And they said, "An Egyptian delivered us from the shepherds, and even drew water for us and watered our

sheep." And Raguel said to his daughters, "Where is he? Why have you left the man? Call him, that he may eat bread."[29] (LXX, Exod 2:18–20)

Here is Josephus's adaptation:

And they, after this beneficent act, went to their father, and, recounting the shepherds' insolence and the assistance which the stranger had given them, urged him not to let such charity go for naught or unrewarded. The father commended his children for their zeal for their benefactor and asked them to bring Moses before him to receive the gratitude that was his due. (*Ant.* 2.261)

The Contours of Josephus's Gentile Noblewoman

In a variety of literary forms, Josephus portrays a number of Gentile noblewomen, both in imperial and biblical times, as advocating Jewish causes with political savvy and financial generosity. More specifically, the benefactions of these women are always bestowed upon Jews or Jewish causes that Josephus himself favors. Antonia champions the cause of Agrippa I, whose character Josephus consistently lauds. Poppaea favors the cause of the Jerusalemites in their conflict with Agrippa II, whom Josephus criticizes in *Antiquities* 20. Often the intercessions of these women come in the middle of volatile political situations;[30] with few exceptions, the intercessions result in improved circumstances for the Jews.[31]

In the case of the imperial women, it is possible that perceptions of them held by his Roman contemporaries served to define the parameters of what Josephus does and does not say about them. The empress with arguably the worst reputation in Josephus's day, Messalina, described by his contemporary Juvenal as "the harlot Augusta" (*meretrix Augusta*) is not mentioned by Josephus.[32] Antonia's reputation as *univira*, a once and only once married woman, remained unscathed by the popular practice of imperial womanbashing. She receives Josephus's special attention as friend of Berenice and political ally and virtual stepmother of Agrippa.[33]

Although Josephus's silence about Messalina and praise of Antonia may reflect his alignment with Roman polarities of the worst and best imperial women, his narrative does not otherwise conform to negative Roman literary stereotypes. He does record the story of Agrippina's murder of her husband Claudius, an incident with multiple attestation in the sources,[34] but his qualification of the story with the phrase, "or so the story goes" [*kathaper ēn logos*] (*Ant.* 20.151), suggests that he doubts its veracity.[35] For Tacitus, Poppaea Sabina was "never sparing of her reputation, and drew no distinctions between husbands and adulterers: vulnerable neither to her own nor to others' passion, where material advantage offered, there she transferred her desires" (*Ann.* 13.45 [Jackson, LCL]). For Josephus, she was *theosebēs*.

A significant exception to this Josephan tendency to depict Gentile noblewomen in heroic postures is his portrait of Cleopatra, which conforms to Roman depictions of her as Antony's master and casts her as bloodthirsty predator seeking the throne of Judea.[36] Given the convergence of his Cleopatra portrait with Roman stereotypes of this most hated, foreign noblewoman, Josephus's depiction of the Egyptian princess Thermuthis as Moses' savior is particularly intriguing. This Egyptian princess of biblical times serves as a prototype for the Julio-Claudian women in his narrative, not for Cleopatra, her royal descendent.

The positive depictions of these Gentile noblewomen stand in stark contrast to the presentation of Jewish noblewomen in the *Antiquities*, including the biblical matriarchs and the women of the Hasmonean and Herodian dynasties. As Betsy Halpern Amaru has demonstrated, Josephus systematically alters stories about "problematic" biblical matriarchs to make them more chaste, more beautiful, and more dependent upon the men around them.[37] The contrast between Josephus's depiction of Jewish and Gentile noblewomen is clear in his adaptation of the biblical story of Moses. Although he is expanding the role of the Pharaoh's daughter in Moses' salvation, he diminishes the role of Moses' mother and sister. In the Bible it is Moses' mother who first conceals the infant and then arranges for the papyrus basket used to set him in the reeds; in the *Antiquities* the decision to do so is attributed to his father (Exod 2:3; *Ant.* 2.219). In rabbinic tradition, Miriam receives the dream predicting Moses' future greatness (Exod *Rab.* 1.22); in the *Antiquities* God sends the dream to Moses' father (*Ant.* 2.212–16).[38]

As for the Hasmonean and Herodian women, the *Antiquities* recognizes them as political figures who exercise a measure of power, but ridicules them for wielding power as women. As one example, the house of Queen Salome Alexandra is said to have been destined to fall "because of her desire for things unbecoming a woman" [*epithumia tōn mē prosēkontōn gynaiki*] (*Ant.* 13.431). Moreover, although Josephus will hold up tales of imperial women attempting to influence emperors as laudatory, such attempts made by a woman of the Herodian house are ridiculed. *Antiquities* 18.240–55 narrates how Agrippa I's sister Herodias, jealous at his success, nags her husband Herod to seek similar reward. When Herod does seek promotion from Gaius, both he and his wife are exiled. The summary sentence reads, "God visited this punishment on Herodias for her envy of her brother and on Herod for listening to a woman's frivolous chatter" [*gynaikeion koupho-logiōn*] (*Ant.* 18.255).[39]

The advocacy of most of these women on behalf of the Jews is best understood within the framework of a personal patronage system. Richard P. Saller has identified three distinguishing characteristics of a personal patronage relationship: (1) it involves the reciprocal exchange of goods and services; (2) as opposed to a commercial transaction in the marketplace, a personal relationship of some duration is required; and (3) these relationships are asymmetrical and not friendships between equals, since the two parties are of unequal status and offer different kinds of goods and services.[40] In many instances Josephus has provided readers with nearly perfect "textbook" cases of how patron-client systems operate.

Josephus does highlight on occasion a Gentile noblewoman's interest in the "religious" aspects of Judaism, but this attraction or conversion to the Jewish religion does not seem to be the necessary prerequisite for their willingness to help secure the rights of the Jewish community. Josephus claims that several offer such assistance without indicating that they engage in Jewish cultic practices.[41]

The Rhetoric of Womanly Influence

Several literary and epigraphic sources from the time of the late Republic and into the second century of the common era suggest that the women of elite Roman families wielded significant public and political influence. This phenomenon has been viewed as something of a paradox, since such sources contend with others portraying idealized Roman matrons as confined solely to domestic roles. Further, both Roman legislation and tradition formally excluded women from political participation.

As one example of the social construct of the ideal Roman matron as confined to domestic duties, consider the following epitaph from the late second century BCE:

> Friend, I have not much to say; stop and read it. This tomb, which is not fair, is for a fair woman. Her parents gave her the name Claudia. She loved her husband in her heart. She bore two sons, one of whom she left on earth, the other beneath it. She was pleasant to talk with, and she walked with grace. She kept the house and worked in wool. That is all. You may go.[42]

That Augustus employed this social construction as part of his propaganda is suggested by Suetonius, who notes Augustus had his daughter and granddaughters taught to spin wool (*Aug.* 64.2). The triteness of this stereotype of the ideal matron in some literary circles by the late first century is indicated by Juvenal's sixth satire, where it is included in a list of platitudes about what made the "good old days" so good: "In days of old, the wives of Latium were kept chaste by their humble fortunes. It was toil and brief slumbers that kept vice from polluting modest homes; hands chafed and hardened by Tuscan fleeces, Hannibal nearing the city, and husbands standing to arms at the Colline tower" (*Sat.* 6.287–91 [Ramsey, LCL]).[43] A consensus has emerged among scholars of women in antiquity that the ability of elite Greco-Roman women to carry out public duties in a staunchly patriarchal system infused with such domesticating portraits of women is due to a general blurring of boundaries between private and public affairs among the elite classes.[44] For example, Suzanne Dixon argues that ventures by Roman matrons of the republican period into the public sphere were necessary and permissible because these matrons were responsible for conducting family business; Riet Van Bremen attributes the increased prominence of civic patronage among elite women in Asia Minor to the Hellenistic system of euergetism which required all members of wealthy families, including women, to be paraded onto the public stage.

However, not unsurprisingly, the fluidity of this boundary concerning legitimate and illegitimate ventures by women into the public sphere provided many Roman writers with opportunities to accuse high-standing women of having transgressed appropriate public behavior. Tom Hillard, whose study focuses on the literary sources for women of the republican period, and Suzanne Fischler, whose study focuses on the imperial women of the Julio-Claudian dynasty, converge in their analyses of the rhetorical aims of negative portrayals of elite women with political influence.[45] Hillard begins by pointing out that most indications of women's political influence in the republican period derive from forensic and political oratory. He argues that in this context the allegation that a woman wielded political power was made primarily for the purposes of effeminizing the male who was purportedly under her influence. After reviewing the rhetorical context of several texts commonly read as evidence for powerful women of the Republic, including Clodia Metelli (Cicero's *Pro Caelio*), Sempronia (Sallust's *Bellum catalinae*), and Terentia (Plutarch's *Cicero*), he concludes:

(1) practically all such information [of women's political activity] is transmitted as allegation, which highlights the unsubstantiated nature of each claim, and the fact that an active political role for women was regarded as undesirable; and (2) the women concerned were politically irrelevant in that they were not the primary targets of this hostile material; rather, their alleged roles were a means of attacking the politically potent, that is, their male kinsfolk or associates.[46]

Fischler does not go so far as to suggest that the women she studies did not wield some measure of political power. She does concur, however, that the negative portrayals of imperial women aimed to insult the men with whom they are involved. Of most interest is her thesis about why these imperial women are so often subject to the slanderous pen. Drawing from Dixon's earlier argument that elite Roman women frequently engaged in public roles to conduct family business, Fischler argues that although this behavior may have been seen as sometimes permissible, in the case of the imperial family, whose "business" was running the state, this public role had unprecedented and threatening political implications:

The proximity of the imperial women to the functioning of the state lent new meaning to normal family activities and granted them the capacity for public acts of a new order. Furthermore, the access this apparently granted the women to the central authority within the Roman state was at odds with the constitutional settlements made between Augustus and the ruling classes at Rome in the early decades of the Principate, for only in a monarchy could women achieve such power within the state. As such . . . the position of the women was a source of tension, graphically revealing the contrast between Republican practice, in which women could never hold power within the state, and the new imperial order, which contained the threat that women might do so.[47]

Therefore, the staining of these women's characters by Roman satirists and historiographers was an anxious response to their unprecedented access to power, as well as a critique of the emperors who were their sons, husbands, or lovers.

As shown above, Josephus presents Gentile noblewomen as effective historical agents with great political acumen, neither constrained by the Roman propagandistic ideal of the virtuous matron as a homebound spinner of wool, nor condemned as transgressors of proper social roles. In analyzing his rhetorical aim in these portraits, it may be useful to consider hypothetically what he could have done instead. If he had decided that such a presentation offended the sensibilities of his audience, he could have easily modified this portrayal. Precedent for such a modification in the biblical paraphrase is found in the *Antiquities*, where he freely alters the narrative to make women from Jewish tradition more submissive. Or, he could have ignored them. It would have been easy for Josephus to have recorded imperial decisions concerning Jews without giving credit to the women involved, because imperial women's ability to change political outcomes depended ultimately on the emperors' goodwill. The decision about when to release Agrippa I from prison was Gaius's, not Antonia's; the emperor Claudius, not his wife Agrippina, had authority to rule in favor of the Jews over the Samaritans; and Nero, not Poppaea, rendered the decision permitting the temple wall to stand. Each of these stories could have moved forward without mentioning the women's intercessions.

The fact that accusing a man of succumbing to the influence of the women around him was a common rhetorical means of calling that man's character into question leads one to consider whether Josephus has similar rhetorical aims. By implying that Roman (and in the Moses cycle, Egyptian) male worthies are influenced by the women of their courts, is Josephus critiquing Roman (and Egyptian) rulers? This is clearly the case in his portrayal of Antony as slave to Cleopatra. Furthermore, his claim that Claudius, when hearing the case of the Jewish aristocrats held responsible for unrest in the province, is pulled in different directions by the advice of his freedmen and wife, could be read as faulting the emperor for having no will of his own.[48] And yet, in the majority of instances of Gentile noblewomen's intercessions discussed above, it does not seem best to read Josephus's rhetorical aim as denigrating Gentile noblemen. With few exceptions, the Gentile noblewomen who use their power to influence their men do so on behalf of Jews whom Josephus favors. It would be difficult to read these stories both as affirmation for these women's intercessions on behalf of the Jews and as insinuations against the men who succumb to womanly wiles. On the whole Josephus does not seem to be highlighting these Gentile women's actions as a critique of Gentile male character and rule.

Because these women wield influence for the good of Josephus's constituents, they have a positive rather than a negative rhetorical function within the narrative. Although she is working with texts having different rhetorical aims than the *Antiquities*, Kate Cooper has also explored the positive rhetorical function a woman may serve in narratives from antiquity.[49] Like Hillard and Fischler, Cooper recognizes the common rhetorical practice of citing a woman's influence as a way to critique a man's character. Cooper argues, however, that this rhetorical figure of womanly influence existed in a positive, as well as a negative, version:

> The negative version styled woman as a seductress, bent on tempting a man by private allurements to a betrayal of public duty. The positive version dwelt on a man's licit relationships with female family members, whose soothing charm would ideally restore him to order when he had strayed, and persuade him to hear the voice of reason. A man represented as being in harmony with his legitimate wife was thus symbolically anchored to duty and to the cause of the common good.[50]

As examples of these negative and positive versions of womanly influence, Cooper cites Plutarch's contrast between the influence of Cleopatra over Antony, with the potential influence of Antony's prospective bride, Octavia. Plutarch views Cleopatra's domination of Antony as emblematic of his utter lack of self-mastery (see, for example, *Anton*. 66.7). But Plutarch also suggests that another woman, Antony's legitimate bride, Octavia, has the potential to restore order to the Roman state: "Everybody tried to bring about this marriage [of Antony to Octavia]. For they hoped that Octavia, who, besides her great beauty, had intelligence and dignity, when united to Antony and beloved by him, as such a woman naturally must be, would restore harmony and be their complete salvation" (*Anton.* 31.3 [Perrin, LCL]). Josephus employs the figure of a Gentile (Roman) woman as one who provides a voice of reason to the men with whom she is involved. Because Josephus is a cultural outsider, writing out of concern for acceptability, his aims are different from Plutarch's. He does not employ the figure principally as a way to judge the man over whom the woman holds influence. Rather, he employs the figure as a way to argue that those on whose behalf the woman advocates are to be judged acceptable. Through these narratives, Josephus says, as the author of Acts will also say, "One of the proofs that we are a legitimate community is that Gentile noblewomen are our advocates."

Reconstructing Imperial Women's Benefaction on Behalf of the Jews

Finally in this chapter I move from tracing the rhetorical function of these gentile noblewomen to asking what the text may indicate about the historical phenomenon of imperial women's benefaction on behalf of the Jews. In light of Josephus's account, and the supporting sources to be discussed below, it does seem that imperial women did on occasion come to the aid of the Jews in their struggles with Rome because they had entered into personal patronage relations with members of the Jewish aristocracy.

The ease with which Josephus describes these incidents of imperial women's patronage suggests that he understands his portraits as verisimilitudinous. He does not offer extended justifications for these women's behavior, nor otherwise indicate that the exchanges between these women and their Jewish clients is something that his readers would view as extraordinary. Although Josephus undoubtedly exaggerates the extent of personal contact between Livia and Salome, or places Antonia in the right place at the right time to heighten the drama of the episode of Agrippa I's imprisonment, I argue that he draws his character portraits in the knowledge that such special relations between imperial *patrona* and Jewish client could and did exist.

Although Josephus is virtually the only source that claims personal patronage relations between imperial women and Jewish clients,[51] there are extra-Josephan sources that support the reliability of his general claim for special ties between the Herodian household and Antonia. Included in the second series of coins minted by King Agrippa I, for example, is one with a bust of Antonia on the obverse with the inscription ANTONIA ΣΕΒΑΣΤΟΥ.[52] Although they do not make reference specifically to the Herodian family, both Suetonius and Dio speak of aristocratic children of other royal houses being raised in the imperial household (Dio *Hist.* 51.16.1–2; *Aug.* 48). Such portraits suggest the plausibility of Josephus's explanation for ties among Berenice, Agrippa, and Antonia.

An inscription from Aphrodisias preserves a letter from Augustus to the people of the island of Samos providing insight into Livia's advocacy on behalf of the Samians. Because the relational dynamics between this imperial woman and a community from the eastern part of the empire are similar to those suggested by Josephus for his community, it serves as a useful comparison to Josephan passages discussed above. In response to their request for freedom, Augustus addresses the people of Samos:

> You yourselves can see that I have given the privilege of freedom to no people except the Aphrodisians, who took my side in the war and were captured by storm because of their devotion to us. For it is not right to give the favor of the greatest privilege of all at random and without cause. I am well-disposed to you and should like to do a favour to my wife who is active on your behalf [*kai bouloimēn an tē gynaiki mou hyper hymōn spoudazousē charizesthai*] but not to the point of breaking my custom. For I am not concerned for the money which you pay towards the tribute, but I am not willing to give the most highly prized privileges to anyone without good cause.[53]

Augustus indicates that Livia took on the cause of the Samian people and attempted to use her influence to convince Augustus to grant them a major political concession. These circumstances parallel Josephus's accounts of Agrippina's intervention on behalf of Agrippa II, Poppaea's advocacy on behalf of the Jerusalemites concerning the temple, and Poppaea's efforts to secure the liberation of captive Judean priests. Such patronage is consistent with the sources that suggest imperial women, especially those of the

Julio-Claudian period, often took on public roles and performed public benefactions.[54]

However, the presentation of imperial women in the *Antiquities* as unhesitating and loyal advocates is best read as an optimistic view of the workings of patron-client relationships, motivated by apologetic purposes. Josephus is attempting to secure good relations between himself and his own patrons in particular, and between Jews and Romans in general, by claiming precedent for those good relations. That the standing of Jewish clients before their patrons was much more precarious than Josephus will allow is poignantly revealed in a comparison of the "edicts of Claudius" concerning the rights of Jews in Alexandria and in "the rest of the world" preserved in *Antiquities* 19.280–91 with the letter of Claudius to the Alexandrians published from a papyrus in 1924.[55] Josephus credits Claudius's upholding of Jewish rights to the influence of his "friends," Kings Agrippa and Herod. Note especially the following portion of the second edict:

> Kings Agrippa and Herod, my dearest friends [*tōn philtatōn moi*], having petitioned me to permit the same privileges to be maintained for the Jews throughout the empire under the Romans as those in Alexandria enjoy, I very gladly consented, not merely in order to please those who petitioned me, but also because in my opinion the Jews deserve to obtain their request on account of their loyalty and friendship to the Romans [*dia tēn pros Rōmaious pistin kai philian*]. (*Ant.* 19.287–88)

Contrast the edicts preserved in *Antiquities* with the letter of Claudius to the Alexandrians. This letter addresses strife-torn relations between Jews and Alexandrians, first by urging Alexandrians to permit the Jews to exercise their traditional worship and observe their traditional customs. Then follows a stern address to the Jews, which includes no mention of long-standing loyalties or personal friendships, and ends with a threat of punishment for suspicious behavior:

> I bid the Jews not to busy themselves about anything beyond what they have held hitherto, and not henceforth, as if you and they lived in two cities, to send two embassies . . . but to profit by what they possess,

and enjoy in a city not their own [*en allotria polei*] an abundance of all good things; and not to introduce or invite Jews who sail down to Alexandria from Syria or Egypt, thus compelling me to conceive the greater suspicion; otherwise I will by all means take vengeance on them as fomenting a general plague for the whole world [*ei de mē, panta tropon autous epexeleusomai kathaper koinēn teina tēs oikoumenēs noson exegeirontas*].[56]

The difference in tone between these two documents is instructive for those reading Josephus's portraits of imperial women. Although imperial women may have occasionally interceded on behalf of their Jewish clients, it is implausible to imagine them on the whole as heroic defenders of Jewish aristocrats and Jewish nationalistic causes. In a way that Claudius's letter to the Alexandrians does not, Josephus's rhetorical portrayal of imperial women's benefaction masks the vulnerabilities and the relative powerlessness of those subject to Roman rule.

Now that the contours of "womanly influence" in Josephus's *Antiquities* have been established, it remains to set Josephus's work within a larger Greco-Roman framework. In the next chapter I identify the pattern of Gentile noblewomen benefactors in Luke's Acts, as well as in other Hellenistic Jewish sources. I will then argue that the rhetorical presentation of highstanding women benefactors in these literary sources is congruent with the historical phenomenon of noblewomen's benefaction in Greco-Roman antiquity.

3 "MORE THAN A FEW GREEK WOMEN OF HIGH STANDING"

"GOD-FEARING" NOBLEWOMEN IN ACTS

JOSEPHUS IS NOT the only apologetic historian attempting to link his community with Gentile noblewomen for positive rhetorical effect. The narrative tendencies in the *Antiquities* that I have identified in the previous chapter are replicated in Acts. The author of Acts, like Josephus, depicts the women from inside his community in subordinate and diminutive roles. But Luke, like Josephus, characterizes Gentile noblewomen differently. Their association with his community is not submerged in his narrative, but rather is highlighted as a prominent feature of Paul's missionary journeys.

Like Josephus, Luke has an apologetic rhetorical goal. The stated intention of the narrator in his preface to the Third Gospel is to write an orderly account of Christian beginnings so that his reader might recognize the movement's "surety" (*asphaleia*).[1] This initial intention is borne out in the rhetoric of Acts. To demonstrate this surety in Acts the author portrays the community of Christ believers as a model community, one with utopian communal practice, harmonious councils, a charismatic leader/philosopher with a gift for powerful oratory, converts and supporters from the upper classes, and respect for the law and social customs of Greco-Roman society.[2]

Because of the peculiar nature of the group for whom he is an advocate, Luke has a task before him that Josephus does not. He must demonstrate that even though the Christian assemblies are dominated primarily by Gentiles, and have abandoned most of the ancestral customs of the Jews, their adherents are not promoting an upstart religion. To the contrary, they are the true heirs of Israelite tradition. Thus, in his trial Paul emphasizes repeatedly that he is a Pharisee, that is, someone who has never transgressed the religion of his ancestors (22:3, 23:1–6, 24:14, 25:8, 26:4–5). References to the belief in the resurrection as Pharisaic (23:6, 23:8, 26:5–6) assure readers that this doctrine is not outlandish, but rather deeply embedded in tradition. The rejection of Christian teaching by the majority of Jews, and its embrace by many Gentiles, is not proof that the new movement has no claim to Israel's heritage. To the contrary, this phenomenon fulfills Israel's own prophetic scriptures (13:47, 28:26–28).[3]

The claim to be truly Israel has not only theological but also social and political implications; through it the author of Acts attempts to appropriate the social and legal privileges accorded to diaspora Jews for his own community.[4] This is especially clear in Acts 19, where the riot against "the Way" in Ephesus is resolved when the town clerk advises the crowd to leave the group alone (19:36–40).[5] As Robert Stoops has argued, the admonishment that adherents of the Way should not be hindered is Luke's attempt to secure a legal privilege of no small account: "That seemingly small request was an extraordinary privilege in the Roman world, one that had set the Jews apart from other groups."[6] This depiction of Christians as worthy of legal privilege is coupled with disparaging portraits of "the Jews" as instigators of violence and sedition. The peace-loving, solid citizen Paul stands in stark relief against "the Jews" who repeatedly incite mob riots. The story of Paul's Thessalonian mission in Acts 17 is typical in this regard. After Paul and Silas have converted devout Greeks and leading women there, the narrative continues: "But the Jews became jealous, and with the help of some ruffians in the marketplaces they formed a mob and set the city in an uproar. While they were searching for Paul and Silas to bring them out to the assembly, they attacked Jason's house. When they could not find them, they dragged Jason and some believers before the city authorities" (17:5–6).[7] Lawrence Wills has rightly noted that these portraits of incendiary Jews play into Roman fear of mob violence. Acts attempts to establish the legitimacy of Christians through calling into question the social conformity and worthiness of "the Jews."[8]

Women Within the Christian Community in Acts

In spite of the multiple indications that Acts is written to present Christianity as nonthreatening to Greco-Roman social order, scholars often credit its author with portraying women in innovative, liberating ways. In his two works, Luke includes more material about women than any other canonical author, and his stories about men are often coupled with stories about women. Thus Luke is read as a champion of women. Helmut Flender explains the frequency of male-female parallelism in Luke and Acts as Luke's expression "that man and woman stand together and side by side before God. They are equal in honor and grace; they are endowed with the same gifts and have the same responsibilities."[9] This argument, based as it is on the assumption that every mention of women is an affirmation of women, does not convince. The same can be said of Ben Witherington's discussion of women's roles in Acts. Noting that women in Acts are assigned roles such as "hostess," "deaconness," and "prophetess," he concludes that Luke's purpose here is to show "how the Gospel liberates and creates new possibilities for women."[10] Witherington does not ask, however, which roles are off-limits for women, nor does he consider the constraints that Acts places on women in the roles they do occupy.

A more convincing analysis is presented by those who recognize that women within the Christian community in Acts are depicted only in diminutive and socially acceptable roles. Turid Karlsen Seim, while identifying both positive and negative portrayals of women in Luke's gospel, has argued that Acts is dominated by masculinization and reduces women to invisibility. Elisabeth Schüssler Fiorenza notes that women in Acts are portrayed in general as disciples and converts rather than as leaders actively shaping the missionary movement.[11] A comparison of women's leadership in the Pauline epistles and in Acts supports these arguments. One looks in vain in this second Lukan work for mention of Phoebe of Cenchreae, or any other female "deacon" (*diakonos*) and "benefactor" (*prostatis*) of Paul (cf. Romans 16:1); for Junia, or any other female "apostle" (*apostolos*, cf. Romans 16:7); for Euodia and Syntyche of Philippi, or any other female "coworker" (*synergos*) of Paul (cf. Philippians 4:2–3). Although Prisca is mentioned in Acts, her first introduction is as Aquila's wife (18:2, cf. Romans 16:3 where she is mentioned before Aquila). She is granted a teaching role in Acts, but it is not a public one. Prisca and Aquila take Apollos aside (*proselabonto auton*) before instructing him (18:26). There is no indication that she might have "risked her neck for Paul's life" and earned the gratitude of all the churches of the Gentiles (cf. Romans 16:4). When viewed against the Pauline epistles, Acts does not appear to be championing the liberation of women, but instead working to diminish their contributions to early Christian communities. The circumscription of women's roles in the Christian community by Luke is consistent with his overarching concern to provide an orderly account of the movement's beginnings.

Prominent Women in Male-Female Pairings
Among Paul's Prospective Converts

Although Acts constricts the depiction and roles of women within the Christian community, it nevertheless highlights the role of prominent Gentile women whom Paul encounters in his missionary journeys. At three points in Paul's travels, prominent Gentile women are singled out in male-female pairs: (1) 13:50, where the Jews of Pisidian Antioch incite "God-fearing women of high standing and leaders of the city" [*tas sebomenas gynaikas tas euschēmonas kai tous prōtous tēs poleōs*], to oppose Paul and his teaching; (2) 17:4, where Paul converts some of the Jews of the Thessalonian synagogue, "as well as many of the God-fearing Greeks and more than a few of the leading women" [*tōn te sebomenōn Hellēnōn plēthos polu, gynaikōn te tōn prōtōn ouk oligai*]; (3) 17:12, where Paul and Silas convert Jews in Beroea, along with "more than a few Greek women of high standing as well as men" [*tōn Hellēnidōn gynaikōn tōn euschēmonōn kai andrōn ouk oligoi*].[12]

These three passages are commonly categorized with other male-female pairings in Acts, but they differ from the formulaic division of a group by gender that occurs in the account of the Christian movement preceding Paul's Gentile mission. In the story of church activity before the Pauline mission, the occasional division of a group by gender is expressed through the simple formula, "men and women," [*andres te kai gynaikes*] (5:14, 8:3, 8:12, 9:2, and 22:4).[13] This formula appears three times as a description of those already believing and twice as a description of those converting to the movement. Once Paul's missionary journeys begin, however, the division of a group by gender occurs only in the context of conversion to Christ belief or, in the case of Pisidian Antioch, resistance to Paul's message.[14] The women in Pisidian Antioch, Thessalonica, and Beroea all receive designations of high status through the use of the modifiers *euschēmōn* and *prōtos*. Twice, this high status designation is given only to the women of the male-female pair (17:4, 17:12). In 13:50 and 17:12, the women precede the men in the pairing. This prominence is granted to the women, at least in 13:50, without reference to their fathers or husbands.[15]

Locating the Prominent Women Among the "God-fearers"[16]

In his well-known essay, "The Disappearance of the 'God-fearers,'" A. Thomas Kraabel argues that the narrative in the second third of Acts (Chapters 9–19) charts the progress of salvation from the Jews to the Gentiles via an intermediary group of "God-fearers."[17] Kraabel has provoked much controversy in his further argument that "God-fearers" are no more than a literary invention of Luke and that no corresponding class actually existed in history. I will return to this aspect of Kraabel's argument in my discussion of Acts and historical reconstruction. Here I consider Kraabel's view of how "God-fearers" function at the level of the narrative in order to situate the prominent women in Acts with respect to this much-disputed category.

According to Kraabel, Cornelius, twice designated as *phoboumenos ton theon* (10:2, 10:22), is the archetypal "God-fearer." He is a well-placed Roman citizen, zealous in his devotion to prayer, and generous in his benefaction to the Jewish people. Luke depicts his conversion to Christianity with dramatic detail. Peter's decision to eat at a table with him and his defense of his baptism serve to legitimate Cornelius's entry into Christian fellowship. Although subsequent references to "God-fearers" are not embedded in narratives of such length and detail, they are nevertheless to be read in light of the Cornelius story. Shortly after the resolution of the Cornelius incident, Paul begins his missionary journeys. In his synagogue visits, Paul addresses both Jews and "God-fearers." Although he makes successful conversion among the former only on rare occasions, he has much success among the latter.

In order to develop his thesis, Kraabel assumes that the participles *phoboumenos/oi* and *sebomenos/oi* in Acts always signify this class of "God-fearers."[18] In so doing, however, Kraabel has presumed what Kirsopp Lake questioned more than fifty years ago, namely, whether in every instance in Acts these participles do function in this way.[19] According to Lake, this terminology in Acts is not technical or quasi-technical terminology for "God-fearers." Rather, these terms are vague indicators of piety used for both Jews and Gentiles. Only in a few instances does Lake allow that Acts has in view a class of pious persons distinct from Jews in the synagogue. He argues that in most cases in which the terminology is used in Acts it is impossible to determine whether those so described are Jewish or Gentile. Max Wilcox, in an even more skeptical view, argues that in only one instance can *sebomenos/oi* be clearly understood as a reference to a group of devout persons distinct from Jews (17:4), and that even Cornelius should not be understood as belonging to a class of "God-fearers."[20]

If Lake's and Wilcox's objections concerning the use of *phoboumenos/oi* and *sebomenos/oi* in Acts are valid, the result is a more radical "disappearance of the 'God-fearers'" than Kraabel himself imagined. Because my argument that the prominent women Paul encounters in his missionary journeys are Gentiles builds on Kraabel's work, I will entertain their objections here. In Luke's rhetorical strategy, do *phoboumenos/oi* and *sebomenos/oi* indicate Gentile synagogue affiliates, or are they such vague designators that, unless the context otherwise indicates, it is impossible to decide?

Luke 1:50: God's mercy is for *those who fear him* [*tois phoboumenois auton*] from generation to generation.

For Wilcox, this verse from the Magnificat is the strongest indication that *phoboumenos/oi* is not an exclusive signifier of Gentile synagogue affiliates. Since, in his view, this reference is to the pious of Israel, further uses of *phoboumenos/oi* in the story of Cornelius's conversion and Paul's synagogue preaching cannot be understood as references to an exclusively Gentile piety.[21] The single use of this term in a hymn adapted from the Septuagint and sung by a character in the first of Luke's works, however, need not bear the same force as its repeated use by the (omniscient) narrator in the second. Moreover, given that prophecies in Luke and Acts are replete with irony concerning the status of Jews and Gentiles in salvation history, it may be best to understand *tois phoboumenois auton* not as a clear referent to the pious of Israel, but as early and ironic intimation of the transfer of grace from the Jews to the "God-fearing" Gentiles.[22]

Acts 13:43a: After the meeting in the synagogue broke up, many Jews and *worshipping proselytes* [*tōn sebomenōn prosēlytōn*] followed Paul and Barnabas.

Lake cites this passage as proof that *sebomenos* in Acts is not exclusively used for non-Jews, since it is paired here with *prosēlytos*, which is generally understood as a technical term for Jewish converts.[23] Assuming that Luke understands proselytes as those fully incorporated into the Jewish community through conversion, several commentators see this verse as an obstacle to understanding *sebomenos* as an exclusively Gentile referent. They argue that its presence here is best explained either as a redactor's interpolation or a Lukan mistake.[24] As Jack Sanders has pointed out, however, it is not necessary to posit a rigid distinction between proselytes and other gentile synagogue affiliates in Acts. Both proselytes and other Gentile synagogue affiliates belong to the periphery through which the salvation of God passes in the narrative method employed in Acts. In this view the phrase *sebomenos prosēlytos* is not the clear indication that *sebomenos/oi* is used of Jews as well as Gentiles, but rather is another instance of the use of the term for those not fully within the Jewish fold.[25]

Before moving to a consideration of passages where the participles *phoboumenos/oi* and *sebomenos/oi* seem to indicate "God-fearers" in the text, I point out that a pattern of Paul encountering two groups in the synagogue, both Jews and "God-fearers," can be established without relying exclusively on these terms. In Iconium (14:1), Thessalonica (17:4), Beroea (17:12), and Corinth (18:4), Paul directs his synagogue message to both Ioudaioi and Hellēnes. The Hellēnes are not a subset of the Ioudaioi, but are instead a distinct group of "Greeks," Gentiles who attend the synagogue.[26]

In some instances it is clear that those designated as *phoboumenos/oi* and *sebomenos/oi* belong to this second, non-Jewish group of synagogue affiliates. Among these one may count Cornelius, the pious Gentile centurion who generously gives alms to the people of Israel and who prays constantly (10:2, 10:22). Peter's use of the term *phoboumenos/oi* in his speech given after his encounter with Cornelius is also a reference to those whom Cornelius typifies (10:35).[27] Furthermore, in Acts 17:4, converts from the synagogue in Thessalonica include Ioudaioi and *sebomenoi* Hellēnes. Because Hellēnes are distinct from Ioudaioi, this is a clear instance in which *sebomenoi* designates this second, non-Jewish group. In Acts 17:17, Paul argues in Athens in the synagogue with *tois Ioudaiois kai tois sebomenois*. Because the article is used with *sebomenois*, it is difficult to argue that there is a hendiadys here.[28] Like the Hellēnes in other cities, the *sebomenoi* in Athens are a group worshipping in the synagogue distinct from the Ioudaioi.

Since it is common for Paul to encounter both Jews and "God-fearers" in the synagogue, and since there are clear instances in which the non-Jewish group is designated with *phoboumenos/oi* or *sebomenos/oi*, the question remains whether to read other instances of this terminology as part of the same pattern. Kraabel and the scholars who agree with him presume such a pattern exists in Luke's narrative method. Lake and Wilcox, who analyze each instance of the term without considering the larger patterns and narrative themes in Luke, do not. Luke's penchant for patterns and his weighting of the narrative with symbolic language stand in sharp relief against Lake's and Wilcox's neglect of larger literary themes in Acts.

These two scholars equivocate about whether Paul's synagogue address in Pisidian Antioch to "you Israelites and you who fear God" [*andres Israēlitai kai hoi phoboumena ton theon*] (13:16), and to "My brothers, descendents of Abraham and those who fear God" [*andres adelphoi huioi genous Abraam kai hoi en hymin phoboumenoi ton theon*] (13:26), are addresses to Israelites alone, or to two groups in the synagogue. For those who recognize the "two group" pattern in Acts, the latter is the better reading.

Reading *phoboumenos/oi* and *sebomenos/oi* as specific to this class of Gentile synagogue affiliates grants a rich symbolic import to the text, but a reading that equivocates about this terminology does not. For example, in Acts 18:7, Paul leaves the synagogue and goes to the house of Titius Justus, a worshipper of God (*sebomenos ton theon*). Although this transition occurs in Corinth immediately after Paul is rejected by the Jews and has pronounced that he is going to the Gentiles (cf. 13:46), Wilcox argues that it is impossible to establish that Titius Justus is not Jewish. (That Paul does not totally abandon the Jews in Corinth, in spite of his pronouncement to go to the Gentiles, is indicated in the next verse, 18:8, where Crispus, "the head of the synagogue" [*ho archisynagōgos*] converts along with his household.[29]) If *sebomenos ton theon* is not read as signifying a status other than Jewish, however, it is difficult to explain why Paul, having first taken up residence with the Jews Aquila and Priscilla in Corinth, announces his "going to the Gentiles," only to move to another Jewish household. If one understands the phrase as designating a "God-fearer," then Paul's otherwise inexplicable departure from the home of Aquila and Priscilla becomes part of the narrative movement in which Paul transfers the mission's base from the household of Jews to that of pious Gentile synagogue affiliates.[30] Acts 16:14 describes "a certain woman named Lydia, a dealer in purple cloth from the city of Thyatira and a worshipper of God" [*tis gynē onomati Lydia, porphoropōlis poleōs Thyateirōn sebomenē ton theon*]. Here is another instance where some scholars have argued that Lydia may be a pious Jew and not a "God-fearer" since the only indication that she is a Gentile synagogue affiliate is the disputed phrase *sebomenos ton theon*. However, as in the case of Titius Justus, if Lydia is a Jew, the text has little symbolic weight. If she is Jewish, then this pericope is the longest narrative devoted to the conversion of a Jew in a section of Acts that is otherwise charting the transfer of Paul's missionary base from Jew to Gentile. As a "God-fearer," however, Lydia becomes the Cornelius of Paul's missionary phase in Macedonia. One can recognize her story along with Cornelius's as a male-female pair of significant Gentile converts. By moving into her house, Paul, like Peter before him, enters into fellowship with a prominent Gentile.[31] As a pious Gentile turned Christian convert, Lydia's story illustrates the dramatic disintegration of boundaries integral to the success of Paul's missionary journey.[32]

The arguments of Lake and Wilcox about reading the participles *phoboumenos/oi* and *sebomenos/oi* in Acts as indeterminate rather than as exclusive designations for a class of "God-fearers," therefore, do not provide the most convincing reading of the text. This is so particularly because these scholars focus on each specific instance of the terminology in isolation, while neglecting the broader narrative patterns of Acts. I hold, with Kraabel, that Luke does manipulate this class of "God-fearers" in his narrative to chart a deliberate progression of salvation history from Jews to Gentiles via this intermediary group.

In addition to the story of the "God-fearing" Lydia, there are three passages concerning prominent women encountered by Paul. I argue that these women too are numbered among the "God-fearers" of Acts. First, according to Acts 13:50, "The Jews stirred up the 'God-fearing' women of high standing and the leaders of the city" [*hoi de Ioudaioi parōtrynan tas sebomenas gynaikas tas euschēmonas kai tous prōtous tēs poleōs*]. Because participial forms of *sebomenos/oi* in Acts designate "God-fearers," these high-standing women in Pisidian Antioch should be considered as part of this class. Furthermore, it is difficult to understand these women as Jews themselves, because they are in this passage distinguished from "the Jews" who encourage their resistance.[33]

The second passage is Acts 17:4, "Some of [the Jews] were persuaded and joined Paul and Silas, as did a great many of the 'God-fearing' Greeks and more than a few of the leading women" [*kai tines ex autōn epeisthēsan kai proseklērōthēsan tō Paulō kai tō Sila, tōn te sebomenōn Hellēnōn plēthos polu, gynaikōn te tōn prōtōn ouk oligai*]. These noblewomen are affiliated in some way with the Thessalonian synagogue, for their conversion follows on Paul's preaching there. The text is more ambiguous concerning whether the women are Jewish or Gentile synagogue affiliates. Understanding them as Gentiles fits well with the male-female parallelism in Acts. It is easier to understand their status as parallel to the "God-fearing Greeks" than to view them as a subset of the Jews whose conversion is recorded in the first line of the verse. Because the women in the third passage, Acts 17:12, are designated as Hellēnides, the status of these women as Gentile synagogue affiliates is unambiguous: "Many of them therefore believed, including more than a few Greek women of high standing as well as men" [*polloi men oun ex autōn episteusan kai tōn Hellēnidōn gynaikōn tōn euschēmonōn kai andrōn ouk oligoi*].

In the narrative of Paul's missionary journeys, Lawrence Wills has identified an important organizing principle, "a repeating cycle of three dramatic moments: positive missionary activity, opposition and constriction, and release and expansion."[34] Although there is some variation in this cycle of events, it is typically fleshed out in the following way: (1) Paul preaches in the synagogue, and successfully wins converts; (2) opposition arises from the Jews who instigate disorderly conduct among the crowds; (3) Paul is forced to leave town, but wins even more converts in the course of new missionary activity.

In view of Kraabel's outline of the progression of salvation in Acts, it is no surprise to find that most often "God-fearers" are mentioned in this first dramatic moment, as prominent among those with whom Paul achieves success (13:43, 14:1, 17:4, 17:12, 18:4). The high-standing women of Thessalonica and Beroea are included among these converts (17:4, 17:12). The conversion of these "God-fearers" sparks the jealous and incendiary reaction of "the Jews."

The exception to the place of "God-fearers" in this cycle of three dramatic moments occurs at 13:50, with the high-standing, "God-fearing" women of Pisidian Antioch. Only here are "God-fearers" singled out not as converts of Paul, but as those whom "the Jews" incite in opposition to the mission. It is not the case, therefore, that all prominent "God-fearing" women are depicted as converting to Christianity. This has implications for historical reconstruction to which I shall return.

The Prominent Gentile Woman as Hellenistic Jewish Topos

In Chapter 2 I showed how Josephus frequently ascribes to prominent Gentile women the role of benefactor to the Jews. Assuming this role are many women of imperial times, including several women of the imperial household, Helena the Queen of Adiabene, and Fulvia (although, of course, in Fulvia's case the story is of benefaction "gone wrong"). This topos also figures in his version of the Moses narrative.

The highlighting of prominent Gentile women is not a Josephan idiosyncrasy, but rather a common topos of Jewish literature. Daniel Schwartz, a leading contemporary source critic of Josephus, argues that Josephus has copied the passages in which Antonia aids Agrippa I (*Ant.* 18.164–67, 18.179–86, 18.202–4) from an earlier Jewish novel. In Schwartz's view the source for the story in which Poppaea comes to the aid of the Jerusalemites in their struggle against Festus and Agrippa II (*Ant.* 20.189–96) is probably a Jerusalemite priest. If Schwartz is correct, then multiple authors, and not Josephus alone, are responsible for narratives of imperial women coming to the aid of Jews in the *Antiquities*.[35]

Tannaitic sources preserve stories of a prominent foreign royal woman, Queen Helena, devoting herself to Jewish practices and benefaction to the temple.[36] A passage from the *Acts of Hermaiscus* also narrates the intercessions of an imperial woman, Plotina, wife of Trajan, on behalf of the Jews. Although this work is not part of a tradition that views her intercession positively, it is best explained as a response to this tradition.[37] Further, in the *Acts of Pilate* there is an indication that the topos of the prominent foreign woman affiliating with the Jews was known among Christians. After hearing of his wife's dream concerning Jesus (cf. Mt. 27:19), Pilate summons the Jews and says to them, "You know that my wife fears God [*theosebēs estin*] and favors rather the customs of the Jews with you" [*kai mallon ioudaizei syn hymin*].[38]

Luke's highlighting of prominent Gentile women affiliated with Judaism in Acts 13:50, 16:11–40, 17:4, and 17:12 is an appropriation of this topos. The involvement of prominent Gentile women with Christian communities in Acts is similar to Josephus's claim that Queen Helena, Poppaea Sabina, and Fulvia expressed interest in the Jewish religion and acted as benefactors.

Traces of Luke's appropriation of this motif are not limited to stories of women religious converts and sympathizers. In light of Josephus's noting several benefactions extended by high-standing women who have no expressed interest in religious aspects of Judaism, it is worthy of note that in Acts, Berenice (25:13, 25:23, 26:30) and Drusilla (24:24), although not converting to Christianity, nevertheless play a role in legitimizing the new religion by hearing the Apostle Paul's defense of Christianity. Strikingly, as Josephus highlights the role of the Pharaoh's daughter in the *Antiquities*, the only woman from biblical history who is mentioned in Acts is not from the people Israel, but is this same Pharaoh's daughter. In Acts 7:21, in Stephen's recitation of salvation history, this prominent Egyptian woman is credited for adopting the infant Moses and raising him as a son. Finally, like Josephus, who underscores the role of the prominent Gentile women in his narrative while simultaneously diminishing or ridiculing the role of Jewish women, Luke also indicates the prominence of Gentile women while playing down in general the contributions of women already within the Christian community.[39]

The Prominent Gentile Woman and the Rhetoric of Apologetics

At first glance, the topos I have just identified may seem to be at cross-purposes with the "rhetoric of surety," the concern of Acts and Josephus to depict their respective communities as unthreatening to Roman order, because it conflicts with the commonly recognized topos in antiquity that condemns the participation of Greco-Roman women in "foreign" cults. I have already spoken of Juvenal's contempt for religions foreign to Rome as preying on gullible women. In his sixth satire, Judaism is doubly denigrated since it not only appeals to, but is also propagated by, a woman (*Sat.* 6.542–47). The well-known exhortation of Plutarch on wifely religious practice is often cited as reflecting Greco-Roman sensibilities concerning "foreign" religions:

> A wife should not make friends of her own, but rather enjoy her husband's friends in common with him. The gods are the first and most important friends. Therefore it is fitting for a wife to worship and know only the gods that her husband believes in, and to shut the front door tightly upon all strange rituals and outlandish superstitions. For with no god do stealthy and secret rites performed by a woman find any favour.[40] (*Conj. praec.* 140D)

Working from general proscriptions like Plutarch's, along with hostile texts aimed specifically at the Isis, Dionysos, and Jewish religions, David Balch argues that these religions foreign to Rome were despised primarily because of their appeal among women of the upper classes.[41] An upper-class woman's affiliation with these religions was suspect because it potentially positioned her outside of the religious customs of her *pater familias.*

Josephus and Luke undoubtedly were aware of this fusion of sexual and religious, household and state disorder in invective toward religions nontraditional to Rome, including Judaism.[42] But if cultural disapproval of all women's participation in "foreign" religions was unvarying, then these two apologists would seem to be needlessly inviting such invective by advertising the association of prominent Gentile noblewomen with their respective communities. Given the sentiment typified in Juvenal or Plutarch concerning women and "foreign" rites, and given the concerns of Acts and Josephus for cultural acceptability, why do they depict the Gentile women who patronize, and sometimes affiliate with, their respective communities?[43]

The answer to this question cannot be that Acts and Josephus simply abandon their apologetic concerns to record the participation of prominent women in their communities. I have argued hypothetically that if Josephus had wanted to modify, or even omit, depictions of high-standing women, he could have done so without sacrificing the forward movement of his narrative. The same could be said of Luke. The repeated return to this topos in these two works is an indication that the prominent Gentile woman associated with a minority community could serve a positive rhetorical function. However strong the sentiment ridiculing Gentile women's involvement in "foreign" religions was, it stands in tension with the view that such involvement was acceptable. I shall elaborate this argument further in Chapter 4. Here I suggest that a partial explanation for the rhetorical presentation of Gentile noblewomen in Josephus and Luke lies in the historical phenomenon of elite women's benefaction. Through highlighting Gentile noblewomen's support for their communities, these authors may be promoting the understanding of their respective communities not so much as "foreign cults" but as political communities modeled to some extent on the Greek city or collegia.[44] In civic society of the eastern provinces, as well as in Rome itself, the phenomenon of public benefactions by prominent women has long been recognized.[45]

Although a few sources suggesting prominent women's involvement in public benefaction date to the late Hellenistic period, the number of extant sources suggesting such benefaction increases dramatically beginning in the first century CE. Riet van Bremen has catalogued and analyzed hundreds of such sources for the Greek East in the Roman period.[46] Scholars concur that this phenomenon owes largely to the fact that the blurring of the public/private distinction among wealthy families required the display of their women on the public stage. One example of the increased acceptance and promotion of prominent women's public benefaction is a set of inscriptions from the beginning of the second century CE commemorating a Plancia Magna of Perge for her renovation of a city gate. Shortly after this renovation, similar types of benefaction appear by prominent women of Perge's neighboring cities, suggesting that intercity rivalry also contributed to women's public involvement.[47]

An important synagogue inscription from Acmonia indicates that the Jewish community within this city both welcomed and freely advertised the public benefactions of the city's leading women on their behalf. Here Julia Severa is acknowledged as donor of the Acmonian synagogue building:

> The building was erected by Julia Severa; P(ublius) Tyrronios Klados, the head-for-life of the synagogue, and Lucius, son of Lucius, head of the synagogue, and Publius Zotikos, archon, restored it with their own funds and with the money which had been deposited, and they donated the murals for the walls and the ceiling, and they reinforced the windows and made all the rest of the ornamentation, and the syn-

agogue honored them with a gilded shield on account of their virtuous behavior, solicitude and zeal for the synagogue.[48]

Julia Severa belonged to a prominent Acmonian family and was active in the 50s and 60s of the first century CE. The inscription does not indicate the precise nature of Julia Severa's affiliation with Judaism. Other inscriptions from the city, however, reveal that her ties to the Jewish community did not prevent her from holding other civic and religious offices, because she is honored as high priestess of the imperial cult, *agōnothetis* (a judge of the games), and eponymous magistrate.[49] Because the synagogue inscription commemorates a renovation of the building, it must be dated at least as late as the end of first century CE. In their acknowledgment of this benefaction from a prestigious Gentile woman, it is evident that class has "trumped" gender. The Jews of Acmonia proclaim publicly the association of Julia Severa with their community.

The acceptability of prominent women's public benefaction helps to account for the place of prominent foreign women in Josephus and Acts. The role of independent high-standing Gentile women in the *Antiquities* and Acts undoubtedly would have been greeted with scorn by Juvenal. Such roles do not conform to Plutarch's opinion that a wife devote herself solely to the gods of her husband. And yet, it would have been unobjectionable to those who publicly acclaimed the civic benefaction of a Livia, or a Plancia Magna, or a Julia Severa. Josephus's narrative reflects affirmation of the public role of imperial women, as Luke's narrative reflects affirmation of the public position of prominent women in the provinces.

The volatility of this apologetic topos of elite noblewoman as benefactor to the Jews is indicated by its function in the text roughly contemporary to Acts and the *Antiquities*, the *Acts of Hermaiscus*.[50] This piece of Alexandrian propaganda is a polemic against both the Alexandrian Jewish community and the Roman Empire. As propaganda fusing civic and religious concerns, its purpose is comparable to both the *Antiquities* and the Acts. According to it, representatives of both Jewish and Alexandrian parties travel to Rome to settle a dispute, "each party carrying its own gods" (lines 17–18). At the close of the disputation, the bust of Serapis carried by the Alexandrians breaks into a sweat, apparently in confirmation of the righteousness of the Alexandrian cause (lines 50–53).[51] In this mix of religious and civic propaganda, the Roman noblewoman figures as a means of slandering the Alexandrians' Roman and Jewish opponents. According to the narrative, Plotina, Trajan's wife, holds much sway over the Roman senators and the emperor himself. Plotina approaches the senators in the court room, "in order that they might oppose the Alexandrians and support the Jews" (lines 26–28). Furthermore, Trajan is said to greet the Jews most cordially when arriving to hear the case, "having already been won over by Plotina" (lines 28–32).

This portrayal of Plotina calls to mind depictions of Poppaea Sabina and Agrippina in the *Antiquities*. In all three instances, the imperial wife's intercessions before the emperor on the Jews' behalf occur in the context of a legal dispute with a third party. But the apologetic effects of the incidents in the *Antiquities* and the *Acts of Hermaiscus* mirror each other inversely. Josephus advertises the influence of Agrippina and Poppaea on behalf of the Jews as a positive indicator of the relationship between these imperial women and the Jewish community. The *Acts of Hermaiscus* also advertises this influential link of the imperial wife and the Jewish community, but as a means of insulting both the emperor and the Jews of Alexandria.[52]

Rhetoric and Reality: Historical Reconstruction and Prominent Female "God-Fearers" in Acts

Having outlined the overarching apologetic aim of Acts, and the specific rhetorical function of the passages highlighting prominent Gentile women affiliated with the synagogue, I turn now to a reconstruction of the historical situation that Acts addresses. This reconstruction begins with the premise that "God-fearers" are not merely a fiction of Luke, but did actually exist in history. In spite of the value of Kraabel's arguments concerning narrative movement in Acts, he is simply wrong on this point. There are ample indications for the historical existence of Gentiles who affiliated with synagogues, or otherwise expressed interest in Jewish religious practices. Scholars writing to refute Kraabel's claim point to several literary sources that he either ignores or minimizes and extend the terminological exploration beyond the participles *phoboumenos/oi* and *sebomenos/oi*.[53] No small amount of support for the theorization of a class of "God-fearers" in antiquity comes from the now-famous Aphrodisias inscription in which such a group, distinct from Jews and proselytes, is recognized.[54]

Moreover, Gentile women, as well as men, became "God-fearers." Scholars who understand the inscriptional reference, *theosebēs*, and its Latin equivalent, *metuens*, as designations for "God-fearers" argue that women numbered prominently among this class, for approximately 80 percent of those so designated in epigraphic sources are women.[55] This means of identifying "God-fearers," however, has been rightly questioned; it is impossible to establish that these were technical terms, always used for Gentile synagogue affiliates, in epigraphic sources.[56] Although the nature of the epigraphic sources is indeterminate, it is reasonable to theorize that women were included among the class of Gentiles affiliated with the synagogue in view of social-historical considerations. Epigraphic sources indicate that Gentile women became proselytes, a commitment to Judaism more complete than the affiliation of a "God-fearer." It is likely that many Gentile women attracted to Judaism could not (or did not wish to) make full conversions, due to restrictions and responsibilities placed upon them by their familial and social ties. For them, a looser affiliation would have been more permissible.[57]

It is not inconceivable that some female "God-fearers" were of relatively high social standing, as Luke suggests in Acts. Epigraphic sources suggest that at least some "God-fearers" were drawn from the upper classes.[58] Among the women of wealth whom some scholars view as "God-fearers" are Capitolina, a woman described as *theosebēs* in an inscription commemorating her donation to the synagogue in Tralles; and Tation, a synagogue donor from Phocaea, Ionia.[59] But Luke's focus on wealthy "God-fearers" should not be read as an indication that interest in Judaism was merely a matter for the upper classes in the provinces. I have suggested that Josephus's focus on the matron Fulvia as a convert to Judaism and his "crucifixion" of the freedwoman Ida are a means of turning attention away from women of lower classes who participated in and helped to shape Jewish religious practice. The same phenomenon will also be seen in Acts 16, where Lydia, the prominent merchant and convert to Christianity, is juxtaposed with a slave girl representing an inferior god. Luke's focus on the upper classes is less a *reflection* of reality than a *deflection* from less-esteemed converts and sympathizers.

Although Kraabel's argument questioning the existence of "God-fearers" cannot stand, he is right to decry historical reconstructions of early Christianity that replicate Luke's apologetical claim that "God-fearers" turned en masse from Judaism to Christianity.[60] The difficulties of reading Acts's depiction of the "God-fearers"' immediate and near-total abandonment of Judaism for Christianity as reflecting a historical phenomenon are many. For one, this description of how the Pauline mission spread does not concur with the history of Christian expansion reconstructed from Paul's letters. As Wayne Meeks has noted, the pattern in Acts of beginning in the synagogue with an address to Jews and "God-fearers" does not concur with Paul's own declaration that he is a missionary primarily, if not exclusively, among the Gentiles.[61] Paul gives no indication that he has presented his gospel before these two groups of synagogue adherents, Jews and "God-fearers"; indeed, nowhere in his letters does he refer to synagogue preaching. A comparison of the description of the Christian mission in Thessalonica in Acts (17:1–9) and Paul's first letter to the Thessalonians provides one example of the incongruities between these two sources. Acts designates the converts of Thessalonica as Jews and "God-fearers"; but Paul's letter suggests that Thessalonian Christians converted directly from paganism (1 Thess 1:9).[62]

Furthermore, several sources indicating the interest of Gentiles—including Gentile *Christians*—in Jewish religious practices are dated well beyond the completion of Acts. Consider, for example, the hostile reaction against both Gentile Christian converts to Judaism and Gentile Christian Judaizers among the church fathers. Writing in the second century CE, Justin Martyr warns that those who have first confessed Christ, but then turn to the observance of Mosaic law while denying Christ, are especially excluded from salvation (*Dialogue with Trypho* 47). John Chrysostom's eight discourses against the Judaizing Christians delivered in the year 386/87 are clear indications of the appeal of Judaism for Christians in Antioch. They are steeped with invective against Christians who observe Jewish law and celebrate Jewish holidays, and decry the fact that Christian women are attending synagogue service.[63] One of the strongest indications that Judaism won the loyalty of non-Christian Gentiles, long after the establishment of Christianity comes from the region of Caria, whose capital city was Aphrodisias. P. W. van der Horst has called attention to the fact that although in all districts of western Asia Minor Christianity is attested in first, second, or at the latest early third century, ancient indications for Christianity's presence in Caria date from 325 or later. By contrast, there exists a clear indication of ties between Jews and their Gentile neighbors in this region—the Aphrodisias inscription singling out "God-fearers" who have contributed to the local synagogue. This Jewish donor inscription from the third century CE acknowledges fifty-four "God-fearers" who have contributed to the local synagogue, including nine who are recognized as city councilors (*bouleutai*). Van der Horst has argued that one explanation for the lack of visible Christian presence in Caria is the strength of the bond between Jews and Gentiles suggested by this inscription.[64]

A reconstruction in which "God-fearers" prefer Christianity to Judaism because of the appeal of Paul's circumcision-free Gospel is also untenable. Those who understand the transfer of loyalty of the "God-fearers" in Acts from Jews to Christians as an accurate reflection of history often attribute this phenomenon to the superiority of Christian ethics over cumbersome Jewish ritual practice. According to this view, "God-fearers" were attracted to Christianity of the Pauline variety because it offered them a sort of "Judaism Lite": same great monotheism, half the ritual demands. For example, Gerd Theissen writes, "Christianity, [unlike Judaism], especially in its Pauline form, offered [God-fearers] the possibility of acknowledging monotheism and high moral principles and at the same time attaining full religious equality without circumcision, without ritual demands, without restraints which could negatively affect their social status."[65] Although for Theissen circumcision is first on the list of ritual demands that "God-fearers" were eager to avoid, for Karl Georg Kuhn it is the sole ritual that leads to Paul's successful mission. After citing each reference in Acts where those designated as *sebomenos/oi* convert to Christianity, including the four that mention women, Kuhn concludes, "[Paul's] success among the *sebomenoi ton theon* is to be explained by the fact that Paul, unlike Jewish Christians of Palestine, did not make conversion to Judaism by circumcision a condition of salvation."[66]

These arguments that "God-fearers" preferred Christian ethics to Jewish ritual are countered by sources that indicate that Gentile Christians were often attracted to such rituals.[67] Furthermore, not even Acts itself, which claims success for Paul's mission to the "God-fearers," locates this success in Paul's stance on the circumcision question. Kuhn's conclusion that this must have been the case can be refuted by consideration of the gender of "God-fearers" in Acts alone. At the risk of stating the obvious, I note that circumcision could not have been of concern to female "God-fearers." If communicating the importance of the circumcision issue for these Gentiles was a primary concern in Acts, it is unlikely that the narrative would single out female "God-fearers" in four instances (13:50, 16:14, 17:4, 17:12).

Reading the three references to "God-fearing" women who transfer their loyalty to Christianity (16:14, 17:4, 17:12) as reflecting a widespread historical phenomenon implies that Christians in general succeeded in luring away wealthy women supporters of the synagogue.[68] But Luke's claim that wealthy "God-fearing" women transferred loyalty from the synagogue to Christian communities, like the claim that "God-fearers" in general did the same, is better read as Luke's attempt to appropriate Jewish cultural acceptability for his own community. Robert Stoops, in an exegesis of Acts 19, has argued that Luke, recognizing a legal privilege of the Jews in the diaspora, attempts to claim that privilege for Christianity.[69] In a similar way, Luke recognizes the social prestige conferred upon Jewish diaspora communities through their association with high-standing women and claims that Christians are now the beneficiaries of their support. It is unlikely, however, that wealthy Gentile women attracted to the synagogue would have opted in large numbers to give up their ties with an established community to affiliate with a cult, which at the time of the composition of Acts, has little prestige.[70] In an otherwise uniform narrative of "God-fearers" turning from Judaism to Christianity, Luke includes one story of high-standing, "God-fearing" women in Pisidian Antioch who, with the Jews, resist the message of Paul (13:50). Although this is an exceptional passage in Acts, it is a stronger indicator of where these women's loyalty would lie.

By constructing his narrative so that each time Christianity gains the support of a high-standing woman, the synagogue loses, Luke lays the groundwork for the oft-repeated scholarly claim that Christianity had more to offer women than Judaism did. Consider, for example, the recent work of Susanne Heine. She acknowledges that Lydia was first attracted to Judaism because of the ethical implications of the law, but she also makes the following assessment of her conversion to Christianity:

> The opening up of the Christian mission to Gentiles resulted in the surrender of many Jewish elements which were impossible for the godfearers: circumcision, the observance of ritual laws and the strict observance of the precepts of the law expounded casuistically by the Jewish scribes. Therefore women like Lydia must have found Christian faith even better and more in accord with their hopes.[71]

In the face of this facile assumption of Christian superiority stand the indications from Chrysostom's *Discourses Against Judaizing Christians* (2.4–6, 4.3) that Christian women were interested in Jewish ceremonies and synagogue services, and the Theodosian Code, 16.8.6, which suggests that large numbers of Christian women even in the fourth century had converted to Judaism.[72]

That women *were* prominent among early Christian converts is suggested by a variety of sources.[73] As I have argued, one of the likely motivations for Luke's appropriation of the topos of the high-standing Gentile woman supporter is his desire to deflect attention from the numerous women of less reputable backgrounds affiliated with Christianity. But it is both possible and necessary to theorize the conversion of Gentile women to Christianity without positing an "inadequate" Judaism as the foil against which these conversions take place.

4 FIRST CONVERTS

ACTS 16 AND THE LEGITIMATING FUNCTION OF HIGH-STANDING WOMEN IN MISSIONARY PROPAGANDA

THE MOTIF OF THE high-standing Gentile woman as benefactor and savior is common to both Josephus and Luke. The practice of rich women's civic benefaction serves as one explanation for the turn to this motif. I now choose another lens for analysis. This chapter focuses on the narrative in Acts 16:11–40 of Lydia, the "God-fearing" dealer in purple dye, and the unnamed mantic slave girl whom Paul encounters in Philippi. These narratives are not explicated by looking to women's civic benefactions, but rather by consideration of their resonance with missionary propaganda in other Hellenistic religions. Missionary religions drew on the topos of high-standing women as one means of mediating between their adherents and the larger culture. This owes in part to the place of women in public religious practices in the Greco-Roman world.

Complete with valiant prisoners singing hymns in jail, the miraculous loosening of chains subsequent to an earthquake, the conversion of the jailer, and the legal vindication of the missionaries newly arrived in Philippi, Acts 16:19–40 has been singled out by many scholars as an exemplary instance of a type of Hellenistic religious propaganda, the divinely effected prison escape.[1] The scene is so closely patterned on the prison escape of Dionysos in Euripides' *Bacchae* that Otto Weinreich argued early in the past century that the redactor of Acts was directly dependent on this classic Athenian drama.[2] Lilian Portefaix has broadened the discussion of the links between the Philippian mission narrative in Acts and the Dionysos tradition by noting that not only the incarceration proper but also the prefatory scene, Acts 16:11–18, resonates with the missionary pattern of the *Bacchae*.[3]

Identifying Acts 16:11–18 as conforming to a pattern of missionary activity present in the *Bacchae* helps to clarify one of the exegetical puzzles in the narrative of Paul's mission to Philippi. Typically in Acts the synagogue visit is integrally connected to Paul's entry *into* a city and preaching to "the Jews."[4] But in 16:11–15, Paul and his companion travel *outside* of the city to search for a synagogue on the sabbath. They do find one, designated with the term προσευχή[5] rather than the typically Lukan συναγωγή. Moreover those congregated are not said to be "Jews and God-fearers," or "Jews and Greeks," but "women":

> On the sabbath day we went outside the gate by the river, where we supposed there was a synagogue, and we sat down and spoke to the women who had gathered there. (16:13)
>
> τῇ τε ἡμέρᾳ τῶν σαββάτων ἐξήλθομεν ἔξω τῆς πύλης παρὰ ποταμὸν οὗ ἐνομίζομεν προσευχὴν εἶναι, καὶ καθίσαντες ἐλαλοῦμεν ταῖς συνελθούσαις γυναιξίν

Also, according to Acts 16:14–15, the first convert of Philippi is Lydia, a woman of some means and a dealer in purple from Thyatira, who is not mentioned in Paul's own letter to the Philippians (I discuss Lydia's status below). This narrative is not typical of Acts's presentation of Paul's synagogue visits.

The visit to the "synagogue of women" and the conversion of Lydia, however, resonate with Dionysiac propagandistic themes. In Euripides' *Bacchae* the prophet/god of the Dionysos cult claims Lydia in Asia Minor as his homeland and travels to Europe to spread his religion accompanied and supported by Lydian women. Although the dramatic movement centers around Pentheus's rejection and persecution of Dionysos, the miraculous escape of Dionysos, and Pentheus's subsequent dismemberment, the story is prefaced by Dionysos's encounter with the women of Thebes, upon whom he imposes maenadic trance states. In Acts 16, Paul, the missionary of a new religion travels from Asia Minor to Philippi, a major city of Macedonia. His first convert there is a woman from Thyatira, a city in Lydia, who bears Lydia as a personal name. Before Paul meets with any male officials of the city, he first brings his message to the women gathered in the synagogue outside the city gate. Both stories, then, center on the reception of the new religion by important male officials of the locality. This dramatic center is prefaced with the new religion's initial reception by women.[6]

Such parallels may be more tantalizing if one could argue for direct dependence of Luke on the *Bacchae*. Weinreich did just that, pointing to verbal idiosyncracies and literary motifs in Acts that he felt were best explained with reference to this text.[7] Without going so far as to suggest that Luke composed the Acts with a text of the *Bacchae* before him, I do posit that the basic pattern of the *Bacchae* was widely known in antiquity and therefore available to Luke.[8]

This pattern—common to the *Bacchae*, several passages in Acts, and the Apocryphal Acts,—has been classified by Richard Pervo as "mission aretalogy" and outlined by him as follows: "(1) Missionaries of a new god appear; (2) They achieve success (*usually with women, foreigners, slaves, or some other less "respectable" group*); (3) The establishment is jealous, and opposition develops; (4) That leads to persecution and punishment (arrests, martyrdoms, suits, etc.); (5) The mission is vindicated by what believers see as a miracle; (6) There follow the defeat and punishment of the opponents, possibly ending with their conversion."[9] Pervo himself did not pursue further the apologetic/propagandistic function of the second element of his proposed aretalogical pattern, the initial encounter of missionaries with a "less respectable" group. I take up that question in this chapter, with respect to the interaction of missionaries and the women of a community. But first, a modification of Pervo's second element is in order. The women who are part of this first missionary encounter are generally women of high standing and will be designated as such below.

This motif of encountering the women first also appears in Josephus's story of the conversion of the royal family of Adiabene in the *Antiquities*. This story lacks several of the aretalogical elements that link Acts 16 and the *Bacchae*, but one sees nevertheless a similar function with respect to gender. In the portion of the narrative devoted to the conversion of Izates, the king of Adiabene, to Judaism, Josephus is careful to note that his conversion is made possible through the missionary's initial contact with the women of the court:

> Now during the time when Izates resided at Charax Spasini, a certain Jewish merchant named Ananias visited the king's wives and taught them to worship God after the manner of the Jewish tradition. It was through their agency that he was brought to the notice of Izates, whom he similarly won over with the cooperation of the women.[10] (*Ant.* 20.34–35 [Feldman, LCL])

The appearance of this motif of the reception of the new religion first by elite women in Acts and Josephus is puzzling if it is read solely in terms of Greco-Roman suspicion of elite women's participation in missionary religions. The problem can be stated as it was in previous chapters: given both the concern of these authors for cultural acceptability and the widely disseminated literary topos that viewed the affiliation of women—especially upper-class women—with nontraditional religions as subversive, why do Josephus and the author of Acts advertise the conversion of prominent women to their communities?

Sexual Immorality, State Subversion, and the Cult of Dionysos

Because of the thematic parallels between the *Bacchae* and the texts from Acts and Josephus, it is worthwhile to consider how gender functions both in polemics against and support for Dionysiac rites.[11] As Dionysos worship evolves from ancient Greece to imperial Rome, the function of women in the cult also changes. Most notably, sources indicate the ecstatic rites of groups made up exclusively of women give way to more sober ceremonies, involving both women and men.[12] But despite the multiform and evolving nature of Dionysiac rites, a polemical topos concerning women's involvement in these rites varies little from the time of Aristophanes to that of Tacitus. Several elite writers throughout the Hellenistic and Roman periods stereotype practitioners of "foreign rites" as primarily women involved in sexual immorality that subverts state order. For many authors, the Bacchic rites epitomize the immorality and subversiveness they loathe.

In Euripides' *Bacchae*, Pentheus, king of Thebes, is chief spokesman for this common prejudice concerning women's participation in Dionysos ritual:

> I happened to be traveling outside this land,
> but now I hear of strange and vile deeds in this city—
> that our women have gone forth from their homes,
> feigning Bacchic rapture, darting among the thickly wooded hills,
> honoring with their dances this new god Dionysos, whoever he is;
> that the wine-bowls stand in the middle of each *thiasos* full to the brim,
> and that one by one they go
> crouching in the wilderness to serve the lechery of men.
> While they profess to be Maenads making sacrifice,
> they honor Aphrodite more than Bacchus.[13] (*Bacchae* 215–25)

As I argue above in Chapter 2, Livy appropriates this topos in his depiction of the Bacchanalia in Rome in 186 BCE.[14] Cicero also identifies Dionysos worship as emblematic of the orgiastic revelry that subverts the Roman state. As precedent for his legislation prohibiting the participation of women in nocturnal cults in his *Leg.* 2.35–37, he first cites the Senate action against the Bacchanalia of 186 BCE: "The strictness of our ancestors in matters of this character is shown by the ancient decree of the Senate with respect to the Bacchanalia, and the investigation and punishment conducted by the consuls with the assistance of a specially-enrolled military force" [*Quo in genere severitatem maiorum senatus vetus auctoritas de Bacchanalibus et consulum exercitu adhibito quaestio animadversioque declarat*]. As further precedent he reminds his dialogue partner that in one of the plays of Aristophanes, Sabazios, a god often confused with Dionysos and who also required nightly vigils by women, is banished from the state.[15]

To these authors' depictions of the Dionysos cult as locus of sexual immorality and subversion can be added Tacitus's early-second-century description of the empress Messalina's Bacchic "garden party." This description follows immediately upon his narration of Messalina's divorce of the emperor Claudius and traitorous marriage to Silius. Tacitus underscores her act of treason by referring to her Bacchic revelry:

> But Messalina had never given voluptuousness a freer reign [*At Messalina non alias solutior luxu*]. It was the height of autumn and she was

celebrating a mimic vintage throughout the household. Presses were being trodden, vats flowed, while women girded in skins were bounding like Bacchanals excited by sacrifice or delirium. She herself was there with flowing hair and waving thyrsus; and next to her, Silius with an ivy crown, wearing the buskins and tossing his head, while around him rose the din of a wanton chorus.[16] (*Ann.* 11.31.2)

Although these texts imply that women's involvement in Dionysos rites was a primary cause for Greco-Roman suspicion of the cult, disapproval of women's Dionysos worship was not unvarying. This condemnation contended with the view that women's participation in this cult—even in its nocturnal, ecstatic rites—was proper. Indications of this alternate perception surface throughout the period in a variety of literary forms.

The Bacchae

Although Pentheus articulates a common prejudice concerning women's involvement in maenadic worship in the *Bacchae*, he is not a hero in the play, but rather a *theomachos*, one who foolishly resists the God who has confronted him.[17] The folly of Pentheus's judgment concerning Dionysos is the source of the downfall of his house. His charges equating Bacchic worship with sexual promiscuity prove unsubstantiated. They are deflected in the play by the prophet Teiresias (314–18) and Dionysos (485–88) and refuted most fully by the herdsman who reports to Pentheus that he has spied the maenads at rest in the high pastures:

[They lay on the ground] modestly [*sōphronōs*], not—as you say— drunk with wine and flute-music, hunting for love in the solitary woods. . . . They were a sight to marvel at for good order [*eukosmias*];[18] women both old and young, girls still unmarried. (686–88, 693–94)

Pentheus does indeed make a conventional assessment of the nature of Bacchic worship. No sharper modifier could be used to refute Pentheus's view, however, than *sōphronōs*, a word difficult to translate, but encompassing self-control, deference, modesty, and—above all for women—chastity. The *Bacchae* challenges its viewers to reconsider standard distinctions between established religions and new, "foreign" cults. Euripides' paradoxical portrait of maenads as chaste and well-ordered is constituent of that challenge.[19]

The Senatus consultum de Bacchanalibus

Although both Livy and Cicero employ the familiar topos of women/foreign religion/sexual misconduct to justify the repression of the Bacchanalia in 186 BCE, another significant source detailing the repression of Dionysiac worship in Rome, the so-called *Senatus consultum de Bacchanalibus* (*ILS* 18), suggests that women's involvement in the cult was not intrinsically problematic. The decree does set severe restrictions on Dionysiac worship, but does not bar women from participating in it. To the contrary, the decree permits women, but not men, to become priests of Bacchus. Furthermore, the decree allows for women to outnumber men in the small congregations permitted to organize around Bacchic worship.[20] These provisions have led Albert Henrichs to conclude that for Roman authorities, Bacchic rites were primarily "women's business."[21]

Cicero's De legibus

Cicero's proposed prohibition of sacrifice by women at night (*Leg.* 2.21) and his dialogue concerning this prohibition (*Leg.* 2.35–37) are often cited as expressions of the unfavorable view of women's involvement in "foreign" religions. Although Cicero himself clearly holds this view, the structure of his dialogue with Atticus indicates his awareness that this universal law he proposes will not meet with universal acceptance. He begins by questioning whether his dialogue partner Atticus can accede to his proposed legislation, "In regard to what follows, I am wondering, Titus, how you can agree with me or how I can attack your position" [*At vero quod sequitur quo modo aut tu adsentiare aut ego reprehendam sane quaero, Tite*]. Atticus responds that he does accede since the law is not without exception, "But I am in agreement with you, especially as the law itself makes an exception of the customary public sacrifice" [*Ego vero adsentior, excepto praesertim in ipsa lege sollemni sacrificio ac publico*]. Cicero presses further, suggesting that his regulation could be detrimental to the widespread and impressive rites of Dionysos and the Eleusinian mysteries, since he is making legislation "not for the Roman people in particular, but for all virtuous and stable nations" [*non enim populo Romano, sed omnibus bonis firmisque populis leges damus*]. Again Atticus responds by assuming that Cicero will make further exceptions, "I take it for granted that you make an exception of those rites into which we ourselves have been initiated" [*Excipis, credo, illa, quibus ipsi initiati sumus*]. After first agreeing that such an exception would be granted, and then praising the divine mysteries, Cicero explains that his general objection to nocturnal rites is due to the potential licentiousness these rites could inspire among the Roman people. Atticus meets this objection by suggesting a further exception to the proposed legislation, "Very well, then; propose such a law for Rome, but do not deprive us of our customs" [*Tu vero istam Romae legem rogato; nobis nostras ne ademeris*]. Cicero concedes, "I will then return to our own enactments" [*Ad nostra igitur revertor*].

This is the only point in his treatise, otherwise concerned with laws for the ideal state, at which Cicero limits the application of a law specifically to Rome. Further, anticipating that some will still find the legislation too harsh in spite of its limited application, he supports it by citing Greek legal precedent, "*That we may not possibly seem too severe*, I may cite the fact that in the very center of Greece, by a law enacted by Diagondas of Thebes, all nocturnal rites were abolished forever" [*atque omnia nocturna*, ne nos duriores forte videamur, *in media graecia Diagondas Thebanus lege perpetua sustulit*] (my emphasis).

When this passage is read as indicating Cicero's apprehension concerning the acceptability of his proposed legislation restricting women's involvement in nocturnal rites, it cannot be held up as an unqualified demonstration that "the fear of women misbehaving with men at nocturnal wine-feasts of some god must be described as general or typical."[22] Cicero is aware that his proposal to restrict women's involvement in such rites would be contested by many of his peers in Rome and especially by educated readers outside of the Roman capital.

Philo

The notion that the association of women, nontraditional gods, nocturnal rites, and ecstatic practices was always perceived negatively in antiquity is called into question by Philo's remarkable description of the fifty-day feast of the Therapeutics in his *On the Contemplative Life*. This treatise extols the

Jewish monastic community of men (Therapeutae) and women (Therapeutrides) living outside of Alexandria as the preeminent example of virtuous contemplative life. Although the literary and religious purposes of this treatise are complex and frequently debated, scholars do agree that Philo aims to portray the Therapeutics in a favorable light.[23] In light of this aim, consider the close of the treatise, in which the sacred vigil celebrated on the feast of Pentecost is recounted:

> After the supper they hold the sacred vigil which is conducted in the following way. They rise up all together and standing in the middle of the refectory form themselves first into two choirs, one of men and one of women. . . . Then they sing hymns to God . . . and brimming with enthusiasm reproduce sometimes the lyrics of the procession, sometimes of the halt and of the wheeling and counter-wheeling of a choric dance. Then when each choir has separately done its own part in the feast, having drunk as in the Bacchic rites of the strong wine of God's love they mix and both together become a single choir [*kathaper en tais bakcheiais akratou spasantes tou theophilous, anamignuntai kai ginontai choros heis ex amphoin*], a copy of the choir set up of old beside the Red Sea in honor of the wonders worked there. (*Contempl. Life* 83–85)

To be sure, this is metaphorical, not literal, language. Philo's "mixing" is a blending of voices in song, not sexual union of male and female. These metaphors would nevertheless exemplify for a Pentheus, or Livy, or Cicero the depravity of ecstatic, Bacchic worship: a nocturnal vigil, dancing, "drunkenness," the mixing of male and female. But for Philo the Therapeutic vigil is paradigmatic of the virtuous life:

> Utterly good/beautiful [*pagkala*] are the thoughts; utterly good/beautiful [*pagkala*] are the words; worthy of reverence are the choristers, and the end and aim of thoughts, words and choristers alike is piety [*eusebeia*]. Thus they continue until dawn, drunk with this honorable drunkenness [*tēn kalēn tautēn methēn*]. (*Contempl. Life* 88)

Philo characterizes the nocturnal mixing of Therapeutae and Therapeutrides with the phrases "most excellent/beautiful" [*pagkala*], "piety" [*eusebia*], and "honorable drunkenness" [*kalē methē*].[24] In so doing he appears to have taken the anti-Bacchanalia tradition and turned it on its head. Hans Lewy has suggested that in *On the Contemplative Life* the honorable drunkenness (*kalē methē*) of the Therapeutics serves as a paradoxical contrast to the wicked drunkenness (*kakē methē*) of those who attend Greek symposia, for before turning to the Therapeutics Philo speaks at length about the depravity of the Greeks at table.[25] Although this contrast is certainly operative, it is not a sufficient explanation for Philo's elaborate and favorable description of the nocturnal mixing of the sexes. It would have been possible to argue for the superiority of Therapeutic over Greek dining practices without resorting to metaphors of ecstatic Bacchic practice. Moreover, it is not necessary for Philo to provide an account of men and women "mixing" at night in order to be true to the scriptures he interprets. Philo speaks of the celebration of the fifty-day feast as modeled on the biblical celebration that ensued after the parting of the Red Sea. But the narrative in Exodus 15 does not speak of a "single choir." Rather, it tells first of Moses leading the singing of the "Israelites" and second of Miriam leading the singing women. At no point does the biblical account speak of the choir of Moses joining together with the choir of Miriam. Philo's use of this bacchanalian imagery suggests he does not view it as damaging to his apologetic aims. He seems, instead, to be working within a tradition that viewed these practices as virtuous.[26]

Plutarch

Approval of women's participation in Dionysiac worship is also apparent in Plutarch's references to maenadic practice.[27] His treatise *Mulierum virtutes* is dedicated to his friend Clea, the priestess of Osiris at Delphi, whom he acknowledges in another work as "the leader of the Delphic maenads" [*archēida en Delphois tōn Thuiadōn*] (*De Iside et Osiride* 364 E). Plutarch offers no indication that his respect for Clea is somehow mitigated by her holding this office.[28] Furthermore, an incident involving women's practice of maenadic rites is singled out in this treatise as an exemplary act of women's virtue. In *Mulierum virtutes* 249 E–F he tells the story of maenads who, in their Bacchic frenzy, wander into a city under enemy control.[29] When they are found sleeping in the marketplace the next morning, the women of the city first provide for their needs and then secure permission from their husbands to escort them safely from the hostile territory. In

Plutarch's telling these nocturnal rites of maenads are neither suspicious nor offensive. The vulnerable sleeping women are protected by the women of the city; the men of the city respect their right to safe passage.

Plutarch's well-known and oft-quoted proscription against women's independent religious practice in his *Conjugalia praecepta* 140 D, then, stands in tension with his own narrative presentation of maenadic rites. His denunciation of "stealthy and surreptitious rites" performed by women there is not brought to bear on his sympathetic description of the maenadic practice of wandering off at night in ecstatic trances in *Mulierum virtutes*.[30]

In a discussion of sexual conduct among Dionysiac worshippers, Albert Henrichs argues that despite the many accusations of sexual licentiousness directed against Dionysos devotees, in reality such practice was not pervasive.[31] In other words, Henrichs proposes (1) a stereotypical propagandistic theme that condemned women's participation in the cult on the grounds of sexual impropriety, often coupled with charges of subversion, and (2) a "historical reality" in which such impropriety cannot be documented on a wide scale. In light of the sources discussed above, I suggest a third factor: a line of argumentation, apparent in the writings of the elite as well as in popular literary forms, that respected, supported, and even promoted women's prominent role in Dionysiac rites. Philo's easy identification of Bacchic with Therapeutic ecstasy is especially noteworthy, since it indicates Hellenistic Jewish use of Dionysian concepts in apologetic presentation of women's cultic worship.[32] That such a line of argumentation can be identified with respect to Dionysos worship helps to clarify why Josephus and Luke include narratives of high-standing women converts.

Women, Religion, and the Public Life

The identification of two lines of argumentation concerning the function of women specifically in missionary religions—one that views their participation as subversive and one that views it as proper—can be set within the discussion of women's functions within the religious sphere in general. Several texts from antiquity deride not only missionary religions but also religion in general, because it is associated with women. Hence, Ross Kraemer's important book on women's religions in antiquity begins with the sentence, "It was a commonplace in Greco-Roman antiquity that religion was women's business, and it was not a compliment."[33] Such a statement requires further nuance. There is high praise in Greek and Roman texts for women's religious activity, along with an understanding that women's public religious function can be exercised positively for the state.

The importance of women's religious or ritual function is given prominent attention from the *Iliad* on in Greek literature. For example, in the *Iliad* Homer assigns the role of making sacrifices and offering supplications to Hecuba and other Trojan noblewomen (6.312–65).[34] The women in Aristophanes' *Lysistrata* justify their takeover of the Acropolis by reference to their roles in the city's most important religious cults.[35] The privileged place of women in the religious sphere is articulated most eloquently in Greek literature by Melanippe, the protagonist of Euripides' *Melanippe Captive*:

> [Women] manage the home, and guard within the house the seaborne wares. No house is clean or prosperous if the wife is absent. And in religion—highest I judge this claim—we play the greatest part. In the oracles of Phoebus, women expound Apollo's will; and at the holy seat of Dodona, beside the sacred oak, woman conveys the will of Zeus to all Greeks who may desire it. As for the holy rites performed for the Fates and the Nameless Goddesses—they are not holy in the hands of men; among women they flourish all. So righteous is woman's part in holy service. How then should her kind be fairly abused?[36]

We find the view that women's public participation in religious practices is for the good of the state in Latin texts as well. In the *Aeneid*, Hecuba and "her hundred daughters," perform religious duties similar to those assigned to them in the *Iliad* (*Aeneid* 2.501–15, 11.477–87). Livy also gives key roles to Roman matrons, who offer supplication at critical junctures. For example, he notes that during Hannibal's march on Rome, the women pour into the streets to offer their prayers at altars and temples of the gods (Livy *Hist.* 26.9.7–8).[37] Arguing against the view that women held only peripheral roles in Roman religion, Ariadne Staples has shown that women's participation is essential to several important public rituals and festivals of the Roman civic calendar, including the cults of Bona Dea, Ceres, Flora, and Venus.[38]

The prominence of women in the civic, religious sphere has been obfuscated in recent scholarship that has adopted the public/private binary to conceptualize the social roles of men and women in antiquity, without attention to how religious obligations functioned to destabilize this binary. These arguments generally posit that since Greco-Roman ideology restricted women to domestic space, and reserved public speech and political action for men, Jews and Christians who wanted to conform to standard mores exhorted their women to stay home.[39] In the case of early Christianity, Karen Jo Torjeson has argued that women's leadership in religious affairs was tolerated only so long as it was confined to the private sphere, and that as the church moved into public space, women were no longer granted leadership roles.[40] The locus classicus for this understanding of how the public/private dichotomy informed Jewish, and later Christian, thinking is Philo's *On the Special Laws* 3.169, which assigns the "open-air life" to men and the home to women:

> Market places and council-halls and law-courts and gatherings and meetings where a large number of people are assembled, and open-air life with full scope for discussion and action—all these are suitable to men both in war and peace. The women are best suited to the indoor life which never strays from the house, within which the middle door is taken by the maidens as their boundary, and the outer door by those who have reached full womanhood [*thēleiais de oikouria kai hē endon monē, parthenois men eisō klisiadōn tēn mesaulon horon pepoiēmenais, teleiais de ēdē gynaixi tēn auleion*]. . . . (*Spec. Laws* 3.169 [Colson, LCL])

Philo's articulation of Greco-Roman public/private ideology, however, cannot be fully analyzed in isolation from a subsequent paragraph, in which he allows for some destabilization of the public/private binary:

> A woman, then, should not be a busybody, meddling with matters outside her household concerns, but should seek a life of seclusion. She should not show herself off like a vagrant in the streets before the eyes of other men, except when she has to go to the temple [*plēn eis hieron hopote deoi badizein*], and even then she should take pains to go, not when the market is full, but when most people have gone home, and so like a free-born lady worthy of the name [*eleutheras*

tropon kai tō onti astēs], with everything quiet around her, make her
oblations, and offer her prayers to avert the evil and gain the good.
(*Spec. Laws* 3.171 [Colson, LCL])

This paragraph is intriguing on several counts. Philo's use of the terms
"freeborn" (*eleutheras*) and "female citizen" (*astēs*) as attributes of "woman"
indicates that his public/private gender ideology pertains only to elite
women.[41] References to local temple worship and the offering of sacrifices
indicate that Philo is adopting the language of Gentile communal worship in
Alexandria. The proscriptive nature of this and subsequent paragraphs (172–
77) is an obvious indication that Philo knows women who are not conforming to the ideology of domestic confinement. Notably, Philo adopts not only
the standard rule concerning elite women's confinement to domestic quar-
ters but also the standard exception to the rule. Even a most rigid formulation of the ideology proscribing elite women's seclusion must allow for
ventures into public space for the performance of religious duties.[42]

In light of the privileged place of elite women in the religious sphere as
promoted in the texts discussed above, it is fitting that apologists for missionary religions, such as Josephus and Luke, would construct narratives
featuring the initial reception of their religions by women. To do so serves as
a gesture of recognition that in Greco-Roman society women were associated with certain public religious functions and, hence, would provide a
bridge between these missionary cults and the larger society. To understand
these apologists as appropriating such a motif is not to say that in Acts 16:11–
15 or in *Antiquities* 20.34–48 the narratives place women at the center of
early Christianity or Judaism. As with the *Bacchae*, so in Acts and Josephus,
the prefatory nature of the material on women's involvement with the new
religion is an expression of the marginal nature of these women's religious
experience in the structure of the narrative. At the center of all three stories
is the resolution of conflict between the male worthies of a locality and the
male missionary/god.

The Status of Lydia as a Rhetorical Strategy in Acts

Acts 16:14 introduces Paul's first convert in Philippi as "a woman named
Lydia, a dealer in purple from the city of Thyatira" [*gynē onomati Lydia,*

porphyropōlis poleōs Thyateirōn]. The narrative indicates further that Lydia is a householder (16:15, 16:40). Given Luke's skill at creating symbolic characters, the string of modifiers attached to Lydia's name is clearly intended to import much about who Lydia is. How precisely to interpret these modifiers with respect to Lydia's status is a question of dispute among scholars. The disagreement stems in part from conflicting views concerning the respectability of merchants in antiquity. Clarification on this issue is further hindered by the tendency among scholars to read the narrative as a window onto the "historical Lydia," without first raising the issue of Luke's rhetorical strategies. Although I devote some attention to historical questions in a later section, here I address the question of Lydia's status only at the level of narrative.

By citing stereotypical views of elite writers who denigrate anyone involved in small-scale trade (for example, Cicero *De officiis* 1.42), some argue that Lydia should be regarded as a member of a despised profession and hence of low status with little wealth.[43] Others hold the view that Lydia, although not from the highest stratum of society, would have amassed enough wealth by virtue of her profession to be considered part of a quasi elite.[44] Still others, pointing both to the wealth needed to deal in purple and the epigraphic sources indicating that some (male) purple-sellers held prominent civic offices, set Lydia squarely among the urban elite.[45] Lydia's name has been taken as an indication that she is a freedwoman, since slaves and freedpersons often bore names reflecting their geographical origin.[46] This argument is called into question, however, in light of first- and second-century inscriptions in which women of the social elite bear the name as well.[47]

It is difficult to ascertain Lydia's status primarily on the basis of four words, *Lydia, porphyropōlis poleōs Thyateirōn*. Drawing from their study of the social history of the dye profession, feminist scholars Luise Schottroff and Ivoni Richter Reimer argue that Lydia should be understood as a member of a despised profession, of humble status and modest means. From this understanding, they have produced liberation readings of the text in which Lydia is emblematic of the "last who become first," and the household that she heads signifies a "contrast society" (*Gegengesellschaft*) within a Roman colony.[48] Although Schottroff and, more extensively, Richter Reimer have provided a valuable social history of work in the manufacture of dye in antiquity, their arguments that trade in purple necessarily involved work in manufacturing it are less than compelling.[49] Most importantly, readings that foreground Lydia's lowliness do not take into account Luke's rhetorical strategies concerning class and status in the Acts.

A dominant theme of Luke's double work is that the privileged members of Jewish society reject the message of Jesus, and those on the margins respond favorably to it. Prominent among those on the margins in the Third Gospel are social outcasts, including tax collectors, sinners, and the poor.[50] In Acts those who are "marginal" and hence the true recipients of God's grace are not the poor, but the Gentiles.[51] Many of these Gentiles are assigned an explicitly prominent social status, including the Ethiopian chamberlain (8:26–40) Cornelius, a centurion and prototypical "God-fearer" (10:1–48), the proconsul Sergius Paulus (13:7–12), the women of high standing in Thessalonica (17:4), the leading men and women of Beroea (17:12), and Dionysius the Areopagite (17:33). Moreover, Asiarchs and Roman governors, even though they do not convert to Christianity, protect its emissaries. The shift in emphasis from *les misérables* in the Third Gospel to the social elite in Acts is a primary reason for Richard Pervo's wry observation: "One would be somewhat hard-pressed to illustrate the Sermon on the Plain (Luke 6:20–49) by reference to Acts."[52] In light of this narrative strategy in which the designation "marginal, yet saved" is transferred from the poor of the Gospels to the (well-placed) Gentiles of Acts, it is not convincing to argue that in Acts Lydia's conversion is a vindication of the "poorest of the poor." Indeed, those who undoubtedly are of this low status, namely, the mantic slave girl (16:16–18) and the prisoners in the Philippian jail (16:25–34), are not recipients of salvation in Luke's narrative. As Yann Redalié notes:

> [The slave girl] is introduced only in order to demonstrate the power of the apostle. . . . Paul enters into a relationship with her only when his patience has been exceeded, and he heals her only in order to get rid of her. . . . The same goes for the prisoners. Freed by the miraculous earthquake, they remain in prison so that the jailer may be converted. The power of God is expressed by Luke not in order to deliver the powerless prisoners, but to convert the officer.[53]

Although elite readers of the status of Cicero or Pliny may have despised a character like Lydia because of her involvement in a trading profession, they would have held the hero of the story, Paul, in at least as much contempt. In spite of his many high-status markers in Acts, Paul is nevertheless involved in the lowly craft of tent-making. That characters involved in trade could be portrayed as having more respectability than Cicero or Pliny would grant them makes sense for an audience that includes neither a Cicero nor a Pliny. The audience for whom Luke writes is more appropriately identified as a group of people with some wealth and education, into which persons of low status with wealth were also included.[54] Such an audience would view a character involved in trade, who has also achieved a measure of respectability, as mirroring their own social and economic aspirations. Lydia's status markers—a dealer in purple who is also a householder—thus positions her at least among the ranks of this same "quasi-elite" class.

In addition to being a merchant of purple from Thyatira, Lydia is also designated in 16:14 as "God-fearing" [*sebomenē ton theon*]. As I have argued in Chapter 3, because of this designation, Lydia may be understood as the Cornelius of the European phase of Paul's missionary activity. Like Cornelius, she converts to Christianity and subsequently extends hospitality to the one who has baptized her (cf. 16:15 and 10:48). But such a comparison requires qualification, since one crucial element of the Cornelius episode is displaced in the story of Lydia.

The issue of table fellowship with a Gentile is central to Peter's baptism of Cornelius, as evident in the twice-narrated vision of unclean animals that Peter is commanded to eat (10:9–16, 11:5–10). The hospitality that Cornelius extends includes table fellowship, as indicated by the question of the circumcised addressed to Peter in 11:3: "Why did you go to the uncircumcised men and eat with them" [*eisēlthes pros andras akrobustian echontas kai synephages autois*]. According to Esler, the issue of table fellowship is of such concern in the Acts that Paul's "going to the Gentiles" can be understood primarily as Paul's public establishment of table fellowship between Jew and Gentile.[55]

Lydia's invitation to Paul to stay in her house may be read as an implicit extension of table fellowship from a Gentile to a Jew.[56] Luke explicitly narrates a story of a common meal shared by Jew and Gentile in Philippi, however, only after Paul baptizes the jailer. "Bringing them into his house, the jailer set food before them. He and his entire household rejoiced that he had become a believer" [*anagagōn te autous eis ton oikon parethēken trapezan kai ēgalliasato panoikei pepisteukōs tō theō*] (Acts 16:34). Luke reserves the acknowledgment of Jewish-Gentile table fellowship in Philippi until after the (male) jailer is baptized in Acts. This coincides with the avoidance of narratives of women at public tables in his Gospel.[57] His hesitancy to acknowledge meal sharing between Paul and a Gentile woman may help to account for the inclusion of this second conversion narrative of the jailer in his story of the founding of the Christian community in Philippi.[58] Lydia is the first convert at Philippi, but she is not the first to share a table with Paul.

The Mantic Slave Girl's Religious Allegiance

The first words of the brief narrative of the mantic slave girl, "and it happened as we were proceeding to the synagogue" [*Egeneto de poreuomenōn hēmōn eis tēn proseuchēn*] (Acts 16:16) link it to the story of Paul's encounter with Lydia in the synagogue (*proseuchē*) of women (16:13). This link is important, for the juxtaposition of these two stories establishes a contrast between the status and demeanor of the female Christian convert and the female pagan missionary. Paul and his companion receive hospitality from the well-to-do purple merchant; they are harassed by a *paidiskē*. The range of meaning for *paidiskē* extends from young female, to servant, to slave, to prostitute.[59] In light of the context here, in which the *paidiskē* is controlled by her owners (*kyrioi*), the girl is undoubtedly a slave. The report that she earns money for her masters by her performance on the city streets also indicates that her work is not clearly differentiated from prostitution.

This narrative also stands in contrast with the depiction of Christian women prophets in Acts. Although the narrative of the Pentecost in Acts includes Joel's promise that both sons and daughters shall prophesy and that even male and female slaves shall receive the Spirit (2:17–18), the only Christian women said to prophesy (*propheteuō*) in Acts are the virgin daughters of Philip in Caesarea (21:9). Although later reports indicate that these four daughters were held in high regard by Christians in Asia Minor (cf. Eusebius *Eccl. Hist.* 3.31), Acts devotes only one verse to them and records none of their prophecies.[60] The only inspired woman's speech recorded in Acts is that of the *paidiskē*, who stands outside of the Christian community and whose words are said to be mantic rather than prophetic.[61]

The narrative has several verbal connections to the exorcism stories found in the synoptics, but this is not a typical exorcism.[62] The slave girl is not depicted as being physically tormented by the possessing spirit (cf. Luke 8:29). No crowd is present to witness in astonishment the miraculous event and no one proclaims the deed (cf. Mark 1:27, 1:45; Mark 5:14–17; Luke 8:35–39). Although Jesus characteristically heals on his first encounter with an unclean spirit, Paul exorcises the slave girl only after he has become annoyed by her continued utterance over the course of several days. Rather than affirming her as healed, the text makes no further mention of the slave girl after the spirit departs from her (cf. Luke 8:35–39).[63] Uncharacteristically for Luke, and for the synoptic tradition, the spirit is not designated as unclean (*pneuma akatharton*) or demonic (*pneuma ponēron*).[64] Rather, the slave girl is said to have a "Pythonian spirit" (*pneuma pythōna*). Finally, unlike those who are possessed in the synoptics, the slave girl is said to earn large sums of money for her owners through her prophesying (*manteuomai*).

Both *pneuma pythōna* and *manteuomai* are hapax legomenona in the New Testament. Ivoni Richter Reimer argues convincingly that the word cluster *pneuma*, *pythōna*, and *manteuomai* evokes associations with the Pythian priestess of Apollo at Delphi.[65] *Pythōn* is the name of the serpent guarding the Delphic oracle who is slain by Apollo. According to Plutarch, the word came to designate a ventriloquist in later usage.[66] However, this does not mean that the initial association of the word with Delphic prophecy would have been lost.[67] The girl is not called a "ventriloquist" *pythōn* herself, but rather is said to have a *pneuma pythōna*. This designation is consistent with the broad tradition that the odor of the snake's decomposed body inspires the Pythia.[68] Synonyms for the Pythia include *mantis* and *pro-mantis*, and *manteuomai* is the verb frequently associated with her oracular utterances.[69] In view of these associations, Acts 16:16 presents for readers, as Werner de Boor argues, a Pythia in miniature.[70]

In this reading, the phrase *pneuma pythōna* serves to indicate the slave girl's cultic allegiance, and the incident in 16:18 represents a religious competition in which the God of Paul prevails over Apollo, the God of the slave girl. The mantic slave girl is best understood not as someone tormented by evil spirits along the lines of the possessed in the Gospels, but as a prophet/missionary of the greatest of the oracular Gods who is compelled to identify Paul and his companion as the slaves of the one true "Most High God" (*theos hypistos*). That Luke reports how the owners of the slave earn much profit through her prophecies also suggests that here is a narrative of missionary competition. Charges that missionary opponents are hucksters motivated by financial gain are a stock feature of invective against religious movements.[71]

Because Luke depicts the only female who speaks prophetically in Acts as a *paidiskē* whose source of inspiration is the *pneuma pythōna*, these verses lie on a trajectory of Christian criticism of female religious functionaries of Apollo articulated most fully in extant literature by Origen (*Cels.* 3.25, 7.3–7). One means by which Origen derides Delphic prophecy is to note that the Pythian priestess receives the spirit of prophecy through her womb after ascending the tripod (*Cels.* 3.25, 7.3). Chrysostom articulates the same criticism:

> This same Pythoness then is said, being a female, to sit at times upon the tripod of Apollo astride, and thus the evil spirit ascending from beneath and entering the lower part of her body, fills the woman with madness, and she with disheveled hair begins to play the bacchanal and to foam at the mouth, and thus being in a frenzy to utter the words of her madness. (*Homiliae in epistulam i ad Corinthios* 29.2)[72]

Origen and Chrysostom show nothing but contempt for the notion, attested much earlier, that sacred intercourse with Apollo is the source of the Pythia's inspiration.[73] If this hostile evaluation of Pythian inspiration was shared by Luke's readers, they would find a slave girl possessed by a *pneuma pythōna* especially unseemly.

But even if the phrase *pneuma pythōna* was not read in this way, Origen's more general criticism of Delphic religion still illuminates the propagandistic function of Luke's story of the slave girl who is Apollo's missionary/prophet:

> If the Delphic Apollo were a god, as the Greeks imagine, shouldn't he have chosen as his prophet some wise man or, if such a man could not be found, at least one who had made progress in that direction? And why did he not prefer to prophesy through a man rather than a woman? If, however, he even preferred the female . . . shouldn't he have chosen a virgin rather than a married woman to prophesy his will? In fact the Pythian Apollo admired by the Greeks did not deem any wise man, or indeed any man at all, to be worthy of what the Greeks take to be divine inspiration. *And from the female sex he did not choose a virgin or a wise person who had been helped by philosophy, but some vulgar woman* [ἀλλ᾽ οὐδ᾽ ἐν τῷ θήλει γένει παρθένον τινὰ ἤ

σοφὴν καὶ ἀπὸ φιλοσοφίας ὠφελημένην ἀλλά τινα γυναῖκα ἰδιῶ-
τιν]. (*Cels*. 7.5–6, my emphasis).[74]

Here Origen's critique is one with Luke's. Unlike the prophecies of the God of Paul, which are delivered in Acts solely by men, the prophets of the Pythian Apollo, both in Luke's time and in Origen's, are women. In Acts this Pythian prophet is depicted not only as a woman, but as a παίδισκν, slave girl, far removed from acceptable categories for women prophets—that is, virgins and educated women.[74]

From Rhetorical Analysis to Historical Situation

This final section devoted to historical reconstruction focuses on the question of the historical religious activity of women in Philippi. But first, a general comment about the legitimate place granted to women in the public religious sphere in the Greco-Roman world: the prominence of women in public religious life cannot be facilely equated with a "liberating" place for women. As Froma Zeitlin notes for Dionysos worship, and Ariadne Staples argues in the case of Roman religion, the ritual categorization of women serves to legitimate the male-defined status of women.[75] By the same token, however, it would be facile to state categorically that women in antiquity did not find liberating possibilities in the religious sphere.[76] Authors of the period repeatedly assert that women's involvement in public religious rites makes possible illicit sexual liaisons. To cite but two examples, in the ancient romance *Chariton* an amorous relationship is ignited at the precise moment when a woman ventures into public space for a religious festival:

> A public festival of Aphrodite took place, and almost all the women went to her temple. Callirhoe had never been out in public before, but her father wanted her to do reverence to the goddess, and her mother took her. Just at that time Chaereas was walking home from the gymnasium; he was radiant as a star. . . . Now, chance would have it that at the corner of a narrow street the two walked straight into each other; the god had contrived the meeting so that each should see the other. At once they were both smitten with love. . . . [77]

Likewise, in Lysias's *On the Murder of Eratosthenes* an adulterous affair is sparked by a wife's departure from the home to attend a funeral (*Eratosthenes* 8). This linking of religious duties and sexual liaison suggests the disruptive potential of women's public religious duties. More than one elite male author operates from the assumption that a woman who participates in public religious activity is potentially out of sexual control.

∾

The stories of Philippian women engaged in religious activity in Acts 16 are part of a larger group of literary sources indicating women's prominence among Christians at Philippi.[78] These include Paul's exhortation concerning Euodia and Syntyche in his letter to the Philippians (4:2–3), Polycarp's exhortation in his letter to the Philippians concerning women's celibacy and discretion (4.1–3), and a fragment from the *Acts of Paul* that speaks of a female Christian martyr named Frontina in Philippi.[79]

Since Acts is the only source for Lydia, it is difficult to make the case that she herself is a historical figure and first convert of Philippi rather than Luke's fictional creation. Factors weighing against the historicity of Lydia include Paul's own letter to the Philippian congregation, in which he addresses several members by name, but does not acknowledge Lydia as first convert of this city.[80] In addition to this argument from silence, I read the symbolic richness of Lydia's name as a further indication that she is a character created by Luke.[81]

This is not to say that Luke invented Lydia because he did not know of women who were prominent in the early church at Philippi. It may be that Luke knows all too well that women were leaders in the Philippian congregation, especially the two women named in Paul's epistle, Euodia and Syntyche (Phil 4:2–3). On the basis of her rhetorical analysis of Philippians, Cynthia Kittredge argues convincingly that these two women hold leadership positions in the community independent of Paul, and that Paul's conflict with these women is an important aspect of the historical situation addressed in his letter.[82] Acts can be read, then, as substituting the narrative of a female convert generously accommodating the Pauline mission for a more conflictual account of Paul's relations with the female leadership in Philippi.[83] Such a reading coincides with Luke's rhetorical aim to portray the early church as unencumbered by conflict.[84]

Although Luke's positioning of the mission's base in the household of Lydia in Philippi may not reflect an actual historical situation, this is not to say that women did not host house churches in early Christianity. Paul's letters reveal that they did.[85] What is most suspect in Acts's depiction of Lydia is not the suggestion that a woman like Lydia could have hosted a house church in Philippi, but rather her portrayal only as a convert accommodating Paul and his mission, and not as a Christian missionary/leader in her own right.[86]

Although the mantic slave girl is not portrayed as a member of the early Christian community, her story can also be read as indicative of tensions concerning the status and roles of women in the early church. Josephus responds to charges that the Jews attract men and women from the lower classes by deflecting those charges onto devotees of Isis. He does so by contrasting the status and demeanor of Fulvia, the Roman matron of senatorial rank and a convert to Judaism, with that of Ida, the cunning, immoral freedwoman whom he places at the heart of the Isis scandal in Rome. A similar act of deflection occurs through the juxtaposition of Lydia and the mantic slave girl in Acts. Lydia is a well-to-do Christian convert and patroness of Paul, who extends hospitality to the missionaries in her house. The enslaved female missionary/prophet openly proclaiming her message on public streets has no place in Luke's presentation of Christianity, but only in an inferior religious practice.

When the accounts of Tacitus and Suetonius are read against the account of Josephus concerning the expulsion of Jews in Rome, one finds indications that, in spite of Josephus's refusal to say so, members of the lower classes were indeed attracted to Judaism in significant numbers. Again, a similar conclusion emerges from reading the apologetic narrative of Luke against the famous letter of his near contemporary, Pliny, to Trajan concerning Christians in Bithynia (*Ep.* 10.96). Although no female slave takes on a leadership role in Acts, Pliny recounts to Trajan how he found it necessary to torture two female slaves, who were deacons of the Christian congregation, for information concerning the cult ("*Quo magis necessarium credidi ex duabus ancillis, quae ministrae dicebantur, quid esset veri et per tormenta quaerere*" [10.96.8]). Here is an indication that slave women took on prominent roles in the early church in Asia Minor, in spite of their absence in Luke's presentation of early Christian officeholders.[87]

Finally, Luke gives just one verse to the Christian prophesying daughters of Philip and attributes the only inspired speech of a female character to the mantic slave girl. By distancing Christian women from prophecy in this way, Acts belies the historical importance of women prophets to the early church. In spite of Acts's near silence about them, Eusebius's preservation of two additional sources on Philip's daughters in his *Eccl. Hist.* 3.31 suggests that they were long revered in Asia Minor.[88] Another text that may be brought to bear on displacement of female prophetic speech onto the missionary of a defeated religion is Revelation 2:20–23. Here the author of the apocalypse derides a Christian female prophet in Thyatira as "Jezebel." The rhetorical strategies of these two authors differ greatly. Acts, which does not wish to portray conflict among Christians, suggests that "unseemly" women's prophecy is a problem only for other religious cults. Revelation, which makes no secret of intra-Christian disputes, vilifies a Christian woman prophet by linking her to an archetypal fornicator.[89] Both sources suggest exalted, if disputed, roles for women prophets in the early church at the turn of the first century CE.

CONCLUSION

THE CONSTRUCTION OF A historical narrative is contingent upon a scholar's angle of vision. If one minimizes the number of sources deemed relevant to the question of Jewish mission, neglects analogies between Hellenistic Judaism and other Hellenistic religions, and defines missionary activity in narrow terms, then it is possible to argue that Judaism in antiquity did not contain a missionary impulse. This study has been undertaken from a different angle, as a means of reaffirming the understanding of Jewish missionary activity in a broad sense, within the general framework of Hellenistic religious propaganda.[1] I have analyzed sources that speak of communicative exchange between Jews and pagans—especially sources that speak of pagan adherence or conversion to Judaism—without assuming that the question of Jewish mission depends on whether their passivity or activity in these exchanges can be established. I have considered texts suggesting early Jewish missionary activity, including early Christian missionary activity, alongside texts of other Hellenistic missionary religions.

I have also attempted to bring the disciplines of gender and women's studies to bear on a debate about mission that, until now, has been framed in androcentric terms. In this endeavor, my hope has been to demonstrate that feminist models of historical reconstruction provide a more adequate history of missionary religions. This is because they account for sources about women that androcentric models minimize or ignore, thereby making visible more of the actors and agents of the past.

Josephus's text concerning the expulsion of Jews and Isis worshippers from Rome in *Antiquities* 18 serves well to illustrate the importance both of understanding Jewish missionary activity alongside other missionary cults and of bringing gender analysis to bear on texts relevant to the mission question. Josephus links these two religious communities for the purpose of comparison and contrast, as a means of deflecting the common criticisms against all "foreign" religions away from the Jewish community and onto Isis worshippers alone. A study of the Jewish incident in isolation from the Isis affair does not do justice to his account, nor to those of Tacitus and Suetonius. These Roman historians, like the xenophobic Juvenal, consider Jews and Isis worshippers together as pollutants of the same sort, spewed "from the river Orontes into the Tiber" (*Sat.* 3.60–80). To consider questions of Jewish mission without placing Hellenistic Jews next to Isis worshippers in this case—or adherents to the cults of Cybele or Dionysos in other cases—is to raise up a fixed boundary around the Jews that many in antiquity did not see. I have shown also that these texts concerning an incident early in the first century CE reflect much about the political situation for practitioners of eastern religions at the end of the first century, when Domitian proclaimed himself "lover of Isis," and anti-Jewish rhetoric reached new heights in the capital city. Attention to the function of gender in *Antiquities* 18 shows that Josephus's careful demarcation of the fates of Isis-worshipping Paulina and Jewish convert Fulvia, so that only the former is sexually violated, would have been found dubious by the conservative Roman elite. In his account of the expulsion, Tacitus groups both Isis and Jewish devotees with Roman matrons who engage in the practice of prostitution. He, like Horace before him, found religious deviation and women's sexual transgression twin perils to the state.

Although no one has previously applied such gender analysis to the expulsion account of *Antiquities* 18, many scholars have long recognized that religious and sexual misconduct are often fused in Greco-Roman reports of wrongdoing. Among biblical scholars, David Balch in particular has been influential in crystallizing the picture of Greco-Roman antipathy toward "foreign" cults as religions of promiscuous women.[2] A significant contribution of my own study has been to show that this topos associating high-standing women with "foreign" religions, sexual misconduct, and state subversion was not the only means of speaking about women's participation in missionary religions. Numerous texts concerning the Dionysos cult, along with the texts of Philo, Josephus, and Luke, suggest that elite women's participation in religious cults was narrated for positive rhetorical effect. A reconstruction of attitudes toward women's participation in missionary religions in antiquity must account not only for the derisive report of the bacchanalia scandal in Livy, but also for Philo's turn to bacchic analogy in his idealized portrait of Therapeutic worship practices.

A more balanced understanding of how high-standing women function in the apologetic narratives of missionary religions has implications for how one interprets the strictures placed upon early Christian women from the end of the first century onward. Intentionally or not, the argument that Greco-Roman men uniformly viewed women's participation in "foreign" cults as subversive has functioned as a sort of apologia for misogynistic texts, such as the exhortation for wives' submission in I Peter. "Christians had no choice but to rein their women in," this line of argument goes, "because of the pressures of pagan opinion." Likewise, the argument that it was the move from private to public space that necessitated the exclusion of women from church offices mistakenly posits an external pagan pressure to keep women out of public religious space. If, however, orthodox Christians had wanted to continue privileging women's participation in and leadership of their communities, they could have pointed to pagan precedent for doing so. When one acknowledges the privileged place of women in the religious sphere in the Greco-Roman world, prohibitions against their officeholding in early Christian communities cannot be so easily accounted for as owing to outside forces.[3]

By utilizing gender analysis, I have been able to show that in the *Antiquities* and Acts the pattern of highlighting Gentile noblewomen's participation in Jewish and Christian communities extends beyond noting those who become religious converts or adherents. In the *Antiquities* the women whose loyalty to Judaism includes religious devotion are a subset of a larger category of Gentile noblewomen patrons, including the Pharaoh's daughter and several women of the imperial house. Although patronage is not stressed equally in Acts, Luke does at least make mention of the Pharaoh's daughter's intercessions on Moses' behalf in Stephen's recitation of Israel's salvation history. These findings lead me to suggest that in future studies of communicative exchange between Jews and pagans the phenomenon of patronage and benefaction should receive more attention.[4] Moreover, because the women Josephus mentions as adherents/converts in the *Antiquities* are without exception Jewish benefactors, I suggest that the performance of benefactions as a means by which women could ritually signify their conversion/adherence to Judaism requires further study. Since circumcision is not an issue for women, scholars have been at a loss to identify ritual acts that signified Gentile women's attachment to Judaism in the first century, except to suggest that marriage to a Jewish man resulted in a de facto conversion by a Gentile woman.[5] Understanding the benefactions of Gentile women converts/adherents as having ritual significance would provide one means for speaking of how Gentile women symbolized their allegiance to Judaism outside of the frameworks of circumcision and marriage.

Although I both identify the pattern of Gentile noblewomen interceding on behalf of Jews and Christians as a literary topos and speak of the noblewoman adherent/convert to Jewish and Christian communities as a rhetorical figure, I have nevertheless argued both for the historicity of imperial women's occasional intercession on behalf of the Jews, and for the prominence of women among religious adherents/converts in early Judaism and Christianity. In spite of the rhetorical nature of historical sources, the convergence of a variety of sources from different genres on this point suggests this to be the best reading of them. Literary and epigraphic sources suggesting imperial women's benefaction on behalf of Rome's client states make it likely that the Jews were occasional recipients of imperial women's favor. Inscriptional evidence, however fragmentary, supports the understanding that women were prominent among those involved in missionary religions, including Isis, Dionysos, and Jewish cults in Rome. The Julia Severa inscription, and perhaps the inscriptions for Tation and Capitolina, suggest the association of high-standing Gentile women with Jewish communities in Asia Minor (as I discussed above in Chapter 3). Literary proscriptions against women's involvement in missionary religions, Juvenal's satire ridiculing such participation, and literary texts affirming it make sense only if these cults did appeal to women.

Yet, reading these texts on high-standing women converts "against the grain" does require modification of the notion that especially women of this status were attracted to missionary cults in antiquity. I have noted that the juxtaposition of the matron Fulvia with the contemptible freedwoman Ida in the *Antiquities* 18, like the juxtaposition of Lydia and the mantic slave girl in Acts 16, serves to deflect attention from lower-class female adherents/converts. That more "Idas" than "Fulvias" were involved in Jewish practice at the turn of the first century CE in Rome is suggested by the expulsion accounts of Tacitus and Suetonius, which target not Roman citizens, but the lower classes. Although the relative respectability of Jewish communities in the diaspora may have attracted prominent female "God-fearers," the majority of women finding their way into the early Christian community would have been of the status of the two female slaves tortured by Pliny, or the *padiskē* in Acts offering her prophecies on the street.

I have also argued that the gendered nature of many of these conversion stories, which posit the missionary as an active male and the convert as a passive female, belie the contributions of women as early Jewish and Christian missionaries. One may look to the many derogatory portraits of "strange women" in the sources—Juvenal's begging Jewish priestess and his Isis devotee who has the audacity to converse with God herself, Josephus's Ida, Acts's mantic slave girl, and Revelation's "Jezebel"—for indications of the powerful roles of women as functionaries and innovators in missionary religions of antiquity.

REFERENCE MATTER

ABBREVIATIONS OF WORKS CITED

AJA	*American Journal of Archaeology*
AJP	*American Journal of Philology*
ANRW	*Aufstieg und Niedergang der römischen Welt: Geshichte und Kultur Roms im Spiegel der neueren Forschung*, ed. H. Temporini and W. Hasse (Berlin: De Gruyter, 1972–)
CBQ	*Catholic Biblical Quarterly*
CII	*Corpus inscriptionum iudaicarum*. Edited by J. B. Frey. 2 vols. (Rome: Pontifical Institute of Christian Archeology, 1936–1952)
CP	*Classical Philology*
HSCP	*Harvard Studies in Classical Philology*
HTR	*Harvard Theological Review*
ILS	*Inscriptiones latinae selectae*. Edited by Hermann Dessau. 3 vols. (Berlin: Weidmann, 1892–1916)
JBL	*Journal of Biblical Literature*
JJS	*Journal of Jewish Studies*
JQR	*Jewish Quarterly Review*
JRS	*Journal of Roman Studies*
JSJ	*Journal for the Study of Judaism in the Persian, Hellenistic, and Roman Periods*
JSNT	*Journal for the Study of the New Testament*
JTS	*Journal of Theological Studies*
LSJ	Liddell, H. G., R. Scott, and H. S. Jones, *A Greek-English Lexicon*, 9th ed., with revised supplement (Oxford: Clarendon, 1996)

MAMA	*Monumenta Asiae Minoris Antiqua* (Manchester: Manchester University Press; London: Longmans, Green & Co., 1928–1993)
NovT	*Novum Testamentum*
NTApoc	Wilhelm Schneemelcher, ed., *New Testament Apocrypha*, rev. ed., vol. 1 (Louisville, Ky.: Westminster/John Knox Press, 1991); Edgar Hennecke, *New Testament Apocrypha*, vol. 2, ed. Wilhelm Schneemelcher (Philadelphia, Pa.: Westminster, 1965)
PW	Pauly, A. F., *Paulys Realencyclopädie der classischen Altertumswissenschaft*, new ed., ed. G. Wissowa, 49 vols. (Munich: Druckenmuller, 1980)
PWSup	Supplement to Pauly, A. F., *Paulys Realencyclopädie der classischen Altertumswissenschaft*, new ed., ed. G. Wissowa, 49 vols. (Munich: Druckenmuller, 1980)
SBLSP	*Society of Biblical Literature Seminar Papers*
Signs	*Signs: Journal of Women in Culture and Society*
TDNT	*Theological Dictionary of the New Testament*, ed. G. Kittel and G. Friedrich, trans. G. W. Bromiley, 10 vols. (Grand Rapids, Mich., 1964–1976)

NOTES

INTRODUCTION

1. Translations are my own, unless otherwise noted. For Juvenal's critique of women's religious practices, see *Sat.* 6.314–46, 6.511–91. For an annotated text of the sixth satire, see Juvenal, *Satura VI*, ed. Amy Richlin (Bryn Mawr, Pa.: Bryn Mawr College, 1986). For discussion, see Amy Richlin, *The Garden of Priapus: Sexuality and Aggression in Roman Humor* (New Haven, Conn., and London: Yale University Press, 1983), 202–7; and Edward Courtney, *A Commentary on the Satires of Juvenal* (London: Athlone, 1980), 252–347.

2. Dieter Georgi, *The Opponents of Paul in Second Corinthians* (Philadelphia, Pa.: Fortress, 1986), 96–117.

3. For a collection of essays on the subject of religious propaganda in antiquity, see Elisabeth Schüssler Fiorenza, ed., *Aspects of Religious Propaganda in Judaism and Early Christianity* (Notre Dame, Ind., and London: University of Notre Dame Press, 1976). For an important study of the apostle Paul within Hellenistic Judaism working from the premise that many Hellenistic Jewish authors, like their pagan contemporaries, were driven by a profound yearning for univocity, see Daniel Boyarin, *A Radical Jew: Paul and the Politics of Identity* (Berkeley, Los Angeles, and London: University of California Press, 1994).

4. Other notable scholars who hold the view of a missionary Judaism include: Adolf von Harnack, *The Mission and Expansion of Christianity in the First Three Centuries* (1904–1905; reprint, New York: Books for Libraries, 1972); Karl Axenfeld, "Die jüdische Propaganda als Vorläuferin und Wegbereiterin der urchristlichen Mission," in *Missionswissenschaftliche Studien: Festschrift zum 70. Geburtstag des Herrn Prof. D. Dr. Gustav Warneck*, ed. Karl Axenfeld et al. (Berlin: Warneck, 1904), 1–80;

George Foot Moore, *Judaism in the First Centuries of the Christian Era: The Age of the Tannaim*, 3 vols. (Cambridge, Mass.: Harvard University Press, 1927–1940); Bernard J. Bamberger, *Proselytism in the Talmudic Period* (Cincinnati, Ohio: Hebrew Union College, 1939); W. G. Braude, *Jewish Proselytizing in the First Five Centuries of the Common Era: The Age of the Tannaim and Amoraim* (Providence, R.I.: Brown University Press, 1940); Peter Dalbert, *Die Theologie der hellenistisch-jüdischen Missionsliteratur unter Ausschluss von Philo und Josephus* (Hamburg: Reich, 1954); Marcel Simon, *Verus Israel: A Study of the Relations Between Christians and Jews in the Roman Empire (135–425)*, Littman Library of Jewish Civilization (Oxford: Oxford University Press, 1986); and Louis H. Feldman, *Jew and Gentile in the Ancient World: Attitudes and Interactions from Alexander to Justinian* (Princeton, N.J.: Princeton University Press, 1993). Cf. Steve Mason, "The *Contra Apionem* in Social and Literary Context: An Invitation to Judean Philosophy," in *Josephus' Contra Apionem: Studies in Character and Context with a Latin Concordance to the Portion Missing in Greek*, ed. L. H. Feldman and J. R. Levison, Arbeiten zur Geschichte des antiken Judentums und des Urchristentums 34 (Leiden: Brill, 1996), 187–228.

5. Scot McKnight, *A Light Among the Gentiles: Jewish Missionary Activity in the Second Temple Period* (Minneapolis, Mn.: Fortress, 1991). Edouard Will and Claude Orrieux, *"Prosélytisme Juif"? Histoire d'une erreur* (Paris: Belles Lettres, 1992). Martin Goodman, *Mission and Conversion* (Oxford: Oxford University Press, 1994). See also his earlier article, "Jewish Proselytizing in the First Century," in *The Jews Among Pagans and Christians in the Roman Empire*, ed. Judith Lieu, John A. North, and Tessa Rajak (London and New York: Routledge, 1992), 53–78.

6. Included among Alf Thomas Kraabel's many articles addressing this issue are: "The Roman Diaspora: Six Questionable Assumptions," *JJS* 33 (1982): 445–64; "Synagoga Caeca: Systematic Distortion in Gentile Interpretations of Evidence for Judaism in the Early Christian Period," in *"To See Ourselves as Others See Us": Christians, Jews, "Others" in Late Antiquity*, ed. Jacob Neusner and E. S. Frerichs (Chico, Calif.: Scholars Press, 1985), 219–46; and "Immigrants, Exiles, Expatriates, and Missionaries," in *Religious Propaganda and Missionary Competition in the New Testament World: Essays Honoring Dieter Georgi*, ed. Lukas Bormann, Kelly Del Tredici, and Angela Standhartinger (Leiden and New York: Brill, 1994), 71–89. In addition to positing a nonmissionary Judaism in several of his articles on conversion, Shaye J. D. Cohen addresses the missionary question directly in "Adolf Harnack's 'The Mission and Expansion of Judaism': Christianity Succeeds Where Judaism Fails," in *The Future of Early Christianity: Essays in Honor of Helmut Koester*, ed. Birger Pearson (Minneapolis, Mn.: Fortress, 1991), 163–69; and "Was Judaism in Antiquity a Missionary Religion?" in *Jewish Assimilation, Acculturation and Accommodation*, ed. Menachem Mor, Studies in Jewish Civilization 2 (Lanham, Md.: University Press of America, 1992), 14–23.

7. Cohen, "Adolf Harnack," 166.

8. See, for example, Shaye J. D. Cohen, "The Origins of the Matrilineal Principle in Rabbinic Law," *Association for Jewish Studies Review* 10, no. 1 (1985): 19–53; idem, "Respect for Judaism by Gentiles According to Josephus," *HTR* 80, no. 4 (1987): 409–30; and idem, "Crossing the Boundary and Becoming a Jew," *HTR* 82, no. 1 (1989): 13–33. These articles are now revised and expanded in a larger work on the question of Jewishness in antiquity. See Shaye J. D. Cohen, *The Beginnings of Jewishness: Boundaries, Varieties, Uncertainties.* Hellenistic Culture and Society 31 (Berkeley, Los Angeles, and London: University of California Press, 1999).

9. See Cohen, "Adolf Harnack"; and Will and Orrieux, 211–89. I take issue, however, with Cohen's conclusion that because Harnack's conceptualization of Jews as missionary was laden with "pro-Christian bias," subsequent work built on the premise that Hellenistic Jews proselytized has no validity. The problem of pro-Christian theological biases of those working with sources on early Judaism is hydra-headed. Scholars with such biases have also conceptualized Judaism as nonmissionary (cf. the historical overview of the question by Will and Orrieux).

10. For Georgi's response to the new proponents of a nonmissionary Judaism, see, "The Early Church: Internal Jewish Migration or New Religion?" *HTR* 88, no. 1 (1995): 35–68, esp. 50–51.

11. For example, Otto Weinreich, "Gebet und Wunder," in *Genethliakon: Wilhelm Schmid zum siebzigstend Geburtstag,* edited by Friedrich Focke et al. (Stuttgart: Kohlhammer, 1929), 200–462; Moses Hadas, *Hellenistic Culture: Fusion and Diffusion* (New York: W. W. Norton, 1959); Morton Smith, "Prolegomena to a Discussion of Aretalogies," *JBL* 90 (1971): 174–98.

12. In arguing that not even Cynic and Epicurean philosophers were interested in proselytizing, Goodman isolates the practice of mission and conversion in Christianity from its Hellenistic milieu more radically than Arthur Darby Nock, who did see similarities between the missionary efforts of these philosophers and Jews and Christians (Arthur Darby Nock, *Conversion: The Old and the New in Religion from Alexander the Great to Augustine of Hippo* [Oxford: Clarendon, 1933], Chap. 11). Likewise, Kraabel speculates that mission was one of the "*nova*" of Christianity, having its genesis "somewhere in those very few years between Jesus and Paul" ("Immigrants, Exiles," 85).

13. In "Was Judaism a Missionary Religion," Cohen separates propaganda from apologetics and argues that Jews were only involved in the latter activity (17). Notice also the passive characterization of Judaism in his conclusion: Judaism was "*open to converts* and did nothing to raise obstacles in their path, but with a few notable exceptions it also *did little or nothing to solicit them*" (21, my emphasis). Will and Orrieux devote a whole chapter to arguing that the term "proselyte" is an intransitive-reflexive verb for one who enters a community and that there is no active term as its counterpart in antiquity (27–46). They argue that although there were proselytes in antiquity, proselytizers simply did not exist.

In arguing against a propagandistic function for Hellenistic Jewish literature, these scholars stand in line with Victor Tcherikover, "Jewish Apologetic Literature Reconsidered," *Eos* 48 (1956): 169–93; and the editors of Emil Schürer's *The History of the Jewish People in the Age of Jesus Christ* (reprint, rev. and ed. Geza Vermes et al., 3 vols. in 4, Edinburgh: T & T Clark, 1973–1986).

14. Goodman, *Mission and Conversion*, esp. 2–19.

15. McKnight, 48.

16. Note the similarities between this description and Josephus's *Antiquities* 18.81–84, where a Jew is said to play the role of an "interpreter of the law of Moses and its wisdom" [*exēgeisthai sophian nomōn tōn Mōuseōs*] for a Roman woman of senatorial rank. This episode is discussed at length in Chapter 1.

17. Harnack, 217–39.

18. See, for example, Ludwig Friedländer, *Roman Life and Manners Under the Early Empire*, 4 vols., trans. L. A. Magnus (London: Routledge, 1908–1913), 1:255; Karl Georg Kuhn and Hartmut Stegemann, "Proselyten," PWSup 9 (1962): 1248–84, esp. 1264.

19. Watershed works in the field of women in early Judaism and Christianity include Elisabeth Schüssler Fiorenza, *In Memory of Her: A Feminist Theological Reconstruction of Christian Origins* (New York: Crossroad, 1983); Bernadette J. Brooten, *Women Leaders in the Ancient Synagogue*, Brown Judaic Series 36 (Atlanta, Ga.: Scholars Press, 1982); Ross Shepherd Kraemer, *Her Share of the Blessings: Women's Religions Among Pagans, Jews, and Christians in the Greco-Roman World* (New York and Oxford: Oxford University Press, 1992).

20. Of the three texts, the dating of Josephus's is most certain, since he speaks of concluding it during the thirteenth year of Domitian, 93–94 CE (*Ant.* 20.267). Juvenal's poems are dated to the first decades of the second century, during the reigns of Trajan and Hadrian. A reference to a comet and an earthquake in connection with Armenian and Parthian affairs (6.407) suggests a date near 115 CE for his sixth satire. I presume a date of at least 90 CE, and possibly as late as the early second century, for the composition of Acts. On this range of dates for Acts, see Hans Conzelmann, *Acts of the Apostles*, Hermeneia (Philadelphia, Pa.: Fortress, 1972), xxxiii; François Bovon, *L'Évangile selon Saint Luc 1–9*, Commentaire du Nouveau Testament 3a (Genève: Labor et Fides, 1991), 28; Helmut Koester, *Introduction to the New Testament*, 2 vols. (New York and Berlin: De Gruyter, 1982), 2:310.

Juvenal's critique of the appeal of foreign religions to gullible women is in line with later second-century pagan critiques directed specifically at Christianity. See Margaret Y. MacDonald, *Early Christian Women and Pagan Opinion: The Power of the Hysterical Woman* (Cambridge: Cambridge University Press, 1996).

21. For my thinking on rhetoric, I am largely indebted to the work of Elisabeth Schüssler Fiorenza. See especially "Text and Reality—Reality as Text: The Problem of a Feminist Historical and Social Reconstruction Based on Texts," *StTh* 43 (1989): 19–

34; *Revelation: Vision of a Just World* (Minneapolis, Mn.: Fortress, 1991); *But She Said: Feminist Practices of Biblical Interpretation* (Boston: Beacon, 1992); "The Rhetoricity of Historical Knowledge: Pauline Discourse and Its Contextualizations," in *Religious Propaganda and Missionary Competition in the New Testament World: Essays Honoring Dieter Georgi*, eds. Lukas Bormann, Kelly Del Tredici, and Angela Standhartinger (Leiden and New York: Brill, 1994), 443–69; *Rhetoric and Ethic: The Politics of Biblical Studies* (Minneapolis, Mn.: Fortress, 1999).

22. For example, as I shall note below in Chapter 2, Josephus's desire for good relations between Romans and Jews results in a narrative in the *Antiquities* in which such positive relations exist. The portrayal in Acts of Christian emissaries receiving the protection of Asiarchs and Roman governors is prompted by a similar motive.

23. See, for example, Elizabeth A. Castelli, "Romans," in *Searching the Scriptures: A Feminist Commentary*, ed. Elisabeth Schüssler Fiorenza with the assistance of Ann Brock and Shelly Matthews (New York: Crossroad, 1994), 272–300, esp. 280–84.

24. Sandra R. Joshel, "Female Desire and the Discourse of Empire: Tacitus's Messalina," *Signs* 21, no. 1 (1995): 50–82, esp. 58–59. See her equally compelling interpretation of Livy's history of Rome, "The Body Female and the Body Politic: Livy's Lucretia and Verginia," in *Pornography and Representation in Greece and Rome*, ed. Amy Richlin (New York and Oxford: Oxford University Press, 1992), 112–30.

25. Kate Cooper, *The Virgin and the Bride: Idealized Womanhood in Late Antiquity* (Cambridge, Mass., and London: Harvard University Press, 1996), 55, her emphasis.

26. Kate Cooper, "Apostles, Ascetic Women, and Questions of Audience: New Reflections on the Rhetoric of Gender in the Apocryphal Acts," *SBLSP* 31 (1992): 147–53, esp. 148, my emphasis.

27. See Kathleen Canning, "Feminist History After the Linguistic Turn: Historicizing Discourse and Experience," in *History and Theory: Feminist Research, Debates, Contestations*, ed. Barbara Laslett et al. (Chicago and London: University of Chicago Press, 1997), 416–52.

28. Schüssler Fiorenza uses the term "kyriocentric," from the Greek *kyrios*, "master, or lord," rather than "androcentric," in recognition that patriarchy is not a dualistic system of gender oppression, but rather a complex interlocking pyramid of gender and status hierarchies, in which the *kyrios*, the lord of the house, rules.

29. Schüssler Fiorenza, "Rhetoricity of Historical Knowledge," 462. For theoretical discussion of reconstructing women's history from androcentric sources by scholars in the classics, see Barbara K. Gold, " 'But Ariadne Was Never There in the First Place': Finding the Female in Roman Poetry," in *Feminist Theory and the Classics*, ed. Nancy Sorkin Rabinowitz and Amy Richlin, Thinking Gender Series (New York and London: Routledge, 1993), 75–101; and Amy Richlin, "The Ethnographer's Dilemma and the Dream of a Lost Golden Age," in *Feminist Theory and the Classics*, Thinking Gender Series, ed. Nancy Sorkin Rabinowitz and Amy Richlin (New York

and London: Routledge, 1992), 272–303; and Mary-Kay Gamel et al., discussion of "Decentering the Text: The Case of Ovid," by Phyllis Culham, *Helios* n.s. 17, no. 2 (1990): 171–262.

30. Gold, "Finding the Female," 84.

31. For discussion of the biblical figure of the "Strange Woman" and the hermeneutical stance of reading "as a strange woman," see Claudia V. Camp, "Feminist Theological Hermeneutics: Canon and Christian Identity," in *Searching the Scriptures: A Feminist Introduction*, ed. Elisabeth Schüssler Fiorenza with the assistance of Shelly Matthews (New York: Crossroad, 1993), 154–71, esp. 166–69.

CHAPTER 1

1. For an overview of the works of Josephus, see Harold W. Attridge, "Josephus and His Works," in *Jewish Writings of the Second Temple Period*, ed. Michael E. Stone (Philadelphia, Pa.: Fortress, 1984), 185–232. On Epaphroditus, see Tessa Rajak, *Josephus: The Historian and His Society* (Philadelphia, Pa.: Fortress, 1984), 223–24.

2. For a recent statement of this apologetic intent, see Gregory E. Sterling, *Historiography and Self-Definition: Josephus, Luke-Acts and Apologetic Historiography*, Novum Testamentum Supplements 6 (Leiden: Brill, 1992), 226–310, esp. 308–10. Cf. also Shaye J. D. Cohen, *Josephus in Galilee and Rome: His Vita and Development as a Historian*, Columbia Studies in the Classical Tradition 8 (Leiden: Brill, 1979), 232–42.

3. Steve Mason, " 'Should Any Wish to Enquire Further' (*Ant.* 1.25): The Aim and Audience of Josephus's *Judean Antiquities/Life*," in *Understanding Josephus: Seven Perspectives*, ed. Steve Mason, Journal for the Study of the Pseudepigrapha Supplement Series 32 (Sheffield, Eng.: Sheffield Academic Press, 1998), 64–103; idem, "Introduction to the *Judean Antiquities*," in *Judean Antiquities 1–4*, translation and commentary by Louis H. Feldman (Leiden: Brill, 2000), xii–xxxv., vol. 3 of *Flavius Josephus: Translation and Commentary*, ed. Steve Mason.

4. Mason, "Introduction to the *Judean Antiquities*," xxii.

5. See, for example, Friedländer, 1:255; Kuhn and Stegemann, cols. 1263–64; Harry J. Leon, *The Jews of Ancient Rome*, updated ed. (Peabody, Mass.: Hendrickson, 1995), 250–56; Brooten, *Women Leaders*, 144–47.

6. A detailing of the discrepancies in the accounts of these four authors, as well as summary of much of the secondary literature on the subject, is supplied in Margaret H. Williams, "The Expulsion of the Jews from Rome in A.D. 19," *Latomus* 48 (1989): 765–84.

7. The translation of the phrase *libertini generis* is widely disputed, and much is at stake in its translation for the "Jews as missionaries" debate. Those who read the phrase as signifying four thousand freedmen in Rome in 19 CE are able to posit a phenomenal number of Jewish proselytes in Rome at this date. See Menachem Stern, *Greek and Latin Authors on Jews and Judaism*, 3 vols. (Jerusalem: Academy of Sciences

and Humanities, 1974–1984), 2:71. Some who view this number as implausible (including the translator for the Loeb Classical Library) have followed Elmer Truesdell Merrill's suggestion that the phrase be translated "freedmen and their descendents" (see his "The Expulsion of Jews from Rome Under Tiberius," *CP* 14 [1919]: 365–72). Williams argues that Tacitus's prejudice against Jewish proselytes has caused him to inflate this number ("Expulsion of Jews," 771–72).

8. E. Mary Smallwood presents the fullest case for missionary activity as the source of the expulsion. See "Some Notes on the Jews under Tiberius," *Latomus* 15 (1956): 314–29. See also Merrill; Georgi, *Opponents of Paul*, 92–96; and Stern, 2:68–73.

Scholars arguing against the paradigm of a missionizing Judaism have paid scant attention to these four texts, neglecting especially Josephus's account in the *Antiquities*. Goodman and Cohen will not consider *Antiquities* 18 as an indication of Jewish proselytizing because Josephus is not explicit in making such a link. Goodman mistakenly conflates the accounts of Josephus and Tacitus (Cohen, "Was Judaism a Missionary Religion?" 22, n. 14; Goodman, "Jewish Proselytizing," 60; idem, *Mission and Conversion*, 68). McKnight devotes a mere two pages of his monograph to all sources indicating Jewish proselytizing in Rome, including *Antiquities* 18 (73–74). In their discussion of the expulsion of Jews from Rome, Will and Orrieux do not mention Josephus's account (106–10).

9. Williams, "Expulsion of Jews," 770.

10. Those who narrowly define missionary activity argue that Romans could take up Jewish and Isis cultic practices without having been proselytized by Jews and Isis worshippers. As I have noted earlier, my concern is not whether representatives of Isis and Jewish cults, or Romans themselves, initiated this exchange, but rather that the exchange takes place.

11. Two additional literary sources support the suggestion that Jews in Rome were sanctioned for missionary activity under Tiberius: (1) a letter of Seneca notes that because foreign rites were suspect during the reign of Tiberius, he was careful to disassociate himself from them (*Epistulae morales* 108.22). Although Seneca makes no explicit reference to Isis or Jewish missionary practices here, he does indicate a general climate of hostility against those who adopted foreign rites. (2) Valerius Maximus, who recounts an expulsion of Jews from Rome in 139 BCE because of missionary activity (*Fact. et dict.* 1.3.3), is a contemporary of Tiberius. I suggest that Valerius's awareness of a crackdown on Jewish proselytizing activity in his lifetime has influenced his construction of historical narrative.

12. Although Martin Goodman does not read the accounts of Tacitus, Suetonius, and Josephus as I do, he does follow the same principle when he suggests that Dio Cassius identifies the expulsion of 19 CE with Jewish proselytizing activity because he is aware of Jewish proselytizing in his own day, the third century CE (Goodman, *Mission and Conversion*, 83, 144).

By the "turn of the first century CE" I mean the period that encompasses the reigns of Domitian (81–96 CE), Nerva (96–98), Trajan (98–117), and the early years of Hadrian, who reigned from 118–138. Josephus completed the *Antiquities* during the thirteenth year of Domitian, 93–94 CE. Quintillian's *Institutio oratoria* was also written under Domitian. The epigrams of Martial span the reigns of Domitian, Nerva, and Trajan. The epigrams I refer to below are generally dated as follows: Book 4 (89 CE); Book 7 (92 CE); Book 11 (96 CE, three months after Domitian's death); and Book 12 (shortly after 100 CE). Tacitus wrote the *Historiae* under Trajan and the *Annales* between 115 and 120 CE. Juvenal's *Satires* were written within the reigns of Trajan and the early years of Hadrian (c. 110–130). Suetonius's *De vita Caesarum* was published in 120 CE under Hadrian.

13. For a discussion of the distinct nature of late-first-century and early-second-century anti-Jewish polemic, see Margaret H. Williams, "Domitian, the Jews and the 'Judaizers,'" *Historia* 39 (1990): 196–211, esp. 205–6; Shaye J. D. Cohen, "Respect for Judaism by Gentiles According to Josephus," *HTR* 80, no. 4 (1987): 409–30, esp. 428–29; John G. Gager, *The Origins of Anti-Semitism: Attitudes Toward Judaism in Pagan and Christian Antiquity* (New York and Oxford: Oxford University Press, 1983), 58–59. See Gager, 55–66, for the argument that anti-Jewish hostility among conservative Romans is closely correlated with successful Jewish proselytizing among the upper classes in Rome.

14. John G. Gager, *Moses in Greco-Roman Paganism*, Society of Biblical Literature Monograph Series 16 (Nashville, Tenn.: Abingdon, 1972), 80–82. On the theory that Quintillian's slander can be explained as an attempt to distance himself from his patron Flavius Clemens, who was convicted of Judaizing, see M. L. Clarke, "Quintillian: A Biographical Sketch," *Greece and Rome* 14 (1967): 24–37, esp. 35.

15. Cf. Martial *Epigr.* 4.4, on the "stench" of fasting Jewish women; 7.30 and 7.55 on the availability of circumcised Judeans as objects of sexual pleasure; 7.35 and 7.82 on the concealment of circumcision; 7.55 on subjugated Judea; 11.94 for the accusation that a Jewish poet has sodomized Martial's own beloved boy; 12.57 on the young Jew taught to beg by his mother.

16. For a recent statement of this view, see Williams, "Domitian, the Jews and the 'Judaizers.'" See also E. Mary Smallwood, "Domitian's Attitude Toward Jews and Judaism," *CP* 51 (1956): 1–13; and idem, *The Jews Under Roman Rule From Pompey to Diocletian* (Leiden: Brill, 1976), 382–83.

17. See Nerva's FISCI IUDAICI CALUMNIA SUBLATA coins in Harold Mattingly and E. A. Sydenham, *The Roman Imperial Coinage*, 10 vols. (London: Spink, 1923–1994), 2:227–28, nos. 58, 72, 82; and Harold Mattingly, *Coins of the Roman Empire in the British Museum*, 8 vols. (London: The British Museum, 1966), 3:15–19, nos. 88, 98, 105–6, pls. 4.7, 5.7; and Dio *Hist.* 68.1.1–2.

18. For Talmudic and Midrashic sources, see Smallwood, *Jews Under Roman Rule*, 382–84. For Christian tradition, see Eusebius *Eccl. Hist.* 3.19–20, 4.26.9.

19. Leonard A. Thompson, *The Book of Revelation: Apocalypse and Empire* (Oxford: Oxford University Press, 1990), 95–115, 133–37, esp. 135.

20. Domitian's relations with Jews in the provinces are not of concern here. For these, see Thompson, 133–45.

21. For the *Acta Pro Judaeis*, see *Ant.* 16.160–78, 19.281–85, 19.287–91, 19.303–11; and discussion in Horst R. Moehring, "The *Acta Pro Judaeis* in the *Antiquities* of Flavius Josephus," in *Christianity, Judaism and other Greco-Roman Cults: Studies for Morton Smith at Sixty,* ed. Jacob Neusner, Studies in Judaism in Late Antiquity 12 (Leiden: Brill, 1975), 124–58; Tessa Rajak, "Was There a Roman Charter for the Jews?" *JRS* 74 (1984): 107–23.

22. Shirley Jackson Case, "Josephus' Anticipation of a Domitianic Persecution," *JBL* 44 (1925): 10–20. Cf. passages concerning Gaius from the *Antiquities* 18.257–308, 19.1–211 with the abbreviated version in *J.W.* 2.184–203.

23. Williams, "Domitian, the Jews and the 'Judaizers,'" 205–6. Cf. Sterling, 299–301.

24. On Vespasian's legendary encounter with Serapis, see Tacitus *Hist.* 4.81; Suetonius *Vesp.* 7.2; Philostratus *Life of Apollonius* 5.27. On Titus's role in the consecration of an Apis bull in Egypt, see Suetonius *Tit.* 1.5.3. Domitian is said to have saved himself in the civil war of 69 CE by disguising himself as a worshipper of Isis (cf. Tacitus *Hist.* 3.74; Suetonius *Dom.* 1.2). That this story conforms to a standard trope is suggested by Valerius Maximus *Fact. et dict.* 7.3.8, which records the same sort of escape by one aedile M. Volusius.

25. For a description of this obelisk, see Michel Malaise, *Inventaire préliminaire des documents égyptiens découverts en italie,* Etudes préliminaires aux religions orientales dans l'empire romain 21 (Leiden: Brill, 1972), 203–7, pls. 20–21.

26. Franz Cumont, *Oriental Religions in Roman Paganism* (New York: Dover, 1956), 85–86.

27. Mattingly and Sydenham, 2:70.

28. Michel Malaise, *Les conditions de pénétration et de diffusion des cultes égyptiens en Italie,* Etudes préliminaires aux religions orientales dans l'empire romain 22 (Leiden: Brill, 1972), 415–16; idem, *Inventaire préliminaire,* 190–91, pl. 16.

29. For another reading, from a different perspective, which also recognizes Josephus's attempts at comparison here, see Horst R. Moehring, "The Persecution of the Jews and the Adherents of the Isis Cult at Rome A.D. 19," *NovT* 3 (1959): 293–304.

30. In fact the husband of each bears the same name, Saturninus. Although an attempt to account for this detail historically has been made (see Robert Samuel Rogers, "Fulvia Paulina C. Sentii Saturnini," *AJP* 53 [1932]: 252–56), it is best to view this phenomenon as further support for understanding these women and their husband(s) as types, not as historical persons.

31. In light of Josephus's care to characterize the leading missionary imposter in

these terms, Williams's suggestion that he serves as a kind of folk hero in the tale is implausible (Williams, "Expulsion of Jews," 777).

32. Otto Weinreich, *Der Trug des Nektanebos: Wandlungen eines Novellenstoffs* (Leipzig and Berlin: Teubner, 1911), 1–48. For more on the Nektanebos episode in the *Alexander Romance*, see Reinhold Merkelbach, *Die Quellen des griechischen Alexanderromans* (Munich: Beck, 1954), 58, 74–75; and Alan B. Lloyd, "Nationalistic Propaganda in Ptolemaic Egypt," *Historia* 31 (1982): 46–50.

33. Their initial encounter:

> After his arrival in Macedonia, Nektanebos became well known to everyone. His calculations were of such accuracy that even the queen, Olympias, heard of him and came to him by night while her husband Philip was away at war. And she learned from him what she had been seeking, and left. A few days later, she sent for him and told him to come to her. When he saw how beautiful she was, Nektanebos was filled with desire for her loveliness, and reaching out his hand, said, "Greetings, Queen of the Macedonians!"
>
> "Greetings to you also, most excellent prophet!" she replied. "Come here and sit down." She continued: "You are the Egyptian teacher whose complete reliability has been established by those who have tried you. Even I have been convinced by you. By what method can you command true predictions?" (From the translation of the text of Pseudo-Callisthenes, *The Greek Alexander Romance* by Ken Dowden in *Collected Ancient Greek Novels*, ed. B. P. Reardon [Berkeley and Los Angeles: University of California Press, 1989], 656–57)

34. See the analysis in Joshel, "Body Female and Body Politic."

35. On asceticism in the Apocryphal Acts as a means of asserting Christian moral superiority, see Cooper, *Virgin and Bride*, esp. 45–67.

In the third century CE representations of women's conversion in terms of sexual allegiance are not limited to Christian literature. Diogenes Laertius represents the "conversion" of the female Hipparchia to Cynic philosophy in terms of her love for the Cynic teacher Crates (6.96–98). In addition to adopting his teachings, she also engages in sexual intercourse with him.

36. Ovid *Amores* 2.2.25–26; *Ars amatoria* 1.77–78, 3.393, 3.635–37.

37. See also Martial *Epigr.* 11.47.3–4, 2.14.7–8; Juvenal *Sat.* 6.535–38, 9.22–25. For convincing rejoinders to the long-held view, based on passages from antiquity cited here, that Isis was a cult of the "demi-monde," see Ilse Becher, "Der Isiskult in Rom— ein kult der Halbwelt?" *Zeitschrift für ägyptische Sprache und Altertumskunde* 96 (1970): 81–90; and Sharon Kelly Heyob, *The Cult of Isis Among Women in the Graeco-Roman World* (Leiden: Brill, 1975), 111–27.

38. See Chapter 4 below for an analysis of writers who defend the women who practice "foreign" religion as chaste. For further discussion of the intertwining of discourse on the well-being of the state and household in terms of religious practice and women's submission, see Schüssler Fiorenza, *In Memory of Her*, Chap. 7.

39. For the entire account, see Livy *Hist.* 39.8–18. Cf. Cicero, who makes reference

to the Bacchanalia as justification for his own legislation concerning women's proper religious practice (*Leg.* 2.35–37).

For a discussion of the complexities involved in using Livy's account as a source for the reconstruction of women's Dionysian devotion, see Kraemer, *Her Share of the Blessings*, 42–46. For the influence of new comedy on Livy's account, see Adele Scafuro, "Livy's Comic Narrative of the Bacchanalia," *Helios* 16, no. 2 (1989): 119–41.

40. John Liebeschuetz, *Continuity and Change in Roman Religion* (Oxford: Clarendon, 1979), 90–100. See also the discussion of Catherine Edwards, *The Politics of Immorality in Ancient Rome* (Cambridge: Cambridge University Press, 1993), 42–47.

41. Edwards, 43.

42. On Tacitus's use of the *Acta Senatus* in these "end of the year" sections of the Annals, see Ronald Syme, *Tacitus*, 2 vols. (Oxford: Clarendon, 1958), 2:278, 296.

43. Williams, "Expulsion of Jews," 775.

44. The only scholar in this century to grant serious consideration to Tacitus's linking of the sanctions against female prostitution with the expulsion of Jews and Isis worshippers was W. A. Heidel in "Why Were the Jews Banished from Italy in 19 A.D.?" *AJP* 41 (1920): 38–48. However, his fanciful proposal that the Romans punished the Jews not because Fulvia was swindled, but because they assumed that the Jews had invited her to become a temple prostitute, led to the dismissal of his arguments in their entirety.

For more analysis of Tacitus's adultery accounts, see Amy Richlin, "Some Approaches to the Sources on Adultery at Rome," in *Reflections of Women in Antiquity*, ed. Helene P. Foley (New York: Gordon and Breach, 1981), 386–88.

45. On the significance of the Vestal's sexual status, see Ariadne Staples, *From Good Goddess to Vestal Virgins: Sex and Category in Roman Religion* (London and New York: Routledge, 1998), 131–56. Cf. the earlier work of Mary Beard, "The Sexual Status of the Vestal Virgins," *JRS* 70 (1980): 12–27; Judith P. Hallett, *Fathers and Daughters in Roman Society* (Princeton, N.J.: Princeton University Press, 1984), 83–89.

46. Cf. Pliny *Ep.* 6.31.4–6; Plutarch *Galba* 12; Cicero *Pro caelio.* 31, 36, 38, 49; Juvenal *Sat.* 6.76–81; Martial *Epigr.* 6.39; Petronius *Satyricon* 69.3, 75.11, 126.5–11. See the related discussion in Edwards, 48–53.

47. This abhorrence of religious practices that allow for class mixing is not limited to the time of Juvenal. John A. North suggests that the Roman senate's disquiet concerning the Bacchists in 186 BCE was caused in part by the unpredictable mixture of social classes that comprised the Bacchic groups (John A. North, "Religious Toleration in Republican Rome," *Proceedings of the Cambridge Philological Society* 205 [1979]: 94).

48. Note also that in the scene immediately preceding the orgy (6.306–13), Juvenal conjures up women of unequal status—a freedwoman and an aristocrat—who

transgress class boundaries to conspire in sacrilege before the altar of Chastity. On textual difficulties here, see Richlin, ed., Juvenal, *Satura VI*, 65–66.

49. Max Radin, *The Jews Among the Greeks and Romans* (Philadelphia, Pa.: Jewish Publication Society, 1915), 304–13.

50. For this typology in new comedy, see Peter P. Spranger, *Historische Unter-suchungen zu den Sklavenfiguren des Plautus und Terenz*, Forschungen zur antiken Sklaverei 17 (Stuttgart: Steiner-Verlag, 1984), 16. On the slave as an extension of the master's self in the ideal novel, see Lawrence Wills, "The Depiction of Slavery in the Ancient Novel," *Semeia* 83 (1998): 113–32.

51. Likewise, the slaves of Plautus have no desire to profit financially from their trickery. On this point, see Erich Segal, *Roman Laughter* (Cambridge, Mass.: Harvard University Press, 1968), 61–63.

52. This is a departure from new comedy, where punishments seldom fit crimes, and the skill of a slave escaping from a threatened punishment is a frequent source of humor. See Spranger, 47–51, 84–87.

53. Tiberius's handling of an adultery case with such leniency has long been recognized as a sign of the fictitious nature of the story. See Robert M. Grant, *The Sword and the Cross* (New York: Macmillan, 1955), 29.

54. For further texts and discussion, see Schüssler Fiorenza, *In Memory of Her*, 176–77; David Balch, *Let Wives Be Submissive: The Domestic Code in I Peter*, Society of Biblical Literature Monograph Series 26 (Atlanta, Ga.: Scholars Press, 1981), 65–80. For a discussion of the texts of Cicero and Plutarch, see Chapter 4, 78–82.

55. For feminist analysis of Romans 16, see Bernadette J. Brooten, "Junia . . . Outstanding Among the Apostles (Romans 16:7)," in *Women Priests*, ed. Leonard S. Swidler and Arlene Swidler (New York: Paulist, 1977), 141–44; Elisabeth Schüssler Fiorenza, "Missionaries, Apostles, Coworkers: Romans 16 and the Reconstruction of Women's Early Christian History," *Word and World* 6 (1986): 420–33; idem, *In Memory of Her*, 168–204; Castelli, 276–80.

For a recent discussion of the status of those greeted in Romans 16, see Stanley K. Stowers, *A Rereading of Romans: Justice, Jews, and Gentiles* (New Haven, Conn., and London: Yale University Press, 1994), 74–82. Stowers argues that most are freedpersons and slaves but suggests that Prisca may be a Roman citizen.

I read Romans 16 as an address to the Roman church, and not, as some scholars have argued, a letter of recommendation to the church in Ephesos. For arguments supporting this reading, see Harry Y. Gamble Jr., *The Textual History of the Letter to the Romans* (Grand Rapids, Mich.: Eerdmans, 1977); Kurt Aland, *Neutestamentliche Entwürfe* (Munich: Kaiser, 1979), 284–301; Wolf-Henning Ollrog, "Die Abfassungs-verhältnisse von Röm 16," in *Kirche: Festschrift für Günther Bornkamm zum 75. Geburtstag*, ed. D. Lührmann and G. Strecker (Tübingen: J. C. Mohr, 1980), 221–44.

56. Of course, as Ross Kraemer cautions, the existing epigraphical material has survived largely due to random chance (Ross Shepherd Kraemer, "Non-Literary

Evidence for Jewish Women in Rome and Egypt" in *Rescuing Creusa: New Method-ological Approaches to Women in Antiquity* = *Helios* 13, no. 2 [1986]: 85–101). Because it is extremely fragmentary, it is difficult to evaluate how representative it is of religious life in Rome. However, given that women tend to be underrepresented in epigraphic sources, due to factors such as women's greater illiteracy and greater lack of material resources, the epigraphic sources indicating the presence of women should receive a privileged place in historical reconstructions.

57. Kraemer, "Non-Literary Evidence," 88.

58. Leon, 253–56. The inscriptions he identifies as signifying women proselytes are *CII* 523, *CII* 462, *CII* 21, *CII* 222, and *CII* 256. See Ross Kraemer's discussion of the problems of *CII* 21 in "On the Meaning of the Term 'Jew' in Greco-Roman Inscriptions," *HTR* 82, no. 1 (1989): 38–42. For further discussion of the epitaph of Beturia Paulla, see Brooten, *Women Leaders*, 58–59.

59. Leon, 254–55. For Kraemer's comments on status, see "Non-Literary Evidence," 88.

60. Heyob, 81–110. This is the thrust of her entire chapter on the participation of women in the cult.

61. See, for example, Wayne A. Meeks, *The First Urban Christians: The Social World of the Apostle Paul* (New Haven, Conn., and London: Yale University Press, 1983), 25; Alan Wardman, *Religion and Statecraft Among the Romans* (Baltimore, Md.: Johns Hopkins University Press, 1982), 120.

62. A point also made by Kraemer, *Her Share of the Blessings*, 75–76.

63. For inscription and commentary, see Franz Cumont, "La grande inscription bacchique du metropolitan museum," *AJA* 37 (1933): 232–63, and pls. 27–29.

64. Albert Henrichs, "Changing Dionysiac Identities," in *Jewish and Christian Self-Definition*, ed. Ben F. Meyer and E. P. Sanders, 3 vols. (Philadelphia, Pa.: Fortress, 1982), 3:137–60, esp. 154–55.

65. Schüssler Fiorenza, *In Memory of Her*, 90. See also Kraemer, *Her Share of the Blessings*, 60, for her argument that the rites of Cybele, Dionysos, and Isis provided a greater measure of autonomy for women than traditional religions of the Roman state. For arguments that Judaism and early Christianity provided avenues of advancement for the "upwardly mobile," see Meeks, 55–63; and Stowers, 74–82.

I concur with this assessment, with the caveat that the appeal of "foreign" religions among elite Roman women must be nuanced by a consideration of class. Domitian's Egypto-philia, expressed in his advertised "love affair" with Isis, is best read as a by-product of colonialism, rather than as an indication of any sympathy for the Egyptian people. The fascination of conquerors for the cultural practices of the conquered was likely shared by elite Roman men and women alike.

66. Roman writers acknowledge that female Isis devotees make ascetic vows, but never without questioning their utility or authenticity. See, for example, Propertius *Eleg.* 2.33.1–4 [Goold, LCL]: "Once more those dismal rites have returned to plague

us: for ten nights Cynthia has sacrificed. And a curse upon the rites which the daughter of Inachus has sent from the warm Nile to the matrons of Italy!" Cf. Tibullus 1.3.23, 25–26; and Ovid *Amores* 3.9.33–35.

On insinuations that such vows are inauthentic, see Propertius *Eleg.* 4.5.33–34 and Ovid *Amores* 1.8.73–74, where chastity vows in connection with the Isis cult are viewed as a means of sexual manipulation. Juvenal suggests that a woman who takes a vow of chastity to Isis inevitably needs absolution for breaking it (*Sat.* 6.535–37).

67. On asceticism as a means of autonomy and religious authority for women in antiquity, see Antionette Clark Wire, *The Corinthian Women Prophets: A Reconstruction Through Paul's Rhetoric* (Minneapolis, Mn.: Fortress, 1990), esp. 90–97; Cooper, *Virgin and Bride*, 73–87; Rosemary Radford Ruether, "Misogynism and Virginal Feminism in the Fathers of the Church," in idem, ed., *Religion and Sexism: Images of Women in the Jewish and Christian Traditions* (New York: Simon and Schuster, 1974), 150–83; Elizabeth A. Clark, "Ascetic Renunciation and Feminine Advancement: A Paradox of Late Ancient Christianity," *Anglican Theological Review* 63 (1981): 240–57.

68. See my analysis of Acts 16 below in Chapter 4, 86–95, for the argument that Luke makes a similar move to suppress the role of women from the lower classes in early Christianity through his juxtaposition of the story of Lydia and that of the mantic slave girl.

CHAPTER 2

1. Josephus refers to Poppaea both in the *Antiquities* and the *Life* as the *gynē* of Nero. Roman sources indicate that she was first Nero's consort (58 CE), and then his wife (62 CE).

2. In this chapter I demonstrate the pattern highlighting the heroic deeds of Gentile noblewomen in the narrative, without pressing the question of whether Josephus himself, or his sources, are responsible for any particular portrait. Later I will suggest that if Josephus's sources feature the Gentile noblewoman as benefactor prior to his redaction of them, then this may be a common motif in Jewish literature, rather than a Josephan idiosyncrasy. See Chapter 3, 61–62.

3. See, for example, Suzanne Dixon, "A Family Business: Women's Role in Patronage and Politics at Rome 80–44 B.C.," *Classica et Mediaevalia* 34 (1983): 91–112, esp. 101–9.

4. See Fergus Millar, *The Emperor in the Roman World* (Ithaca, N.Y.: Cornell University Press, 1977) on gifts, 139–44, and on inheritances and legacies, 153–58.

5. Cf. Philo *Against Flaccus* and *On the Embassy to Gaius*; Dio *Hist.* 59.8.2, 59.24.1, 60.8.2–3; *Acts of Isidorus*; Yaakov Meshorer, *Ancient Jewish Coinage*, 2 vols. (Dix Hills, N.Y.: Amphora Books, 1982), 2:51–54, pl. 9.

6. Daniel R. Schwartz assigns the Antonia passages in the *Antiquities* to a source

that he designates as *Vita Agrippa* and categorizes as a Jewish novel. *Agrippa I: The Last King of Judaea* (Tübingen: Mohr/Siebeck, 1990), 1–37.

7. Schwartz, *Agrippa I*, 34. For a study of other Hellenistic adaptations of the Joseph motif, see Lawrence M. Wills, *The Jew in the Court of the Foreign King: Ancient Jewish Court Legends*, Harvard Dissertations in Religion 26 (Minneapolis, Mn.: Fortress, 1990).

8. For the entire incident, see *Ant.* 20.118–36. The parallel account in *J.W.* 2.232–46 is similar on several points, but it does not suggest the participation of Agrippina in the matter.

9. For example, Suetonius *Claud.* 25.5 [Rolfe, LCL]: "But these and other acts, and in fact almost the whole conduct of his reign, were dictated not so much by his own judgment as that of his wives and freedmen, since he nearly always acted in accordance with their interests and desires." Cf. Suetonius *Claud.* 29.1; Tacitus *Ann.* 12.1.1; Dio *Hist.* 60.2.4–5.

E. Mary Smallwood notes that Josephus "paints a typical literary picture of Claudius as the tool of his wives and freedmen," but she conflates the accounts in the *Antiquities* and the *Jewish War* (see Smallwood, *Jews Under Roman Rule*, 267–68).

10. *J.W.* 2.245 [Thackeray, LCL]: "At Rome Ceasar gave his hearing to Cumanus and the Samaritans in the presence of Agrippa, who made a spirited defense on behalf of the Jews, while Cumanus on his side was supported by many eminent persons. The emperor condemned the Samaritans, ordered three of their most prominent men to be executed, and banished Cumanus."

11. For discussions of the anti-Agrippa II tendency of *Antiquities* 20, see Cohen, *Josephus in Galilee and Rome*, 177–78; and Daniel R. Schwartz, "ΚΑΤΑ ΤΟΥΤΟΝ ΤΟΝ ΚΑΙΡΟΝ: Josephus' Source on Agrippa II," *JQR* 72, no. 4 (1982): 241–68, esp. 241–42.

12. Schwartz suggests that Josephus relies on a source written by a Jerusalemite priest for *Antiquities* 20.189–96 ("ΚΑΤΑ ΤΟΥΤΟΝ ΤΟΝ ΚΑΙΡΟΝ," 241–68).

13. On this particular translation of θεοσεβής, see discussion below.

14. Friedländer, 1:257.

15. E. Mary Smallwood, "The Alleged Jewish Tendencies of Poppaea Sabina," *JTS* n.s., no. 10 (1959): 329–35, esp. 333. Smallwood reaches this conclusion by accepting at face value the testimony of Suetonius, Tacitus, and Dio on Poppaea's hedonism.

16. Margaret H. Williams, "θεοσεβὴς γὰρ ἦν—The Jewish Tendencies of Poppaea Sabina," *JTS* n.s., no. 39 (1988): 97–111, esp. 106–8.

17. Richard A. Horsley, "High Priests and the Politics of Roman Palestine: A Contextual Analysis of the Evidence of Josephus," *JSJ* 17, no. 1 (1986): 23–55, esp. 33. As examples of this tendency, he cites the passage concerning the High Priest Joazar (*Ant.* 17.206–8) and John the Baptist (*Ant.* 18.116–19). For Josephus's spiritualization of the political aspects of John the Baptist's ministry, see also John Dominic Crossan, *Jesus: A Revolutionary Biography* (San Francisco: HarperSanFrancisco, 1994), 33–34.

18. That Josephus's rhetoric is effective, even for modern readers, is clear from

Williams's conclusions; she is content to isolate Poppaea's motives as stemming from personal piety, arguing: "For Josephus, her intervention on the Jews' behalf was directly attributable to her reverence for their God." Citing Poppaea's benefaction described in the *Life* 13–16, she continues, "This Jewish dimension to her 'θεοσέβεια' would also account for her other intervention on the Jews' behalf that [Josephus] records" (Williams, "θεοσεβὴς γὰρ ἥν," 107). For a discussion of events described in the *Life* 13–16, see below.

19. Reading Josephus's highlighting of Poppaea's piety as a rhetorical cover for the political implications of her actions calls into question the argument that although in the *Jewish War* Josephus understands Judaism as a national and political entity, in *Antiquities* he understands it more as a religion (see discussion of this distinction in Cohen, "Respect for Judaism," 427, n. 53). Josephus may in fact describe Judaism primarily in religious terms in this later work, but if one reads his descriptions as rhetorical arguments, rather than mirror reflections of his knowledge of the actual workings of Judaism, one must conclude that Josephus knows more about the political implications of having sympathy for Judaism than he readily admits.

20. Cohen, *Josephus in Galilee and Rome*, 61.

21. See, for example, Cohen, "Respect for Judaism," 424–25; Lawrence H. Schiffman, "The Conversion of the Royal House of Adiabene in Josephus and Rabbinic Sources," in *Josephus, Judaism, and Christianity*, ed. Louis H. Feldman and Gohei Hata (Detroit, Mich.: Wayne State University Press, 1987), 293–312. Mason, "Should Any Wish to Enquire Further," 90–95.

22. Artapanus names the Pharaoh's daughter Merris (Eusebius *Preparation for the Gospel* 9.27.1–16). On Thermuthis as the traditional name for this woman, see Tessa Rajak, "Moses in Ethiopia: Legend and Literature," *JJS* 29 (1978): 111–22, esp. 119.

23. *Exod Rab.* 1.26; *Deut Rab.* 11.10; *Yashar Exod* 131b–32b.

24. In the rabbinic tradition it is the angel Gabriel, not the Pharaoh's daughter, who intercedes to save him from death. For further discussion of this passage, see Louis H. Feldman, "Josephus' Portrait of Moses," *JQR* 82, nos. 3–4 (1992): 285–328, esp. 305–6.

25. A reference to Moses' brush with death in infancy is referred to above.

26. Martin Braun, *History and Romance in Graeco-Oriental Literature* (1938; reprint, New York and London: Garland, 1987), 97–102; cf. also Mielentz, "Tarpeius," PW n.s., no. 4 (1932): 2330–43, esp. 2337–38.

27. Numbers 12:1 (LXX), "And Mariam and Aaron spoke against Moses, because of the Ethiopian wife whom Moses took; for he had taken an Ethiopian wife."

28. Ezekiel the Tragedian solves the problem of Numbers 12:1 by making Midian one and the same place with Ethiopia (*Exodus* 60, trans. and ed. R. G. Robertson, in *The Old Testament Pseudepigrapha*, ed. James Charlesworth, 2 vols. [New York:

Doubleday, 1983–1985], 2:807–19); in Artapanus, the Ethiopian wife disappears altogether. See Rajak, "Moses in Ethiopia," 118; and Braun, 97–98.

29. Philo follows the tradition that the daughters have slighted Moses and dishonored their father. Cf. *On the Life of Moses* 1.58 [Colson, LCL]:

> The girls went home in high glee, and told the story of the unexpected event to their father, who thence conceived a strong desire to see the stranger, which he showed by censuring them for their ingratitude. "What possessed you," he said, "to let him depart? . . . Did you ever have to charge me with unsociable ways? Do you not expect that you may again fall in with those who would wrong you? Those who forget kindness are sure to lack defenders. Still, your error is not yet past cure . . ."

30. Such is the case with Antonia, Agrippina, Poppaea, Thermuthis, and Tharbis.

31. The glaring exception to this pattern is, of course, the story of Fulvia, whose willingness to offer up benefactions has disastrous consequences for the Jews.

32. For his pornographic depiction of Messalina, see Juvenal *Sat.* 6.114–35. For some allegations of her adulterous affairs, see Tacitus *Ann.* 11.12, 11.31.2, 11.36, 13.11.2.

33. Plutarch's praise of Antonia in *Anton.* 87.3 is representative of her reputation. On her image in art, see Katherine Patricia Erhart, "A Portrait of Antonia Minor in the Fogg Art Museum and Its Iconographical Tradition," *AJA* 82 (1978): 193–212.

34. Due, no doubt, to the sensational character of the purported means of the crime—poisoned mushrooms. Cf. Suetonius *Claud.* 44.2–6; Juvenal *Sat.* 5.147, 6.620–21; Tacitus *Ann.* 12.66–67; Pliny *Natural History* 22.92.

35. Cf. also his reference to the death of Claudius in *Ant.* 20.148, "It was reported by some [*logos ēn para tinōn*] that he had been poisoned by his wife Agrippina."

36. For example, *J.W.* 1.243, 1.359; and *Ant.* 15.93. On the function of Cleopatra in Augustan propaganda, see Lucy Hughes-Hallett, *Cleopatra: Histories, Dreams and Distortions* (New York: Harper and Row, 1990), 36–69. Paul Zanker, *The Power of Images in the Age of Augustus*, trans. Alan Shapiro, Jerome Lectures 16 (Ann Arbor: University of Michigan Press, 1988), 57–60.

37. Betsy Halpern Amaru, "Portraits of Biblical Women in Josephus' *Antiquities*," *JJS* 39, no. 2 (1988): 143–70.

38. Feldman, "Josephus' Portrait of Moses," 299–300.

39. Tal Ilan has argued that the portraits of domineering Hasmonian and Herodian women are the literary creations of Josephus's source, Nicolaus of Damascus, and that Josephus himself, when working without sources, has little to say about women. See "Josephus and Nicolaus on Women," in *Geschichte—Tradition—Reflection: Festschrift für Martin Hengel zum 70. Geburtstag*, ed. Hubert Cancik, Herman Lichtenberger, and Peter Schäfer, 3 vols. (Tübingen: Mohr/Siebeck, 1996), 1:221–62.

40. Richard P. Saller, *Personal Patronage Under the Early Empire* (Cambridge and New York: Cambridge University Press, 1982), 1.

41. In this sense, they function like the Asiarchs in Acts, prominent public offi-

cials who do not convert to Christianity, but who nevertheless befriend the Apostle Paul and protect him at a time when his security is jeopardized (Acts 19:31).

42. H. Dessau, *Inscriptiones Latinae Selectae* (Berlin: Weidmann, 1892–1916), 8403. For English translation, see Mary R. Lefkowitz and Maureen B. Fant, eds., *Women's Life in Greece and Rome: A Sourcebook in Translation*, 2d ed. (Baltimore, Md.: Johns Hopkins University Press, 1992), 16, n. 39.

43. With David S. Wiesen, I read these cliches as ironic, rather than as evidence of Juvenal's moral indignation (David S. Wiesen, "The Verbal Basis of Juvenal's Satiric Vision," *ANRW* 2, no. 33.1 [1989]: 708–33).

44. Dixon, 91; Susan Fischler, "The Public Position of Women in the Imperial Household in the Julio-Claudian Period" (Ph.D. diss., Oxford University, 1989), 7–30; Hallett, 29–30; Tom Hillard, "On the Stage, Behind the Curtain," in *Stereotypes of Women in Power: Historical Perspectives and Revisionist Views*, ed. Barbara Garlick, Suzanne Dixon, and Pauline Allen, Contributions to Women's Studies 125 (New York: Greenwood Press, 1992), 37–63; Riet van Bremen, "Women and Wealth," in *Images of Women in Antiquity*, ed. Averil Cameron and Amelie Kuhrt (Detroit, Mich.: Wayne State University Press, 1985), 223–42; idem, *The Limits of Participation: Women and Civic Life in the Greek East in the Hellenistic and Roman Periods*, Dutch Monographs on Ancient History and Archaeology (Amsterdam: Gieben, 1996). Mary Taliaferro Boatwright, "Plancia Magna of Perge: Women's Roles and Status in Roman Asia Minor," in *Women's History and Ancient History*, ed. Sarah B. Pomeroy (Chapel Hill: University of North Carolina Press, 1991), 249–72.

45. Fischler, "Public Position of Women"; and Susan Fischler, "Social Stereotypes and Historical Analysis: The Case of Imperial Women at Rome," in *Women in Ancient Societies: An Illusion of the Night*, ed. Léonie J. Archer, Susan Fischler, and Maria Wyke (London: Macmillan, 1994), 115–33; Tom Hillard, "Republican Politics, Women, and the Evidence," *Helios* 16, no. 2 (1989): 165–82.

46. Hillard, "Republican Politics," 176.

47. Fischler, "Social Stereotypes," 122.

48. This seems also to be the case in the *Acts of Isidorus*, where the women of the court are said to be in attendance when Claudius hears the case of Isidorus. See *The Acts of the Pagan Martyrs: Acta Alexandrinorum*, ed. Herbert A. Musurillo (Oxford: Clarendon, 1954), 18–27, 117–40.

49. Kate Cooper, "Insinuations of Womanly Influence: An Aspect of the Christianization of the Roman Aristocracy," *JRS* 82 (1992): 150–64. See now the expansion of this argument in idem, *Virgin and Bride*.

50. Cooper, "Womanly Influence," 153.

51. I do not include here the *Acts of Hermaiscus*, which portrays Plotina as interceding before Trajan on behalf of the Jews. On this text, see Chapter 3, 65–66.

52. Meshorer, 2:51–54, 2:247, pl. 9. Drusilla, Gaius's favorite sister, is depicted standing on the reverse of this coin. The only other member of the imperial house-

hold appearing on the obverse of Agrippa I's coinage is Gaius. Meshorer identifies the figure depicted on the reverse of this coin as Germanicus (Meshorer, 2:52–54, pl. 9).

53. Joyce Reynolds, *Aphrodisias and Rome* (London: Society for the Promotion of Roman Studies, 1982), 104.

54. On Livia's unprecedented public and political role, see Nicholas Purcell, "Livia and the Womanhood of Rome," *Proceedings of the Cambridge Philological Society* n.s., no. 32 (1986): 75–105. This article is especially noteworthy for his conclusion that in many important ways Livia's "activity and status are public and political in the full male sense to which we are used in the Roman world" (96). For more on the roles of imperial women who succeeded Livia, see also Mary Taliaferro Boatwright, "Imperial Women of the Early Second Century A.C.," *AJP* 112 (1991): 513–40; Fischler, "Public Position of Women."

55. H. Idris Bell, ed., *Jews and Christians in Egypt: The Jewish Troubles in Alexandria and the Athanasian Controversy* (Oxford: Oxford University Press, 1924), 1–37. For more on the tenuous nature of Jewish privilege under Roman rule due to the insecurity of patron-client relations, see Rajak, "Was There a Roman Charter," 107–23.

56. Lines 88–100 of the edict, from Bell, 25.

CHAPTER 3

1. On Luke's preface, see H. J. Cadbury "Commentary on the Preface of Luke," in *The Beginnings of Christianity Part 1: The Acts of the Apostles*, ed. F. J. Foakes-Jackson and Kirsopp Lake, 5 vols. (London: Macmillan, 1919–1933), 2:489–510. On the range of meaning for *asphaleia*, see LSJ, 266; J. H. Moulton and G. Milligan, *The Vocabulary of the Greek Testament* (London: Hodder and Stoughton, 1930; reprint, Peabody, Mass.: Hendrickson, 1997), 88; and Robert Maddox, *The Purpose of Luke-Acts*, Forschungen zur Religion und Literatur des Alten und Neuen Testaments 126 (Göttingen: Vandenhoeck & Ruprecht, 1982), 27, n. 54.

2. For discussion of the apologetic thrust of Acts, see Koester, *Introduction*, 2:319–23; Eckhard Plümacher, *Lukas als hellenistischer Schriftsteller: Studien zur Apostelgeschichte*, Studien zur Umwelt des Neuen Testaments 9 (Göttingen: Vandenhoeck & Ruprecht, 1972), 16–27; Hans Conzelmann, *Theology of St. Luke*, trans. Geoffrey Boswell (New York: Harper, 1961; reprint, Philadelphia, Pa.: Fortress, 1982), 138–44; Wills, "The Depiction of the Jews in Acts," *JBL* 110, no. 4 (1991): 631–54; Philip Francis Esler, *Community and Gospel in Luke-Acts*, Society for New Testament Studies Monograph Series 57 (Cambridge: Cambridge University Press, 1987), 205–17; Maddox, 91–99.

For scholars taking issue with this characterization of Acts, see, for example, Jacob Jervell, *Luke and the People of God: A New Look at Luke-Acts* (Minneapolis, Mn.: Augsburg, 1972); and Richard J. Cassidy, *Society and Politics in the Acts of the Apostles* (Maryknoll, N.Y.: Orbis, 1987), esp. 145–55.

3. On Paul's defense as a Pharisee, see Koester, *Introduction*, 2:323; on this explanation for why belief in the resurrection is shown to have Pharisaic roots, see Esler, 216–17.

4. On the question of Jewish legal status in diaspora communities, see S. Applebaum, "The Legal Status of the Jewish Communities in the Diaspora," in *The Jewish People in the First Century*, ed. S. Safrai and M. Stern, 2 vols. (Philadelphia, Pa.: Fortress, 1974–1976), 1:420–63; and Smallwood, *Jews Under Roman Rule*. For Asia Minor specifically, see Paul R. Trebilco, *Jewish Communities in Asia Minor*, Society for New Testament Studies Monograph Series 69 (Cambridge: Cambridge University Press, 1991), 5–36, 167–85.

5. Cf. the closing verse of Acts 28:31, where Paul is said to be proclaiming the kingdom of God, "in all boldness, without hindrance" [*meta pasēs parrēsias akōlutōs*].

6. Robert F. Stoops, "Riot and Assembly: The Social Context of Acts 19:23–41," *JBL* 108, no. 1 (1989): 73–91, esp. 88–89.

7. Cf. also Acts 6:8–15; 13:50; 14:1–7; 17:10–15; 18:5–17.

8. Wills, "Depiction of Jews," 634–38. His conclusion is worth quoting in full:

> The narrative method of Acts in regards to the Jews is not to state the salvation-history dogma that their theology makes them wrong and lost . . . but to *show* that the Jews are every bit as disorderly and rebellious as one would expect from the fact that they were involved in three bloody rebellions in seventy years. . . . Luke has gone beyond Paul, Mark, and Matthew in at least one important respect: the split between Luke's fellow Christians and Judaism appears to be complete and past. But what is disturbing about Luke's view of the Jews is that it is seen from the ruling Roman perspective, graphically and tendentiously realized in the Jewish mob scenes. Theological controversies no longer hold center stage, but the real issue is citizenship and acceptance in the Roman worldview. (653–54)

9. Helmut Flender, *St. Luke: Theologian of Redemptive History* (Philadelphia, Pa.: Fortress, 1967), 10.

10. Ben Witherington, *Women in the Earliest Churches*, Society for New Testament Studies Monograph Series 58 (Cambridge: Cambridge University Press, 1988), 143–57, esp. 156. See also Cassidy, 57–59.

11. Turid Karlsen Seim, *The Double Message: Patterns of Gender in Luke-Acts* (Edinburgh: T & T Clark, 1994), esp. 249–60. Schüssler Fiorenza, *But She Said*, 52–76; 210–14; idem, "A Feminist Critical Interpretation for Liberation: Martha and Mary (Luke 10:38–42)," *Religion and Intellectual Life* 3 (1986): 16–36; and idem, *In Memory of Her*, 167–68. Others who argue that Luke's portrayal of women in Acts is generally negative include Jacob Jervell, "The Daughters of Abraham: Women in Acts," in his *The Unknown Paul: Essays on Luke-Acts and Early Christian History* (Minneapolis, Mn.: Augsburg, 1984), 149–90; Mary Rose D'Angelo, "Women in Luke-Acts: A Redactional View," *JBL* 109, no. 3 (1990): 441–61. Ivoni Richter Reimer, in her recent monograph-length treatment of women in Acts, presumes Acts is an

androcentric document, but takes no particular stand on the question of Luke's narrative tendencies in depicting women, except to argue that, unlike the Pastorals, "Acts reflects no particular tendency to keep women at home and subject them to men" (see Ivoni Richter Reimer, *Women in the Acts of the Apostles: A Feminist Liberation Perspective* [Minneapolis, Mn.: Fortress, 1995], 267).

12. The ambiguity of the genitive plural in 17:4 makes equally possible the reading, "wives of the prominent," rather than "leading women." Likewise, 17:12 can be read as "Greek wives of the high-standing," rather than "Greek-women of high standing."

Codex D eliminates the ambiguity of 17:4 by substituting the nominative plural *gynaikes* for the genitive gynaikōn, thereby clearly defining the women in relation to their husbands. This codex also emends 17:12 with the effect of playing down the women's prominence. On the antiwoman tendency of the "Western" text, see Richard I. Pervo, "Social and Religious Aspects of the 'Western' Text," in *The Living Text: Essays in Honor of Ernest W. Saunders*, ed. Dennis E. Groh and Robert Jewett (Lanham, Md.: University Press of America, 1985), 229–41; esp. 235–40. Cf. also Ben Witherington, "The Anti-Feminist Tendencies of the 'Western' Text in Acts," *JBL* 103, no. 1 (1984): 82–84.

13. The last of these passages, from Paul's defense before the authorities, is a reference to his life preceding the Gentile mission.

14. The singling out of Dionysius and Damaris as Athenian converts in 17:34 is also an instance of male-female pairing. I shall not consider this passage here because Damaris receives no special distinction by class or status. That Acts does not stress the prominence of women among Athenian converts is also signified through the inclusion of Damaris among the "men" [*andres*] who believe "some of the men joined him and became believers, including Dionysios the Areopagite and a woman named Damaris and others with them" [*tines de andres kollēthentes autō episteusan, en hois kai Dionysios ho Areopagitēs kai gynē onomati Damaris kai heteroi syn autois*].

15. On the possibility of reading the genitive plurals in 17:4 and 17:12 as either "leading women" or "wives of the prominent," see note 12, above.

16. I adopt the term "God-fearers" because it is one most frequently used in the secondary literature. The phrase is problematic because it translates only *phoboumenos/oi ton theon* and not *sebomenos/oi ton theon*, a phrase used in Acts, and *theosebēs*, a frequent designation in inscriptions. In my discussion I will signal the inadequacy of the term by enclosing it with quotation marks.

A body of literature seeks to distinguish degrees of affiliation for Gentiles attracted to Judaism. See, for example, Folkert Siegert's discussion of the distinction between "God-fearers" and Sympathizers ("Gottesfürchtige und Sympathisanten," *JSJ* 4, no. 2 [1973]: 109–64); and Shaye J. D. Cohen's numbering of seven ways "a gentile can show respect or affection for Judaism" ("Crossing the Boundary and Becoming a Jew," *HTR* 82, no. 1 [1989]: 13–33). While recognizing the importance of this work, the arguments I make here do not hinge on assigning degrees of affiliation with such specificity.

17. A. Thomas Kraabel, "The Disappearance of the 'God-Fearers,'" *Numen: International Review for the History of Religions* 28 (1981): 113–26. See also "Greeks, Jews, and Lutherans in the Middle Half of Acts," *HTR* 79, no. 1–3 (1986): 147–57.

18. Kraabel limits his discussion of "God-fearers" to those desginated with participial forms of *phoboumenos/oi* and *sebomenos/oi* (*phoboumenos/oi*: 10:2, 10:22, 10:35, 13:16, 13:26; *sebomenos/oi*: 13:43, 13:50, 16:14, 17:4, 17:17, 18:7). He adopts the view of Marcel Simon that the transition from the former to the latter is a literary device, with *phoboumenos/oi* reflective of biblical language and *sebomenos/oi* more reflective of pagan piety. So argues Simon: "The transition from the one to the other almost corresponds to that very moment at which the apostolic mission of Paul turns from the Jews toward the Gentiles" (see Marcel Simon, "Gottesfürchtiger," *Reallexikon für Antike und Christentum*, ed. T. Kluser et al. [Stuttgart, 1950–], 11 [1981]: 1060–70, esp. 1063, my translation).

19. Kirsopp Lake, "Proselytes and God-Fearers," in *The Beginnings of Christianity Part I: The Acts of the Apostles*, ed. F. J. Foakes-Jackson and Kirsopp Lake, 5 vols. (London: MacMillan, 1919–1933), 5:74–96.

20. Max Wilcox, "The 'God-Fearers' in Acts—A Reconsideration," *JSNT* 13 (1981): 102–22.

21. Wilcox, 104, 115.

22. For a discussion of prophetic ambiguity in the Third Gospel and Acts, see François Bovon, "The Effect of Realism and Prophetic Ambiguity in the Works of Luke," in his *New Testament Traditions and Apocryphal Narratives*, Princeton Theological Monograph Series 36 (Allison Park, Pa.: Pickwick, 1995), 97–104. The utilization of prophetic irony in Luke's treatment of Jews and Gentiles is further analyzed in the dissertation of Marianne Palmer Bonz, "The Best of Times, the Worst of Times: Luke-Acts and Epic Tradition" (Th.D. diss., Harvard University, 1996), 165–222.

23. Lake, 88.

24. Ernst Haenchen, *The Acts of the Apostles: A Commentary* (Philadelphia, Pa.: Westminster, 1971), 413, n. 5; Kazimierz Romaniuk, "Die 'Gottesfürchtigen' im Neuen Testament," *Aegyptus* 44 (1964): 66–91, esp. 81; Conzelmann, *Acts of the Apostles*, 106; Karl Georg Kuhn, "προσήλυτος," *TDNT* 6 (1986): 727–44, esp. 743.

25. Jack T. Sanders, *The Jews in Luke-Acts* (Philadelphia, Pa.: Fortress, 1987), 137–53.

26. Trebilco, *Jewish Communities*, 150–51; Siegert, 138.

27. Wilcox's attempt to distinguish between Cornelius's piety and his "belongingness to a group" is strained. Furthermore, his hesitant concession that Cornelius is *probably* a Gentile indicates his argument to be an exercise in understatement (Wilcox, 104).

28. Trebilco, *Jewish Communities*, 151; Lake, 87; G. H. R. Horsley, *New Documents*

Illustrating Early Christianity, 7 vols. (North Ryde, New South Wales, Australia: Ancient History Documentary Research Centre, Macquarie University, 1981–1994), 3:54.

29. Wilcox, 113–14. See also Trebilco, *Jewish Communities*, 249, n. 30.

30. Esler, 40.

31. For discussion of Lydia's status, see Chapter 4 below.

32. Richard I. Pervo, *Luke's Story of Paul* (Minneapolis, Mn.: Fortress, 1990), 56; Esler, 40.

33. *Pace* Wilcox who argues, "There is nothing in the text to compel us to conclude that the women in question . . . were or were not Jews or proselytes" (Wilcox, 110).

34. Wills, "Depiction of the Jews," 639.

35. On Antonia, see Schwartz, *Agrippa I*, 1–37; on the Poppaea story, see Schwartz, "KATA TOYTON TON KAIPON," 241–68.

36. For Helena's observance of Nazarite laws, see *m. Naz.* 3:6. For discussion of her *sukkah*, see *m. Sukkah* 1:1. For her temple benefaction, see *m. Yoma* 3:10 and *t. Yoma* 2:3. Cf. Eusebius *Eccl. Hist.* 2.12.

The benefaction for which Josephus claims that Helena will be "famous forever" among his people, her largess during a Jerusalem famine (*Ant.* 20.49–52), is not acknowledged in rabbinic sources. Rather, the assistance during the famine from the royal family of Adiabene is attributed to King Monobazus: *t. Pe'ah* 4:18, quoted in *y. Pe'ah* 1:1 and *b. B.Bat.* 11a.

For the argument that Helena's conversion was to Pharisaic Judaism, see Tal Ilan, "The Attraction of Aristocratic Women to Pharisaism During the Second Temple Period," *HTR* 88, no. 1 (1995): 1–33, esp. 15–16. See also the discussion of Schiffman.

37. This passage will be discussed further below, 65–66.

38. *Acts of Pilate* 2.1. For Greek text, see Constantin von Tischendorf, *Evangelia Apocrypha* (1876; reprint, Hildesheim: Olms, 1966), 223. For English translation, see *NTApoc* 1:507–8. According to Felix Scheidweiler, the document dates as late as the fourth century, but arises from an earlier *Grundschrift* (*NTApoc* 1:501–3).

39. One sees a similar phenomenon in Philo, whose misogynism is well known, but who speaks of the empress Livia as if she were in a category apart from women in general. In *On the Embassy to Gaius* 319–20, he asks first how she could have been pious enough to send gifts to the Jerusalem temple, "for the judgments of women as a rule are weaker" [*asthenesterai gar pōs eisin hai gnōmai tōn gynaikōn*]. His own answer is that "she excelled all her sex in this as in everything else, for the purity of the training she received supplementing nature gave virility [maleness] to her reasoning power" [*hē de ge kathaper en tois allois holon to genos kan toutō diēnegken, hypo paideias akratou physei kai meletē perigegenēmenēs, arrenōtheisa ton logismon*]. See also Dorothy Sly, *Philo's Perception of Women*, Brown Judaic Studies 209 (Atlanta, Ga.: Scholars Press, 1990).

40. For other texts and discussion, see Balch, 65–116.

41. Balch, 65–80.

42. This topos is articulated with particular vehemence at the end of the first and the beginning of the second century in Rome, as evident from Martial, Juvenal, Josephus, Tacitus, and Suetonius. It also can be traced in Roman literature back to the writings of Livy and Cicero, and in Greek drama, to the plays of Aristophanes and Euripides. For more on this topos, and how Josephus recognizes and responds to it, see my discussion of the expulsion of Jews and Isis worshippers from Rome in Chapter 1 above.

43. This question was not asked by Balch in his study, which identifies the "anti-women and foreign cults" topos, but then fails to account for the place of prominent women in the apologetic rhetoric of Josephus and Luke. He cites passages speaking of women converts in the *Antiquities* and Acts only to argue that *in spite* of the topos, women converted to Judaism and Christianity (Balch, 85).

44. This characterization of Jewish communities in the diaspora as modeled to some extent on civic society or collegia rather than on any form of cult is made by Trebilco (*Jewish Communities*, 114). It prompts him to account for the prominence of Jewish women in synagogues in Asia Minor by looking to women's roles in the social system of the city, rather than in the religious cults. While I adopt this distinction from him, I recognize that it is not a precise one since, of course, neither the social system of the city nor collegia were devoid of cultic aspects.

45. Two early contemporary articles on the general phenomenon of women's benefaction are Ramsay MacMullen's "Women in Public in the Roman Empire," *Historia* 29 (1980): 208–18; and Anthony J. Marshall's "Roman Women and the Provinces," *Ancient Society* 6 (1975): 109–27. The most comprehensive study of women's benefaction in the Greek East is van Bremen's *The Limits of Participation*. For more on benefaction in the Greek East, see also van Bremen, "Women and Wealth"; and Boatwright, "Plancia Magna." For discussions specific to Ephesos, see Steve Friesen, "Ephesian Women and Men in Public Religious Office in the Roman Period," in *100 Jahre Österreichische Forschungen in Ephesos. Akten des Symposions Wien 1995*, ed. Herwig Friesinger and Friedrich Krinzinger (Vienna: Austrian Archaeological Institute, 1999), 107–13; G. M. Rogers, "The Constructions of Women at Ephesos," *Zeitschrift für Papyrologie und Epigraphik* 90 (1992): 215–23. For a discussion specific to the Latin West, see Elizabeth P. Forbis, "Women's Public Image in Italian Honorary Inscriptions," *AJP* 111 (1990): 493–512.

46. van Bremen, *Limits of Participation*.

47. Boatwright, "Plancia Magna," 261–62; van Bremen, *Limits of Participation*, 104–8.

48. B. Lifshitz, *Donateurs et fondateurs dans les synagogues juives*, Cahiers de la revue biblique 7 (Paris: Gabalda, 1967) 34, no. 33 = *CII* 766 = *MAMA* 6:264. English translation in Brooten, *Women Leaders*, 158.

49. *MAMA* 6:153, 6:263, 6:265. For further discussion of Julia Severa, see

A. Thomas Kraabel, "Judaism in Asia Minor" (Th.D. diss., Harvard University, 1968), 74–80; Ross Shepherd Kraemer, "Hellenistic Jewish Women: The Epigraphic Evidence," *SBLSP* (1986): 183–200, esp. 196–97; Trebilco, *Jewish Communities*, 58–60; Brooten, *Women Leaders*, 144; Lifshitz, 35–36.

50. For text and commentary, see *Acts of the Pagan Martyrs*, 44–48, 161–78.

51. *Acts of the Pagan Martyrs*, 163–64.

52. Rabbinic tradition does not view Plotina as benefactor to the Jews, but rather as urging Trajan to attack the Jews in Alexandria. See *y. Sukkah* 5.1 and the discussion in Hildegard Temporini, *Die Frauen am Hofe Trajans* (Berlin and New York: De Gruyter, 1978), 96–100.

53. Important responses to Kraabel include Louis Feldman, "The Omnipresence of the God-Fearers," *Biblical Archaeology Review* 12, no. 5 (1986): 59–69; Thomas M. Finn, "The God-Fearers Reconsidered," *CBQ* 47 (1985): 75–84; John G. Gager, "Jews, Gentiles, and Synagogues in the Book of Acts," *HTR* 79, nos. 1–3 (1986): 91–99; Trebilco, *Jewish Communities*, 145–66.

Passages frequently mentioned as indicators of "God-fearers" outside Acts include Juvenal *Sat.* 14.96–106; Josephus *Ant.* 3.217, 14.110, 20.34–35; *Against Apion* 2.123; *J.W.* 7.45; Philo *Questions and Answers on Exodus* 2.2; Epictetus *Dissertationes* 2.9.19–21; the Miletus theater inscription, *CII* 748; and the Julia Severa inscription, *CII* 766.

Kraabel also ignores rabbinic references to "fearers of heaven" [*yire shamayim*]. See among others, Lake, 80–82; and Feldman, *Jew and Gentile*, 353–56.

54. Joyce Reynolds and Robert Tannenbaum, *Jews and God-fearers at Aphrodisias: Greek Inscriptions with Commentary*, Cambridge Philological Society, Suppl. 12 (Cambridge: Cambridge University Press, 1987). For further important discussion of the Jewish Donor Inscriptions, see Marianne Palmer Bonz, "Questions Concerning the Jewish Donor Inscriptions from Aphrodisias," *HSCP* 96 (1994): 281–99; and Pieter W. van der Horst, "Jews and Christians in Aphrodisias in the Light of their Relations to Other Cities of Asia Minor," *Nederlands Theologisch Tijdschrift* 43, no. 2 (1989): 106–21.

55. Cf. the discussions of Pieter W. van der Horst, *Ancient Jewish Epitaphs*, Contributions to Biblical Exegesis and Theology 2 (Kampen, The Netherlands: Kok Pharos, 1991), 109–11, 136–37; Richter Reimer, 97–98.

56. See especially the discussion of Gager, "Jews, Gentiles, and Synagogues," 95–98.

57. See, for example, Cohen's discussion ("Respect for Judaism," 417) of *J.W.* 2.559–61, which speaks of the women of Damascus having "gone over to the Jewish religion." He argues that they must be considered "adherents" rather than true "converts" since they remain married to Gentile husbands.

58. For the argument that "God-fearers" were socially well placed, see Kuhn and Stegemann, 1265–66. Van der Horst notes that nine of the fifty-four "God-fearers" from the Aphrodisias inscription are recognized as city councillors (see van der

Horst, "Jews and Christians in Aphrodisias," 106–21). For a counterargument, see Richter Reimer, 96–98.

59. For Tation, see *CII* 738 = Lifshitz, 21 no. 13. For the Capitolina inscription, see *Corpus inscriptionum graecarum*, ed. A. Boeckh, 4 vols. (Berlin, 1828–1877), 2924 = Lifshitz, 32, no. 30. On Capitolina as an elite Gentile, see L. Robert, *Etudes anatoliennes: recherches sur les inscriptions grecques de l'Asie Mineure* (Paris: Boccard, 1937), 409–12; cf. Trebilco, *Jewish Communities*, 157–58; Irina Levinskaya, *The Book of Acts in its Diaspora Setting*, The Book of Acts in its First Century Setting 5 (Grand Rapids, Mich.: Eerdmans, 1996), 65–66. Cf. also the discussion of Kraemer, "Hellenistic Jewish Women," 197–98.

60. The argument that "God-fearers" became Christians in droves finds its way into several New Testament introductory textbooks. See Norman Perrin and Dennis C. Duling, *The New Testament: An Introduction*, 2d ed. (New York: Harcourt Brace Jovanovich, 1982), 5, 80, and esp. 138; F. F. Bruce, *New Testament History* (Garden City, N.Y.: Doubleday, 1969), 145–47; Hans Conzelmann, *History of Primitive Christianity* (Nashville, Tn.: Abingdon, 1973), 66–67, 95.

61. Cf. Gal. 1:16, 2:7–9; Rom. 1:5, 1:13–15, 11:13, 15:15–25; and Meeks, 26–29.

62. For more on the discrepancy between what is known of Paul and his mission from his own letters, and how Paul's mission is portrayed in Acts, see Koester, *Introduction*, 2:321–23.

63. See, for example, Chrysostom *Discourses Against Judaizing Christians* 1.1, 1.5, 2.4–6, 4.3, 8.4; Wayne A. Meeks and Robert Wilken, *Jews and Christians in Antioch in the First Four Centuries of the Common Era*, Society of Biblical Literature Sources for Biblical Study 13 (Missoula, Mont.: Scholars Press, 1978), 83–127; Robert Wilken, *John Chrysostom and the Jews: Rhetoric and Reality in the Late 4th Century* (Berkeley, Los Angeles, and London: University of California Press, 1983), esp. 66–94.

64. Van der Horst, "Jews and Christians in Aphrodisias," 106–21.

65. Gerd Theissen, *The Social Setting of Pauline Christianity: Essays on Corinth* (Philadelphia, Pa.: Fortress, 1982), 103–4.

66. Kuhn, 743–44.

67. See, for example, Ignatius *To the Magnesians* 10.3; and again, Chrysostom *Discourses Against Judaizing Christians* 2.4–6, 4.3. Note the contrast between Kuhn's "ethics over ritual" view and van der Horst's attempt to account for the continuing interest of Gentiles in Judaism ("Jews and Christians in Aphrodisias," 118–19):

> The rather detailed code of behaviour that Scripture and halakha contained must have been envisioned as a stabilizing factor in life by a good many people. . . . For many Christians, the argument that the commandments in the Torah were after all God's words may have carried more weight than the often tortuous argumentations to the effect that God had abolished his own Law.

68. Siegert, 136. Siegert argues further that this transfer of affiliation provoked a

jealous response of the Jews. Although I contest this entire argument, Siegert must be given credit as one of the few scholars involved in the "God-fearer" debate who has recognized and attempted to account for the high frequency of female "God-fearers" in Acts. For further discussion of this passage, see also Richter Reimer, 96–97.

69. Stoops, 73–91. For a reading of this entire chapter as religious missionary propaganda and apologetics, see Elisabeth Schüssler Fiorenza, "Miracles, Mission, and Apologetics: An Introduction," in *Aspects of Religious Propaganda in Judaism and Early Christianity*, ed. Elisabeth Schüssler Fiorenza, University of Notre Dame Center for the Study of Judaism and Christianity in Antiquity 2 (Notre Dame, Ind., and London: University of Notre Dame Press, 1976), 1–25.

70. For discussion of the ethnic composition of early Christian communities, see the analysis of Romans 16 by Helmut Koester, "Ephesos in Early Christian Literature," in *Ephesos: Metropolis of Asia*, ed. Helmut Koester (Valley Forge, Pa.: Trinity Press International, 1995), 119–40, esp. 123–24. For discussion of the likely status of women leaders in early Christian communities, with specific reference to the slave women deacons in Pliny's famous letter to Trajan concerning Christians, see Chapter 4, 93–95, below.

71. Susanne Heine, *Women in Early Christianity: Are the Feminist Scholars Right?* (London: SCM, 1987), 83–86, esp. 84.

72. Brooten, *Women Leaders*, 146–47.

73. See, for example, the Pauline correspondence, especially Romans 16 and the first letter to the Corinthians. Consider also the prominence of women in the canonical Gospel accounts, and the reference to "Jezebel," a Christian female prophet in Revelation 2:20–23. Pliny's famous letter to Trajan concerning Christians in Bithynia includes a reference to two Christian slave women, called "ministers" [*ministrae*]. Early Christian apologists were frequently defending themselves from the charges that their congregations were composed primarily of women. See, for example, Origen *Cels.* 3.44, 3.50, 3.55; and M. Y. MacDonald.

CHAPTER 4

1. The classic discussion of the prison escape as a topos of Hellenistic religious propaganda is found in Weinreich, "Gebet und Wunder," 309–41. See also W. Nestle, "Anklänge an Euripides in der Apostelgeschichte," *Philologus* 13 (1900): 46–57; and, for a recent discussion, Richard I. Pervo, *Profit with Delight: The Literary Genre of the Acts of the Apostles* (Philadelphia, Pa.: Fortress, 1987), 18–24.

2. Weinreich, "Gebet und Wunder," 309–41, esp. 332–41. Pervo, in his recent discussion of sacred incarcerations in Acts, does not argue for textual dependence, but rather speaks more generally of the Dionysos tradition as the "apparent home" of this type (Pervo, *Profit*, 21).

3. Lilian Portefaix, *Sisters Rejoice: Paul's Letter to the Philippians and Luke-Acts as*

Seen by First-Century Philippian Women, Coniectanea biblica: New Testament Series 20 (Stockholm: Almqvist & Wiksell, 1988), 169–71.

4. Cf. 13:14–16, 14:1, 17:1–2, 17:10, 18:4, 18:19, 19:8.

5. Throughout this chapter I will translate προσευχή in Acts 16:13 as synagogue, a well-attested meaning for the term. Many scholars have suggested the word be translated here more loosely as "house of prayer," or "informal meeting place," primarily because only women appear to be in attendance (cf. W. Bauer, W. F. Arndt, and F. W. Gingrich, *Greek-English Lexicon of the New Testament and Other Early Christian Literature* [Chicago: University of Chicago Press, 1957], s.v. προσευχή, 2, and most commentaries). Such an argument employs circular—or what I prefer to call *ad mulierem*—reasoning: because women could not possibly be the sole attendees at a synagogue, a synagogue attended solely by women cannot be a synagogue. For further discussion of this translation, see Brooten, *Women Leaders*, 139–40; and Richter Reimer, 78–92.

6. My outline of parallels differs somewhat from Portefaix's (see Portefaix, 170).

7. Weinreich, "Gebet und Wunder," 326–41. One of Weinreich's most compelling arguments for the "Dionsysian feel" of the prison escapes in Acts is the association between them and the *Bacchae* made by Origen in *Cels.* 2.34. In this work, "Celsus' Jew" quotes a line from the *Bacchae* spoken by the imprisoned Bacchus: "The god himself will free me, whenever I wish" (*Bacchae* 498), and asks why Jesus could not do the same. Origen responds by noting that his God could and did free the imprisoned Peter (Acts 12:6–9), and the imprisoned Paul and Silas (Acts 16:24–26).

8. Indications of the popularity of the *Bacchae* include: a papyrus fragment from Oxyrynchus preserving the initial lines of the *Bacchae* as part of a school exercise (Roger A. Pack, *Greek and Latin Literary Texts from Greco-Roman Egypt*, 2d ed [Ann Arbor: University of Michigan Press, 1965], 40); a reference in Lucian to an uneducated person (*apaideutos*) reading through the *Bacchae* (*The Ignorant Book Collector* 19); Plutarch's *Crassus* 33.1–4, which speaks of an actor's performance of the *Bacchae* at a banquet at which the audience is presumed to know the plot of the story; references in Artemidorus to people dreaming of slave women and poor people reciting passages from Euripides (4.59) as well as to people dreaming of Dionysiac figures belonging to the *Bacchae* (4.39); cf. also the passage from Origen's *Cels.* in the note above.

In her study, focusing on the question of the reception of Acts 16 by women in Philippi, Portefaix argues that those hearing the text in this locale would have known the *Bacchae*, because of the enduring popularity of Euripides in that region, and the mythic associations of Dionysos with neighboring Mt. Pangaion (Portefaix, 98–114).

For indications of the general popularity of Euripides in the Roman era, see Lucian *Quomodo Historia Conscribenda Sit* 1; Dio Chrysostom *Discourses* 18.6.7; the discussions in Louis H. Feldman, *Josephus's Interpretation of the Bible*, Hellenistic Culture and Society 27 (Berkeley and Los Angeles: University of California Press,

1998), 175, n. 20; P. E. Easterling, "From Repertoire to Canon," in *The Cambridge Companion to Greek Tragedy*, ed. P. E. Easterling (Cambridge: Cambridge University Press, 1997), 211–27, esp. 225.

9. Pervo, *Profit*, 19, my emphasis. For his expanded definition of aretalogy as encompassing not only hymns but also "various literary media and structures employed for proclaiming the virtues of a god or divine figure," see ibid., 146, n. 11.

10. For a discussion of the story of the Royal Family of Adiabene as a historical novel, see Lawrence Wills, *The Jewish Novel in the Ancient World*, Myth and Poetics (Ithaca, N.Y., and London: Cornell University Press, 1995), 206–11.

11. In fact, the Dionysos cult and Jewish and Christian cults were frequently conflated in antiquity. See especially the dialogue in Plutarch's *Quaest. conv.* 671C–672C; and commentary in Stern, 2:558–62. On confusion of Dionysian and Christian practice, see Robert Wilken, *The Christians as the Romans Saw Them* (New Haven, Conn., and London: Yale University Press, 1984), 17.

12. Ross Kraemer, *Her Share of the Blessings*, 36–49. Cf. conclusions of Albert Henrichs, "Greek Maenadism from Olympias to Messalina," *HSCP* 82 (1978): 121–60. Both of these scholars are concerned primarily with the task of reconstructing historical maenadic practice, which involves complex questions of the relationship between myth and cult. My study here is limited to the narrower question of how maenadic practice is evaluated in polemics against and support for the cult.

13. See also *Bacchae* 233ff., 260, 352.

14. See also Livy *Hist.* 39.15.9.

15. Scholars assume that the Sabazios incident to which Cicero refers was contained in Aristophanes' comedy, *Horae*, which is no longer extant. See E. R. Dodds, introduction to Euripides' *Bacchae*, ed. E. R. Dodds, 2d ed (Oxford: Clarendon, 1960), xxiv. On the close correlation and even confusion between rites of Dionysos and Sabazios, see Ross Kraemer, "Ecstasy and Possession: The Attraction of Women to the Cult of Dionysus," *HTR* 72 (1979): 55–80, esp. 61–63. For further discussion of Cicero's *De legibus* 2.35–37, see below.

16. While Henrichs cautions that Tacitus's account is an "inseparable blend of fact and fiction," he does assume that this historian correctly assigns to Messalina a flair for Bacchic ostentation (Henrichs, "Greek Maenadism," 156–59). For the difficulties in reconstructing imperial women's history from anything Tacitus says about them, see Joshel, "Female Desire," 50–82.

17. Although there are modern interpreters who resist this characterization of Pentheus, and argue for his virtue, it must be noted that Pentheus is notorious in antiquity for his impiety. Cf. Horace *Odes* 2.19.14–15; Pausanias, *Description of Greece* 2.2.7; and Diodorus Siculus, *Bibliotheca historica* 4.3.4.

18. On the meaning of this term here, see Barbara K. Gold, "Εὐκοσμία in Euripides' Bacchae," *AJP* 98 (1977): 3–15.

19. For further discussion of gender in the *Bacchae*, see the articles of Helene P.

Foley, "The Conception of Women in Athenian Drama," in *Reflections of Women in Antiquity*, ed. Helene P. Foley (New York: Gordon and Breach, 1981), 127–68, esp. 142–45; and Froma I. Zeitlin, "Cultic Models of the Female: Rites of Dionysos and Demeter," *Arethusa* 15 (1982): 129–57. See also the important study of H. S. Versnel, *Inconsistencies in Greek and Roman Religion* 1, Studies in Greek and Roman Religion, 6 (Leiden: Brill, 1990), 156–205.

20. *CIL* 1² 581, lines 10, 19–20: "No man shall be priest of, nor shall any man or woman be master of, such an organization. . . . No one in a company of more than five persons altogether, men and women shall perform such rites; nor in that company shall more than two men or three women be present, unless it is in accordance with the opinion of the urban praetor and the Senate . . ." (translation, Lefkowitz and Fant, 275).

21. Henrichs, "Greek Maenadism," 135. Balch does not consider this inscription when he concludes "the main problem [with the Dionysos cult in Rome] was that Roman women joined the cult" (Balch, 69).

22. This is the argument of Balch, 66.

23. See, for example, the recent statement of David M. Hay, "Things Philo Did and Did Not Say about the Therapeutae," *SBLSP* (1992): 673–93, esp. 677. Ross Shepherd Kraemer, "Monastic Jewish Women in Greco-Roman Egypt: Philo on the Therapeutrides," *Signs* 14, no. 1 (1989): 342–70.

24. Philo makes frequent use of the paradoxical phrase "sober drunkenness" (*methē nēphalios*) in his writings. See *On Drunkenness* 145–46; *On Flight and Finding* 31, 166; *Special Laws* 1.82–83, 3.82; *That Every Good Person is Free* 12–13; *On the Creation of the World* 70; *Moses* 1.187. For discussion, see Hans Lewy, *Sobria Ebrietas: Untersuchungen zur Geschichte der Antiken Mystik* (Gießen: Töpelmann, 1929), esp. 3–41. That Philo is stressing the virtue of the Therapeutics here is apparent in his shift from the typical pairing, sober/drunken, to virtuous/drunken.

25. Lewy, 31–34.

26. Plato, for example, speaks of Dionysian frenzy as a blessing (*Phaedrus* 244B). For discussion, see Ivan M. Linforth, "The Corybantic Rites in Plato," *University of California Publications in Classical Philology* 13, no. 5 (1946): 121–62; idem, "Telestic Madness in Plato, Phaedrus 244DE," *University of California Publications in Classical Philology* 13, no. 6 (1946): 163–72. See also Sze-Kar Wan, "Charismatic Exegesis: Philo and Paul Compared," *Studia Philonica* 6 (1994): 54–82. That Philo is working with Platonic ideals here is evident from his description of the choirs of men and women dissolving finally into "one choir." The Platonic ideal of the dissolution of male and female into oneness is most often discussed by biblical scholars within the context of the baptismal formula in Galatians 3:28. See, for example, Dennis Ronald Mac-Donald, *There Is No Male and Female: The Fate of a Dominical Saying in Paul and Gnosticism*, Harvard Dissertations in Religion 20 (Philadelphia, Pa.: Fortress, 1987). For discussion of Gal. 3:28 in relation to Philo's Therapeutics, see Boyarin, 188–89.

27. In addition to the passages discussed here, cf. *Mulierum virtutes* 251–53; *De primo frigido* 953C; and *Quaestiones romanae et graecae* 293C–F.

28. For more on Clea, one of Plutarch's highly educated female friends, see Philip A. Stadter, "*Philosophos kai Philandros*: Plutarch's View of Women in the Moralia and the Lives," in *Plutarch's Advice to the Bride and Groom and A Consolation to His Wife*, ed. Sarah B. Pomeroy (New York and Oxford: Oxford Univeristy Press, 1999), 173–82, esp. 173–75.

29. On this passage, see also Henrichs, "Greek Maenadism," 136.

30. This inconsistency can be explained in part by the different focus of each work. In *Conjugalia praecepta*, Plutarch lauds the private virtue of women. Only in *Mulierum virtutes* does he consider the subject of women's public virtue. See Kathleen O'Brien Wicker, "*Mulierem Virtutes (Moralia 242E–263C)*," in *Plutarch's Ethical Writings and Early Christian Literatures*, ed. Hans D. Betz (Leiden: Brill, 1978), 106–34. For another instance of Plutarch's inconsistency on a wife's place in private/public, see Sarah B. Pomeroy, "Reflections on Plutarch, *Advice to the Bride and Groom*," in *Plutarch's Advice to Bride and Groom and a Consolation to his Wife*, ed. Sarah B. Pomeroy (New York and Oxford: Oxford University Press, 1999), 33–42.

31. Henrichs, "Changing Dionysiac Identities," 147–48.

32. A second source interpreting female cultic activity in Judaism by analogy to Bacchic worship is Plutarch's *Quaestionum convivialum*. Here Plutarch provides a detailed discussion of Jewish identity, including a speech by the Athenian Moiragenes linking the Dionysos and Jewish cults. As Moiragenes details the Dionysian character of Jewish ritual, he notes that in both Jewish and Dionysian festivals, female "nurses of the God," take on liturgical roles. Plutarch *Quaest. conv.* 672A: "[The Jews] also have noise as an element in their nocturnal festivals, and call the nurses of the god 'bronze rattlers' " [*psophois de chrōntai peri ta nyktelia, kai chalkokrotous tas tou theou tithēnas prosagoreuousin*]. Notably, Plutarch does not link female Jewish and Bacchic cultic activity in derision, but rather makes the analogy while drawing a sympathetic portrait of Jewish cultic practice. For discussion of this dialogue, see Stern, 2:545–62. Stern does not comment on this particular line.

33. Kraemer, *Her Share of the Blessing*, 3.

34. Consider especially Hector's reply to his mother Hecuba, after she exhorts him to make libations to the gods on his return to Troy:

> I'd be ashamed to pour a glistening cup to Zeus with unwashed hands. I'm splattered with blood and filth—how could I pray to the lord of storm and lightning? *No, mother, you are the one to pray.* Go to Athena's shrine . . . go with offerings, gather the older noble women and take a robe . . . and spread it out across the sleek-haired goddess' knees. Then promise to sacrifice twelve heifers in her shrine . . . if only she'll pity Troy. . . . (*Iliad* 6.315–25, trans. Robert Fagels, my emphasis)

35. For further discussion of these texts, see Helene P. Foley, "The Female 'In-

truder' Reconsidered: Women in Aristophanes' *Lysistrata* and *Ecclesiazusae*," *CP* 77, no. 1 (1982): 1–21; idem, "Women in Athenian Drama"; Froma I. Zeitlin, "The Dynamics of Misogyny: Myth and Mythmaking in the Oresteia," *Arethusa* 11, no. 2 (1978): 149–83, esp. 172–73; and Jeffrey Henderson, "*Lysistrate*: The Play and its Themes," *Yale Classical Studies* 26 (1980): 153–218.

36. D. L. Page, *Select Papyri* III (LCL), 113–14.

37. Cf. 22.1.18, 27.37.8–10. For further citation and discussion of Latin texts which privilege women's public religious function, see Wardman, 37–39.

38. See Staples.

39. See, for example, Léonie J. Archer, *Her Price Is Beyond Rubies: The Jewish Woman in Graeco-Roman Palestine*, Journal for the Study of the Old Testament: Supplement Series 60 (Sheffield, Eng.: Sheffield, 1990), 85–86, 113–22; Deborah F. Sawyer, *Women and Religion in the First Christian Centuries* (London and New York: Routledge, 1996), 36–40, 76–77; Balch, 52–56. Cf. also Jerome Neyrey's rigid adherence to the public/private binary in arguing that the Johannine community defied standard mores in "What's Wrong with This Picture? John 4, Cultural Stereotypes of Women, and Public and Private Space," *Biblical Theology Bulletin* 24, no. 2 (1994): 77–91.

There are several other scholars who provide more nuanced discussions of public/private ideology in antiquity. For the widely accepted argument that approval of elite Hellenistic women's benefaction owed to the extension of the private sphere into the public, see van Bremen, "Women and Wealth." For discussion of social innovation in the Roman period that allowed for women's participation in public meals, see Kathleen E. Corley, *Private Women/Public Meals: Social Conflict in the Synoptic Tradition* (Peabody, Mass.: Hendrickson, 1993); cf. also Carolyn Osiek, "The Family in Early Christianity: 'Family Values' Revisited," *CBQ* 58, no. 1 (1996): 1–24, and Carolyn Osiek and David Balch, *Families in the New Testament World: Households and Churches*, The Family, Religion, and Culture Series (Louisville, Ky.: Westminster/John Knox Press, 1997), 43–47, 54–56. For a useful critique of public/private models in terms of the conceptualization of the family in antiquity, see Miriam Peskowitz, " 'Family/ies' in Antiquity: Evidence from Tannaitic Literature and Roman Galilean Architecture," in *The Jewish Family in Antiquity*, ed. Shaye J. D. Cohen, Brown Judaic Studies 289 (Atlanta, Ga.: Scholars Press, 1993), 9–36, esp. 24–28. See also the insightful comments on public rhetoric of "private" life in Cooper, *Virgin and Bride*, 1–19.

40. Karen Jo Torjeson, *When Women Were Priests: Women's Leadership in the Early Church and the Scandal of Their Subordination in the Rise of Christianity* (San Francisco: HarperSanFrancisco, 1993), 126–28.

41. On the connotation of *astē* in Philo, see Sly, 95–97.

42. Cf. Philo's public/private formulation with the treatise attributed to Phintys, a female member of the Pythagorean community in southern Italy, third to second century BCE, which also provides for prominent women to leave the house in order

to make sacrifice. Holger Thesleff, ed., *The Pythagorean Texts of the Hellenistic Period* (Abo, Finland: Abo Akademi, 1965), 151–54, esp. 54; and English translation in Lefkowitz and Fant, 163–64.

43. This view of trade as "dirty work" provides the basis for the readings of Schottroff and Richter Reimer to be discussed further below. Richard L. Rohrbaugh also stresses the low status of merchants by arguing that all but the largest-scale traders were outcasts who lived on the edges or outside of the city (see Richard L. Rohrbaugh, "The Pre-Industrial City in Luke-Acts: Urban Social Relations," in *The Social World of Luke-Acts: Models for Interpretation*, ed. Jerome H. Neyrey [Peabody, Mass.: Hendrickson, 1991], 125–49, esp. 133–37). For a view of social and spatial relations between the urban elite and merchants that is more nuanced than Rohrbaugh's, see Andrew Wallace-Hadrill, "Elites and Trade in the Roman Town," in *City and Country in the Ancient World*, ed. John Rich and Andrew Wallace-Hadrill (London and New York: Routledge, 1991), 241–69.

44. Bonz, "Best of Times, Worst of Times." In support of this view, Bonz cites John H. D'Arms (*Commerce and Social Standing in Ancient Rome* [Cambridge, Mass.: Harvard University Press, 1981]), for whom the freedman Trimalchio from Petronius's *Satyricon* serves as the fictional paradigm of this quasi elite.

45. David W. J. Gill, "Acts and the Urban Elites," in *The Book of Acts in Its Graeco-Roman Setting*, ed. David W. J. Gill and Conrad Gempf (Grand Rapids, Mich.: Eerdmans, 1994), 105–18, esp. 114–17. Gill builds on the work of H. W. Pleket, "Urban Elites and Business in the Greek Part of the Roman Empire," in *Trade in the Ancient Economy*, ed. P. Garnsey et al. (London: Chatto & Windus, 1983), 131–44, esp. 141–43.

46. G. H. R. Horsley, *New Documents*, 2.27; Meeks, 203, n. 93.

47. Thus from Sardis comes the well-placed Julia Lydia, and from Ephesus, Julia Lydia Laterane. See discussion in Gill, 114.

48. Luise Schottroff, "Lydia: A New Quality of Power," in her *Let the Oppressed Go Free: Feminist Perspectives on the New Testament*, trans. Annemarie S. Kidder (Louisville, Ky.: Westminster/John Knox Press, 1993), 131–37. Richter Reimer, 98–130.

49. For arguments concerning the respectability of purple sellers, see note 43 above.

50. The prominent place of social outcasts in the Third Gospel owes much to their prominence in Luke's sources for this first work, Mark and Q.

51. Cf. Sanders, 132–53.

52. Mikeal C. Parsons and Richard I. Pervo, *Rethinking the Unity of Luke and Acts* (Minneapolis, Mn.: Fortress, 1993), 39. Cassidy glosses over this shift in tone in part by arguing that in its affirmation of "women," Acts still shows concern for "less regarded groups" (57–59). This argument fails to take into account the high status of women in this second work.

Note also Pervo's argument that this focus on the elite is best understood as "propagandistic fiction" rather than mere apologetics: "The upward mobility of many new religions encourages fictional propaganda about their adherents' social status" (*Profit*, 79).

53. Yann Redalié, "Conversion ou libération? Notes sur Actes 16, 11–40," *Bulletin du centre protestant d'etudes* 26, no. 7 (1974): 6–17, esp. 12.

54. On the presentation of class in Acts, see Pervo, *Profit*, 79. For further insightful comments concerning "rich" Christians of late first and early second century, see Richard I. Pervo, "Wisdom and Power," *Anglican Theological Review* 67 (1985): 307–25.

55. Esler, 93–109.

56. This is Esler's reading, 99–100.

57. Corley, 108–46.

58. This reading suggests a different reason for the double foundation story in Philippi than that posed by Gottfried Schille, *Die Apostelgeschichte des Lukas*, Theologischer Handkommentar zum Neuen Testament 5 (Berlin: Evangelische Verlagsanstalt, 1983), 340–49. Schille argues that, since including two foundation stories for one community is superfluous, the story of Lydia's conversion must be understood as a secondary addition to the conversion of the jailer, which he views as the original foundation story for Philippi.

59. LSJ, s.v. παιδίσκη.

60. François Bovon reads 21:8–9 as suggesting the strength of the Christian community in Caesarea and its independence from Paul (see François Bovon, "Der Heilige Geist, die Kirche und die menschlichen Beziehungen nach Apostelgeschichte 20, 36–21, 16," in his *Lukas in neuer Sicht*, Biblisch-Theologische Studien 8 [Neukirchen-Vluyn: Neukirchener Verlag, 1985], 181–204).

61. For an important discussion of women prophets in Luke-Acts, see Seim, 164–84; although I disagree with her argument that gender plays no explicit role in Acts 16:16–18 (Seim, 174). See also D'Angelo, who argues, as I do, that women are distanced from prophetic roles by Luke (451–53).

62. For example, the narrative incorporates the words *hypantaō*, a verb commonly used to describe the meeting of the exorcist and the possessed; (*ana*)*krazō*, associated with the possessing spirit's cry; and *exerchomai*, associated with the exorcist's command. Further, like the demons in the synoptics who proclaim publicly the true identity of Jesus of Nazareth, the spirit in the girl utters a recognition oracle on meeting Paul. There are especially close connections between this story and the report of the exorcism of the Gerasene demoniac in Luke 8:26–39, because both share all of the verbal parallels mentioned above, and in both cases the possessed is a Gentile who uses the epithet "Most High God" (*theos hypistos*) in the recognition oracle. Robert Tannehill, *The Narrative Unity of Luke-Acts: A Literary Interpretation*, 2 vols. (Minneapolis, Mn.: Fortress, 1990), 2:197.

63. For discussion of this story in relation to synoptic exorcisms, see Richter Reimer, 154–74, esp. 171–74.

64. Cf., for example, Mark 1:23, 3:11, 5:2; Matt. 8:32, 17:18; Luke 7:21, 8:2; Acts 8:7, 19:13.

65. Richter Reimer, 154–56.

66. Plutarch, *De defectu oraculorum* 414E. Cf. Conzelmann, *Acts of the Apostles*, 131.

67. *Pace* Werner Foerster, "πύθων," *TDNT* 6 (1968): 917–20.

68. Pierre Amandry, *La mantique apollinienne à Delphes: Essai sur le fonctionnement de l'oracle*, Bibliothèque des écoles françaises d'Athènes et de Rome (Paris: Boccard, 1950), 65.

69. Wolfgang Fauth, "Pythia," *PW* 24 (1963): 515–48, esp. 516–17.

70. Werner de Boor, *Die Apostelgeschichte*, Wuppertaler Studienbibel (Wuppertal: Brockhaus, 1965), 298, n. 364; cf. also Otto Bauernfeind, *Kommentar und Studien zur Apostelgeschichte*, Wissenschaftliche Untersuchungen zum Neuen Testament 22 (Tübingen: Mohr, 1980), 208–9.

71. The critique of religious practice motivated by profit occurs in Acts 19 as well as in Acts 16:16–18. For further examples of this kind of accusation, see Lucian's *Alexander the False Prophet*; the depiction of the female religious functionary Oenothea in Petronius's *Satyricon* 134–38; Juvenal's begging Jewess in *Sat* 6.543–47 and the discussion of Georgi, *Opponents of Paul*, 98–101; the apostle Paul's attempts to distinguish himself from popular philosophers who seek monetary gain in 1 Thess 2; and the discussion of Abraham J. Malherbe, " 'Gentle as a Nurse,' the Cynic Background to I Thessalonians 2," *NovT* 12 (1970): 203–17; reprinted in *Paul and the Popular Philosophers* (Minneapolis, Mn.: Fortress, 1989), 35–48.

Because of the way it varies from a traditional exorcism account, and the manner in which Paul triumphs over the rival spirit, Pervo is right to note the entertainment value of the story (*Profit*, 63). Scholars who do not appreciate Luke's humor here can construct elaborate theories to explain Paul's rationale for the exorcism. See, for example, Paul R. Trebilco, "Paul and Silas—'Servants of the Most High God' (Acts 16.16–18)," *JSNT* 36 (1989): 51–73.

72. John Chrysostom, "Homilies on the Epistles of Paul to the Corinthians," in *A Select Library of the Nicene and Post-Nicene Fathers of the Christian Church*, trans. and ed. Philip Schaff (Grand Rapids, Mich.: Eerdmans, 1982), 12:170.

73. Cf. Herodotus *Hist.* 1.182; Strabo *Geographica* 9.3.5; and the discussions of Arthur Bernard Cook, *Zeus: A Study in Ancient Religion* (1914–1940; reprint, 3 vols. in 2, New York: Biblo and Tannen, 1965), 2:207–10; and Hermann Kleinknecht, "πνεῦμα, πνευματικός," *TDNT* 6 (1968): 332–451, esp. 345–46.

74. Origen, *Contra Celsum*, translated into the French by Marcel Borret, *Sources chretiennes*, nos. 132, 136, 147, 150, 227 (5 vols; Paris: Editions du Cerf, 1967–1976), 3:26.

75. Zeitlin, "Cultic Models of the Female"; and Staples.

76. See especially Kraemer's discussion of women's religious devotion in antiquity in *Her Share of the Blessing*; and Schüssler Fiorenza, *In Memory of Her*.

77. Reardon, *Collected Ancient Greek Novels*, 22.

78. Valerie Abrahamsen, "Women at Philippi: The Pagan and Christian Evidence," *Journal of Feminist Studies in Religion* 3, no. 2 (1987): 17–30. Portefaix, 169–73.

79. *NTApoc*, 2:373–78.

80. Cf. Paul's acknowledgment of the household of Stephanas as the first converts of Achaia in 1 Cor 16:15.

81. Here I read with Bonz, who argues:

> The felicitous combination of [Lydia's] name, occupation, and place of origin suggests that Luke is presenting the reader with a symbolic character. . . . A felicitous combination in the sense that Lydia is the name of a region of western Asia Minor, fabled for its wealth ever since the days of its sixth century BCE king Croesus. Thyatira is a city within the region of Lydia that was famous for its purple dye industry. (Bonz, "Best of Times, Worst of Times," 203).

82. Cynthia Briggs Kittredge, *Community and Authority: The Rhetoric of Obedience in the Pauline Tradition*, Harvard Theological Studies 45 (Harrisburg, Pa.: Trinity, 1998), 105–8.

83. My reading coincides with Valerie A. Abrahamsen, "Women at Philippi and Paul's Philippian Correspondence" (a paper delivered at the Society of Biblical Literature Meeting, 1987), cited in Richter Reimer, 128. Richter Reimer herself dismisses the possibility that Lydia could be a fictional creation of Luke.

84. Consider, for example, the conformity of the speeches of Peter, Stephen, and Paul in Acts's narrative, and the argument of Koester, *Introduction*, 2:318–23.

85. Cf. mention of Apphia in Phlm 2; Prisca in 1 Cor 16:19 and Rom 16:15; Nympha in Col 4:15, and discussion of Schüssler Fiorenza, *In Memory of Her*, 175–84. While Lydia herself may be Luke's fictional creation, the mention of Prisca and Aquilla in both the Pauline letters and Acts 18 shows that Luke knows of women who hosted house churches.

86. For one argument concerning the leadership role the host of a house church expected to assert, see 3 John 9–10, and the reading of it by Abraham J. Malherbe, "Hospitality and Inhospitality in the Church," in *Social Aspects of Early Christianity*, 2d ed. (Philadelphia, Pa.: Fortress, 1983), 92–112; originally published as "The Inhospitality of Diotrephes," in *God's Christ and His People: Studies in Honour of Nils Alstrup Dahl*, ed. Jacob Jervell and Wayne A. Meeks (Oslo: Universitetsforlaget, 1977).

In an effort to read Luke's depiction of Lydia as reflecting her active leadership in Philippi, Richter Reimer has stressed the report in 16:15 that she "prevailed upon" [*parabiazomai*] the missionaries to stay in her house (117–25). Richter Reimer then suggests that in view of Roman disapproval of Jewish missionary activity in Philippi, Lydia puts herself at risk by making this invitation. A similar argument is made by Luise Schottroff, *Lydia's Impatient Sisters: A Feminist Social History of Early Christianity*, trans. Barbara and Martin Rumscheidt (Louisville, Ky.: Westminster/John

Knox Press, 1995), 109–111; and Wolfgang Stegemann, *Zwischen Synagoge und Obrigkeit: Zur historischen Situation der lukanischen Christen*, Forschungen zur Religion und Literatur des Alten und Neuen Testaments 152 (Göttingen: Vandenhoeck & Ruprecht, 1991), 213–14.

87. For general discussion of this letter, see Wilken, *Christians as the Romans Saw Them*, 1–30; and Koester, *Introduction*, 2:334–38.

88. Eusebius's sources are somewhat contradictory. One, a letter of Polycrates, speaks of Philip, "who sleeps at Hierapolis with his two daughters who grew old as virgins and his third daughter who lived in the Holy Spirit and rests in Ephesus." The other, a dialogue of Gaius and Proclus, says that all four daughters rest at Hierapolis with their father.

89. For discussion, see Schüssler Fiorenza, *Revelation*, 132–35.

CONCLUSION

1. I would argue, *pace* Cohen ("Adolf Harnack") and Miriam S. Taylor (*Anti-Judaism and Early Christian Identity: A Critique of the Scholarly Consensus*, Studia Post-Biblica 46 [Leiden, New York, and Köln: Brill, 1995]) that such a conceptualization need not be implicated in anti-Jewish and/or Christian supersessionist programs. The best recent visions of Judaism as missionary are articulated in positive terms. Cf. Georgi, "Early Church," esp. 50; cf. also Mason, "Aim and Audience"; and idem, "*Contra Apionem*."

2. Balch, 65–80. Fifteen years after the publication of Balch's work, Margaret McDonald still praises it without qualification and characterizes it as "an important complement" to her own (*Early Christian Women and Pagan Opinion*, 49–50).

3. For an important discussion of women's religious leadership offices in early Christianity, which does acknowledge the acceptability of such offices in Greco-Roman culture, see Kraemer, *Her Share of the Blessing*, 191–98.

4. For a brief discussion of benefaction as one means "to transfer . . . from one side of the boundary [between Jews and Gentiles] to the other," see Tessa Rajak, "The Jewish Community and Its Boundaries," in *The Jews Among Pagans and Christians in the Roman Empire*, ed. Judith Lieu, John A. North, and Tessa Rajak (London and New York: Routledge, 1992), 9–28, esp. 22–24.

5. See the various attempts of Shaye J. D. Cohen to speak of rituals marking women's conversion, in "Respect for Judaism," 430; and "Beginnings of Jewishness," 169–71, 271–73, 306–7. See also the suggestion of Martin Goodman that the majority of conversions to Judaism must have been for the purpose of facilitating marriage (Goodman, "Jewish Proselytizing," 65–66). The focus on marriage as either the means of, or the purpose for, Gentile women's conversion to Judaism is unfortunate, given the number of sources suggesting Gentile women's conversion outside of the framework of marriage.

WORKS CITED

Abrahamsen, Valerie. "Women at Philippi: The Pagan and Christian Evidence."
Journal of Feminist Studies in Religion 3, no. 2 (1987): 17–30.

Acts of the Pagan Martyrs: Acta Alexandrinorum. Edited by Herbert A. Musurillo.
Oxford: Clarendon, 1954.

Acts of Pilate. In *Evangelia Apocrypha.* Edited by Constantin von Tischendorf.
1876. Reprint, Hildesheim: Olms, 1966.

Aland, Kurt. *Neutestamentliche Entwürfe.* Munich: Kaiser, 1979.

Amandry, Pierre. *La mantique apollinienne à Delphes: Essai sur le fonctionnement
de l'oracle.* Bibliothèque des écoles françaises d'Athènes et de Rome. Paris: Boccard, 1950.

Amaru, Betsy Halpern. "Portraits of Biblical Women in Josephus' *Antiquities.*" *JJS*
39, no. 2 (1988): 143–70.

Applebaum, S. "The Legal Status of the Jewish Communities in the Diaspora." In
The Jewish People in the First Century, edited by S. Safrai and M. Stern, 1:420–
63. 2 vols. Compendia rerum iudaicarum ad Novum Testamentum 1. Philadelphia, Pa.: Fortress, 1974–1976.

Archer, Léonie J. *Her Price Is Beyond Rubies: The Jewish Woman in Graeco-Roman
Palestine.* Journal for the Study of the Old Testament: Supplement Series 60.
Sheffield, Eng.: Sheffield, 1990.

Attridge, Harold W. "Josephus and His Works." In *Jewish Writings of the Second
Temple Period,* edited by Michael E. Stone, 185–232. Compendia rerum
iudaicarum ad Novum Testamentum Sec. 2. Philadelphia, Pa.: Fortress, 1984.

Axenfeld, Karl. "Die jüdische Propaganda als Vorläuferin und Wegbereiterin der
urchristlichen Mission." In *Missionswissenschaftliche Studien: Festschrift zum 70.*

Geburtstag des Herrn Prof. D. Dr. Gustav Warneck, edited by Karl Axenfeld et al., 1–80. Berlin: Warneck, 1904.

Balch, David L. *Let Wives Be Submissive: The Domestic Code in I Peter*. Society of Biblical Literature Monograph Series 26. Atlanta, Ga.: Scholars Press, 1981.

Bamberger, Bernard J. *Proselytism in the Talmudic Period*. Cincinnati, Ohio: Hebrew Union College, 1939.

Bauernfeind, Otto. *Kommentar und Studien zur Apostelgeschichte*. Wissenschaftliche Untersuchungen zum Neuen Testament 22. Tübingen: Mohr, 1980.

Beard, Mary. "The Sexual Status of the Vestal Virgins." *JRS* 70 (1980): 12–27.

Becher, Ilse. "Der Isiskult in Rom—ein Kult der Halbwelt?" *Zeitschrift für ägyptische Sprache und Altertumskunde* 96 (1970): 81–90.

Bell, H. Idris, ed. *Jews and Christians in Egypt: The Jewish Troubles in Alexandria and the Athanasian Controversy*. Oxford: Oxford University Press, 1924.

Boatwright, Mary Taliaferro. "The Imperial Women of the Early Second Century A.C." *AJP* 112 (1991): 513–40.

———. "Plancia Magna of Perge: Women's Roles and Status in Roman Asia Minor." In *Women's History and Ancient History*, edited by Sarah B. Pomeroy, 249–72. Chapel Hill: University of North Carolina Press, 1991.

Bonz, Marianne Palmer. "Questions Concerning the Jewish Donor Inscriptions from Aphrodisias." *HSCP* 96 (1994): 281–99.

———. "The Best of Times, the Worst of Times: Luke-Acts and Epic Tradition." Ph.D. diss., Harvard University, 1996.

Boor, Werner de. *Die Apostelgeschichte*. Wuppertaler Studienbibel. Wuppertal: Brockhaus, 1965.

Bovon, François. "Der Heilige Geist, die Kirche und die menschlichen Beziehungen nach Apostelgeschichte 20, 36–21, 16." In *Lukas in neuer Sicht*. Biblisch-Theologische Studien 8. Neukirchen-Vluyn: Neukirchener Verlag, 1985.

———. *L'Évangile selon Saint Luc 1–9*. Commentaire du Nouveau Testament 3a. Genève: Labor et Fides, 1991.

———. "The Effect of Realism and Prophetic Ambiguity in the Works of Luke." In *New Testament Traditions and Apocryphal Narratives*. Princeton Theological Monograph Series 36. Allison Park, Pa.: Pickwick, 1995.

Boyarin, Daniel. *A Radical Jew: Paul and the Politics of Identity*. Contraversions 1. Berkeley, Los Angeles, and London: University of California Press, 1994.

Braude, W. G. *Jewish Proselytizing in the First Five Centuries of the Common Era: The Age of the Tannaim and Amoraim*. Providence, R.I.: Brown University Press, 1940.

Braun, Martin. *History and Romance in Graeco-Oriental Literature*. 1938. Reprint, New York and London: Garland, 1987.

Bremen, Riet van. "Women and Wealth." In *Images of Women in Antiquity*, edited by Averil Cameron and Amelie Kuhrt, 223–42. Detroit, Mich.: Wayne State University Press, 1983.

——. *The Limits of Participation: Women and Civic Life in the Greek East in the Hellenistic and Roman Periods.* Dutch Monographs on Ancient History and Archaeology 15. Amsterdam: Gieben, 1996.

Brooten, Bernadette J. "Junia . . . Outstanding Among the Apostles (Romans 16:7)." In *Women Priests,* edited by Leonard S. Swidler and Arlene Swidler, 141–44. New York: Paulist, 1977.

——. *Women Leaders in the Ancient Synagogue.* Brown Judaic Series 36. Atlanta, Ga.: Scholars Press, 1982.

Brown, Peter. *The Body and Society: Men, Women, and Sexual Renunciation in Early Christianity.* Lectures on the History of Religions, n.s. 13. New York: Columbia University Press, 1988.

Bruce, F. F. *New Testament History.* Garden City, N.Y.: Doubleday, 1969.

Cadbury, H. J. "Commentary on the Preface of Luke." In *Beginnings of Christianity Part 1: The Acts of the Apostles,* edited by F. J. Foakes-Jackson and Kirsopp Lake, 2:489–510. 5 vols. London: Macmillan, 1919–1933.

Camp, Claudia V. "Feminist Theological Hermeneutics: Canon and Christian Identity." In *Searching the Scriptures: A Feminist Introduction,* edited by Elisabeth Schüssler Fiorenza, with the assistance of Shelly Matthews, 154–71. New York: Crossroad, 1993.

Canning, Kathleen. "Feminist History After the Linguistic Turn: Historicizing Discourse and Experience." In *History and Theory: Feminist Research, Debates, Contestations,* edited by Barbara Laslett et al., 416–52. Chicago and London: University of Chicago Press, 1997.

Case, Shirley Jackson. "Josephus' Anticipation of a Domitianic Persecution." *JBL* 44 (1925): 10–20.

Cassidy, Richard J. *Society and Politics in the Acts of the Apostles.* Maryknoll, N.Y.: Orbis, 1987.

Castelli, Elizabeth A. "Romans." In *Searching the Scriptures: A Feminist Commentary,* edited by Elisabeth Schüssler Fiorenza, with the assistance of Ann Brock and Shelly Matthews, 272–300. New York: Crossroad, 1994.

Clark, Elizabeth A. "Ascetic Renunciation and Feminine Advancement: A Paradox of Late Ancient Christianity." *Anglican Theological Review* 63 (1981): 240–57.

Clarke, M. L. "Quintillian: A Biographical Sketch." *Greece and Rome* 14 (1967): 24–37.

Cohen, Shaye J. D. *Josephus in Galilee and Rome: His Vita and Development as a Historian.* Columbia Studies in the Classical Tradition 8. Leiden: Brill, 1979.

——. "The Origins of the Matrilineal Principle in Rabbinic Law." *Association for Jewish Studies Review* 10, no. 1 (1985): 19–53.

——. "Respect for Judaism by Gentiles According to Josephus." *HTR* 80, no. 4 (1987): 409–30.

——. "Crossing the Boundary and Becoming a Jew." *HTR* 82, no. 1 (1989): 13–33.

——. "Adolf Harnack's 'The Mission and Expansion of Judaism': Christianity Succeeds Where Judaism Fails." In *The Future of Early Christianity: Essays in Honor of Helmut Koester*, edited by Birger Pearson, 163–69. Minneapolis, Mn.: Fortress, 1991.

——. "Was Judaism in Antiquity a Missionary Religion?" In *Jewish Assimilation, Acculturation and Accommodation*, edited by Menachem Mor, 14–23. Studies in Jewish Civilization 2. Lanham, Md.: University Press of America, 1992.

——. *The Beginnings of Jewishness: Boundaries, Varieties, Uncertainties*. Hellenistic Culture and Society 31. Berkeley, Los Angeles, and London: University of California Press, 1999.

Conzelmann, Hans. *Acts of the Apostles*. Hermeneia. Philadelphia, Pa.: Fortress, 1972.

——. *History of Primitive Christianity*. Nashville, Tenn.: Abingdon, 1973.

——. *Theology of St. Luke*. 1961. Reprint, Philadelphia, Pa.: Fortress, 1982.

Cook, Arthur Bernard. *Zeus: A Study in Ancient Religion*. 3 vols. 1914–1940. Reprint, 3 vols. in 2, New York: Biblo and Tannen, 1965.

Cooper, Kate. "Apostles, Ascetic Women, and Questions of Audience: New Reflections on the Rhetoric of Gender in the Apocryphal Acts." *SBLSP* 31 (1992): 147–53.

——. "Insinuations of Womanly Influence: An Aspect of the Christianization of the Roman Aristocracy." *JRS* 82 (1992): 150–64.

——. *The Virgin and the Bride: Idealized Womanhood in Late Antiquity*. Cambridge, Mass., and London: Harvard University Press, 1996.

Corley, Kathleen E. *Private Women, Public Meals: Social Conflict in the Synoptic Tradition*. Peabody, Mass.: Hendrickson, 1993.

Courtney, Edward. *A Commentary on the Satires of Juvenal*. London: Athlone, 1980.

Crossan, John Dominic. *Jesus: A Revolutionary Biography*. San Francisco: HarperSanFrancisco, 1994.

Culham, Phyllis. "Decentering the Text: The Case of Ovid." *Helios* n.s. 17, no. 2 (1990): 161–69.

Cumont, Franz. "La grande inscription bachique du Metropolitan Museum." *AJA* 37 (1933): 232–63.

——. *Oriental Religions in Roman Paganism*. New York: Dover, 1956.

Dalbert, Peter. *Die Theologie der hellenistisch-jüdischen Missionsliteratur unter Ausschluss von Philo und Josephus*. Hamburg: Reich, 1954.

D'Angelo, Mary Rose. "Women in Luke-Acts: A Redactional View." *JBL* 109, no. 3 (1990): 441–61.

D'Arms, John H. *Commerce and Social Standing in Ancient Rome.* Cambridge, Mass.: Harvard University Press, 1981.

Dio Cassius. *Roman History.* Translated by Earnest Cary. 9 vols. Loeb Classical Library. Cambridge, Mass.: Harvard University Press, 1954–1955.

Dixon, Suzanne. "A Family Business: Women's Role in Patronage and Politics at Rome 80–44 B.C." *Classica et Mediaevalia* 34 (1983): 91–112.

Easterling, P. E. "From Repertoire to Canon." In *The Cambridge Companion to Greek Tragedy,* edited by P. E. Easterling, 211–27. Cambridge: Cambridge University Press, 1997.

Edwards, Catherine. *The Politics of Immorality in Ancient Rome.* Cambridge: Cambridge University Press, 1993.

Erhart, Katherine Patricia. "A Portrait of Antonia Minor in the Fogg Art Museum and Its Iconographical Tradition." *AJA* 82 (1978): 193–212.

Esler, Philip Francis. *Community and Gospel in Luke-Acts.* Society for New Testament Studies Monograph Series 57. Cambridge: Cambridge University Press, 1987.

Euripides. *Bacchae.* Edited by E. R. Dodds. 2d ed. Oxford: Clarendon, 1960.

——. *Melanippe Captive,* frag. In *Select Papyri,* translated and edited by D. L. Page, 3:108–16. 4 vols. Loeb Classical Library. 1941. Reprint, Cambridge, Mass., and London: Harvard University Press/William Heinemann, 1980.

Ezekiel the Tragedian. *Exodus.* Translated and edited by R. G. Robertson. In *The Old Testament Pseudepigrapha,* edited by James Charlesworth, 2:807–19. 2 vols. New York: Doubleday, 1983–1985.

Fauth, Wolfgang. "Pythia." PW 24 (1963): 515–48.

Feldman, Louis H. "The Omnipresence of the God-Fearers." *Biblical Archaeology Review* 12, no. 5 (1986): 59–69.

——. "Josephus' Portrait of Moses." JQR 82, nos. 3–4 (1992): 285–328.

——. *Jew and Gentile in the Ancient World: Attitudes and Interactions from Alexander to Justinian.* Princeton, N.J.: Princeton University Press, 1993.

——. *Josephus's Interpretation of the Bible.* Hellenistic Culture and Society 27. Berkeley and Los Angeles: University of California Press, 1998.

Finn, Thomas M. "The God-fearers Reconsidered." CBQ 47 (1985): 75–84.

Fischler, Susan. "The Public Position of Women in the Imperial Household in the Julio-Claudian Period." Ph.D. diss., Oxford University, 1989.

——. "Social Stereotypes and Historical Analysis: The Case of the Imperial Women at Rome." In *Women in Ancient Societies: An Illusion of the Night,* edited by Léonie J. Archer, Susan Fischler, and Maria Wyke, 115–33. London: Macmillan, 1994.

Flender, Helmut. *St. Luke: Theologian of Redemptive History.* Philadelphia, Pa.: Fortress, 1976.

Foakes-Jackson, F. J., and Kirsopp Lake, eds. *The Beginnings of Christianity Part 1: Acts of the Apostles.* 5 vols. London: Macmillan, 1919–1933.

Foerster, Werner. "πύθων." *TDNT* 6 (1968): 917–20.

Foley, Helene P. "The Conception of Women in Athenian Drama." In *Reflections of Women in Antiquity*, edited by Helene P. Foley, 127–67. New York: Gordon & Breach, 1981.

———. "The Female 'Intruder' Reconsidered: Women in Aristophanes' *Lysistrata and Ecclesiazusae.*" *CP* 77, no. 1 (1982): 1–21.

Foley, Helene P., ed. *Reflections of Women in Antiquity.* New York: Gordon & Breach, 1981.

Forbis, Elizabeth P. "Women's Public Image in Italian Honorary Inscriptions." *AJP* 111 (1990): 493–512.

Friedländer, Ludwig. *Roman Life and Manners Under the Early Empire.* Translated by A. Magnus. 4 vols. London: Routledge, 1908–1913.

Friesen, Steve. "Ephesian Women and Men in Public Religious Office in the Roman Period." In *100 Jahre Österreichische Forschungen in Ephesos. Akten des Symposions Wien 1995*, edited by Herwig Friesinger and Friedrich Krinzinger, 107–33. Vienna: Austrian Archaeological Institute, 1999.

Gager, John G. *Moses in Greco-Roman Paganism.* Society of Biblical Literature Monograph Series 16. Nashville, Tenn.: Abingdon, 1972.

———. *The Origins of Anti-Semitism: Attitudes Toward Judaism in Pagan and Christian Antiquity.* New York and Oxford: Oxford University Press, 1983.

———. "Jews, Gentiles, and Synagogues in the Book of Acts." *HTR* 79, nos. 1–3 (1986): 91–99.

Gamble, Harry Y. *The Textual History of the Letter to the Romans.* Grand Rapids, Mich.: Eerdmans, 1977.

Gamel, Mary-Kay, et al. Discussion of "Decentering the Text: The Case of Ovid," by Phyllis Culham. *Helios* n.s. 17, no. 2 (1990): 171–262.

Georgi, Dieter. *The Opponents of Paul in Second Corinthians.* Philadelphia, Pa.: Fortress, 1986.

———. "The Early Church: Internal Jewish Migration or New Religion?" *HTR* 88, no. 1 (1995): 35–68.

Gill, David W. J. "Acts and the Urban Elites." In *The Book of Acts in Its Graeco-Roman Setting*, edited by David W. J. Gill and Conrad Gempf, 105–18. The Book of Acts in Its First Century Setting 2. Grand Rapids, Mich.: Eerdmans, 1994.

Gold, Barbara K. "εὐκοσμία in Euripides' Bacchae." *AJP* 98 (1977): 3–15.

———. " 'But Ariadne Was Never There in the First Place': Finding the Female in Roman Poetry." In *Feminist Theory and the Classics*, edited by Nancy Sorkin Rabinowitz and Amy Richlin, 75–101. Thinking Gender Series. New York and London: Routledge, 1993.

Goodman, Martin. "Jewish Proselytizing in the First Century." In *The Jews Among Pagans and Christians in the Roman Empire*, edited by Judith Lieu, John A. North, and Tessa Rajak, 53–78. London and New York: Routledge, 1992.

——. *Mission and Conversion*. Oxford: Oxford University Press, 1994.

Grant, Robert M. *The Sword and the Cross*. New York: Macmillan, 1955.

Hadas, Moses. *Hellenistic Culture: Fusion and Diffusion*. New York: W. W. Norton, 1959.

Haenchen, Ernst. *The Acts of the Apostles: A Commentary*. Philadelphia, Pa.: Westminster, 1971.

Hallett, Judith P. *Fathers and Daughters in Roman Society*. Princeton, N.J.: Princeton University Press, 1984.

Harnack, Adolf von. *The Mission and Expansion of Christianity in the First Three Centuries*. 1904–1905. Reprint, New York: Books for Libraries, 1972.

Hay, David M. "Things Philo Said and Did Not Say About the Therapeutae." *SBLSP* (1992): 673–83.

Heidel, W. A. "Why Were the Jews Banished from Italy in 19 A.D.?" *AJP* 41 (1920): 38–48.

Heine, Susanne. *Women in Early Christianity: Are the Feminist Scholars Right?* London: SCM, 1987.

Henderson, Jeffrey. "*Lysistrate*: The Play and Its Themes." *Yale Classical Studies* 26 (1980): 153–218.

Henrichs, Albert. "Greek Maenadism from Olympias to Messalina." *HSCP* 82 (1978): 121–60.

——. "Changing Dionysiac Identities." In *Jewish and Christian Self-Definition*, edited by Ben F. Meyer and E. P. Sanders, 3:137–60. 3 vols. Philadelphia, Pa.: Fortress, 1982.

Heyob, Sharon Kelly. *The Cult of Isis Among Women in the Graeco-Roman World*. Etudes préliminaires aux religions orientales dans l'empire romain 51. Leiden: Brill, 1975.

Hillard, Tom. "Republican Politics, Women, and the Evidence." *Helios* 16, no. 2 (1989): 165–82.

——. "On the Stage, Behind the Curtain." In *Stereotypes of Women in Power: Historical Perspectives and Revisionist Views*, edited by Barbara Garlick, Suzanne Dixon, and Pauline Allen, 37–63. Contributions in Women's Studies 125. New York: Greenwood Press, 1992.

Homer. *Iliad*. Translated by Robert Fagels. New York: Viking, 1990.

Horace. *Odes and Epodes*. Translated by C. E. Bennett. Loeb Classical Library. Cambridge, Mass.: Harvard University Press, 1914.

Horsley, G. H. R. *New Documents Illustrating Early Christianity*. 7 vols. North Ryde, New South Wales, Australia: Ancient History Documentary Research Centre, Macquarie University, 1981–1994.

Horsley, Richard A. "High Priests and the Politics of Roman Palestine: A Contextual Analysis of the Evidence of Josephus." *JSJ* 17, no. 1 (1986): 23–55.

Horst, Pieter W. van der. "Jews and Christians in Aphrodisias in the Light of their Relations to Other Cities of Asia Minor." *Nederlands Theologisch Tijdschrift* 43, no. 2 (1989): 106–21.

——. *Ancient Jewish Epitaphs*. Contributions to Biblical Exegesis and Theology 2. Kampen, The Netherlands: Kok Pharos, 1991.

Hughes-Hallet, Lucy. *Cleopatra: Histories, Dreams and Distortions*. New York: Harper & Row, 1990.

Ilan, Tal. "The Attraction of Aristocratic Women to Pharisaism During the Second Temple Period." *HTR* 88, no. 1 (1995): 1–33.

——. "Josephus and Nicolaus on Women." In *Geschichte—Tradition—Reflection: Festschrift für Martin Hengel zum 70. Geburtstag*, edited by Hubert Cancik, Herman Lichtenberger, and Peter Schäfer, 1:221–62. 3 vols. Tübingen: Mohr/ Siebeck, 1996.

Jervell, Jacob. *Luke and the People of God: A New Look at Luke-Acts*. Minneapolis, Mn.: Augsburg, 1972.

——. "The Daughters of Abraham: Women in Acts." In *The Unknown Paul: Essays on Luke-Acts and Early Christian History*. Minneapolis, Mn.: Augsburg, 1984.

John Chrysostom. "Homilies on the Epistles of Paul to the Corinthians." In *A Select Library of the Nicene and Post-Nicene Fathers of the Christian Church*. Vol. 12. Translated and edited by Philip Schaff. Grand Rapids, Mich.: Eerdmans, 1982.

Josephus. *Works*. Translated by H. St. J. Thackeray et al. 10 vols. Loeb Classical Library. Cambridge, Mass.: Harvard University Press, 1926–1965.

Joshel, Sandra R. "The Body Female and the Body Politic: Livy's Lucretia and Verginia." In *Pornography and Representation in Greece and Rome*, edited by Amy Richlin, 112–30. New York and Oxford: Oxford University Press, 1992.

——. "Female Desire and the Discourse of Empire: Tacitus's Messalina." *Signs* 21, no. 1 (1995): 50–82.

Juvenal. *The Satires of Juvenal*. Translated by G. G. Ramsay. Loeb Classical Library. Cambridge, Mass.: Harvard University Press, 1918.

——. *Satura VI*. Edited by Amy Richlin. Bryn Mawr Latin Commentaries. Bryn Mawr, Pa.: Bryn Mawr College, 1986.

Kittredge, Cynthia Briggs. *Community and Authority: The Rhetoric of Obedience in the Pauline Tradition*. Harvard Theological Studies, 45. Harrisburg, Pa.: Trinity International Press, 1998.

Kleinknecht, Hermann. "πνεῦμα, πνευματικός." *TDNT* 6 (1968): 332–451.

Koester, Helmut. *Introduction to the New Testament*. 2 vols. New York and Berlin: De Gruyter, 1982.

——. "Ephesos in Early Christian Literature." In *Ephesos: Metropolis of Asia*, edited by Helmut Koester, 119–40. Harvard Theological Studies, 41. Valley Forge, Pa.: Trinity Press International, 1995.

Kraabel, Alf Thomas. "Judaism in Asia Minor." Th.D. diss., Harvard University, 1968.

———. "The Disappearance of the 'God-Fearers.' " *Numen: International Review for the History of Religions* 28 (1981): 113–26.

———. "The Roman Diaspora: Six Questionable Assumptions." *JJS* 33 (1982): 445–64.

———. "Synagoga Caeca: Systematic Distortion in Gentile Interpretations of Evidence for Judaism in the Early Christian Period." In *"To See Ourselves as Others See Us": Christians, Jews, "Others," in Late Antiquity*, edited by Jacob Neusner and E. S. Frerichs, 219–46. Chico, Calif.: Scholars Press, 1985.

———. "Greeks, Jews, and Lutherans in the Middle Half of Acts." *HTR* 79, no. 1–3 (1986): 147–57.

———. "Immigrants, Exiles, Expatriates, and Missionaries." In *Religious Propaganda and Missionary Competition in the New Testament World: Essays Honoring Dieter Georgi*, edited by Lukas Bormann, Kelly Del Tredici, and Angela Standhartinger, 71–89. Leiden and New York: Brill, 1994.

Kraemer, Ross Shepherd. "Ecstasy and Possession: The Attraction of Women to the Cult of Dionysus." *HTR* 72 (1979): 55–80.

———. "Hellenistic Jewish Women: The Epigraphic Evidence." *SBLSP* (1986): 183–200.

———. "Non-Literary Evidence for Jewish Women in Rome and Egypt." *Rescuing Creusa: New Methodological Approaches to Women in Antiquity = Helios*, edited by Marilyn Skinner, 13, no. 2 (1986): 85–101.

———. "Monastic Jewish Women in Greco-Roman Egypt: Philo on the Therapeutrides." *Signs* 14, no. 1 (1989): 342–70.

———. "On the Meaning of the Term 'Jew' in Greco-Roman Inscriptions." *HTR* 82, no. 1 (1989): 38–42.

———. *Her Share of the Blessings: Women's Religions Among Pagans, Jews, and Christians in the Greco-Roman World*. New York and Oxford: Oxford University Press, 1992.

Kuhn, Karl Georg. "προσήλυτος." *TDNT* 6 (1968): 727–44.

Kuhn, Karl Georg, and Hartmut Stegemann. "Proselyten." PWSup 9 (1962): 1248–84.

Lake, Kirsopp. "Proselytes and God-fearers." In *The Beginnings of Christianity Part 1: The Acts of the Apostles*, edited by J. F. Foakes-Jackson and Kirsopp Lake, 5:74–96. 5 vols. London: Macmillan, 1919–1933.

Lefkowitz, Mary R., and Maureen B. Fant, eds. *Women's Life in Greece and Rome: A Sourcebook in Translation*. 2d ed. Baltimore, Md.: Johns Hopkins University Press, 1992.

Levinskaya, Irina. *The Book of Acts in Its Diaspora Setting*. The Book of Acts in Its First Century Setting 5. Grand Rapids, Mich.: Eerdmans, 1996.

Leon, Harry J. *The Jews of Ancient Rome*. Updated ed. Peabody, Mass.: Hendrickson, 1995.

Lewy, Hans. *Sobria Ebrietas: Untersuchungen zur Geschichte der antiken Mystik*. Gießen: Töpelmann, 1929.

Liebeschuetz, John. *Continuity and Change in Roman Religion*. Oxford: Clarendon, 1979.

Lifshitz, B. *Donateurs et fondateurs dans les synagogues juives*. Cahiers de la revue biblique 7. Paris: Gabalda, 1967.

Linforth, Ivan M. "The Corybantic Rites in Plato." *University of California Publications in Classical Philology* 13, no. 5 (1946): 121–62.

———. "Telestic Madness in Plato, Phaedrus 244DE." *University of California Publications in Classical Philology* 13, no. 6 (1946): 163–72.

Livy. *History of Rome*. Vol. 11. Translated by Evan T. Sage. Loeb Classical Library. Cambridge, Mass.: Harvard University Press, 1936.

Lloyd, Alan B. "Nationalistic Propaganda in Ptolemaic Egypt." *Historia* 31 (1982): 46–50.

MacDonald, Dennis Ronald. *There is No Male or Female: The Fate of a Dominical Saying in Paul and Gnosticism*. Harvard Dissertations in Religion 20. Philadelphia, Pa.: Fortress, 1987.

MacDonald, Margaret Y. *Early Christian Women and Pagan Opinion: The Power of the Hysterical Woman*. Cambridge: Cambridge University Press, 1996.

MacMullen, Ramsay. "Women in Public in the Roman Empire." *Historia* 29 (1980): 208–18.

Maddox, Robert. *The Purpose of Luke-Acts*. Forschungen zur Religion und Literatur des Alten und Neuen Testaments 126. Göttingen: Vandenhoeck & Ruprecht, 1982.

Malaise, Michel. *Inventaire préliminaire des documents égyptiens découverts en italie*. Etudes préliminaires aux religions orientales dans l'empire romain 21. Leiden: Brill, 1972.

———. *Les conditions de pénétration et de diffusion des cultes égyptiens en Italie*. Etudes préliminaires aux religions orientales dans l'empire romain 22. Leiden: Brill, 1972.

Malherbe, Abraham J. "Hospitality and Inhospitality in the Church." In *Social Aspects of Early Christianity*. 2d ed. Philadelphia, Pa.: Fortress, 1983. Originally published as "The Inhospitality of Diotrephes," in *God's Christ and His People: Studies in Honour of Nils Alstrup Dahl*, edited by Jacob Jervell and Wayne A. Meeks, Oslo: Universitetsforlaget, 1977.

———. " 'Gentle as a Nurse,' the Cynic Background to I Thessalonians 2." *NovT* 12

(1970): 203–17. Reprinted in *Paul and the Popular Philosophers*, Minneapolis, Mn.: Fortress, 1989, 35–48.

Marshall, Anthony J. "Roman Women and the Provinces." *Ancient Society* 6 (1975): 109–27.

Mason, Steve. "The *Contra Apionem* in Social and Literary Context: An Invitation to Judean Philosophy." In *Josephus' Contra Apionem: Studies in Character and Context with a Latin Concordance to the Portion Missing in Greek*, edited by L. H. Feldman and J. R. Levison, 187–228. Arbeiten zur Geschichte des antiken Judentums und des Urchristentums 34. Leiden: Brill, 1996.

———. "Should Any Wish to Enquire Further (*Ant.* 1.25): The Aim and Audience of Josephus's *Judean Antiquities/Life*." In *Understanding Josephus: Seven Perspectives*, edited by Steve Mason, 64–103. Journal for the Study of the Pseudepigrapha Supplement Series 32. Sheffield, Eng.: Sheffield Academic Press, 1998.

———. "Introduction to the *Judean Antiquities*." In *Judean Antiquities 1–4*, translation and commentary by Louis H. Feldman, xiii–xxxv. Vol. 3 of *Flavius Josephus: Translation and Commentary*, edited by Steve Mason. Leiden: Brill, 2000.

Mattingly, Harold. *Coins of the Roman Empire in the British Museum*. 8 vols. London: The British Museum, 1966.

Mattingly, Harold, and E. A. Sydenham. *The Roman Imperial Coinage*. 10 vols. London: Spink, 1923–1994.

McKnight, Scot. *A Light Among the Gentiles: Jewish Missionary Activity in the Second Temple Period*. Minneapolis, Mn.: Fortress, 1991.

Meeks, Wayne A. *The First Urban Christians: The Social World of the Apostle Paul*. New Haven, Conn., and London: Yale University Press, 1983.

Meeks, Wayne A., and Robert Wilkin. *Jews and Christians in Antioch in the First Four Centuries of the Common Era*. Society of Biblical Literature Sources for Biblical Study 13. Missoula, Mt.: Scholars Press, 1978.

Merkelbach, Reinhold. *Die Quellen des griechischen Alexanderromans*. Munich: Beck, 1954.

Merrill, Elmer Truesdell. "The Expulsion of Jews from Rome Under Tiberius." *CP* 14 (1919): 365–72.

Meshorer, Yaakov. *Ancient Jewish Coinage*. 2 vols. Dix Hills, N.Y.: Amphora Books, 1982.

Mielentz. "Tarpeius." PW n.s. 4 (1932): 2330–42.

Millar, Fergus. *The Emperor in the Roman World*. Ithaca, N.Y.: Cornell University Press, 1977.

Moehring, Horst R. "The Persecution of the Jews and the Adherents of the Isis Cult at Rome A.D. 19." *NovT* 3 (1959): 293–304.

———. "The *Acta Pro Judaeis* in the *Antiquities* of Flavius Josephus." In *Christianity,*

Judaism and the Other Greco-Roman Cults: Studies for Morton Smith at Sixty, edited by Jacob Neusner, 124–58. Studies in Judaism in Late Antiquity 12. Leiden: Brill, 1975.

Moore, George Foot. *Judaism in the First Centuries of the Christian Era: The Age of the Tannaim*. 3 vols. Cambridge, Mass.: Harvard University Press, 1927–1940.

Nestle, W. "Ankläge an Euripides in der Apostelgeschichte." *Philologus* 13 (1900): 46–57.

Neyrey, Jerome. "What's Wrong with This Picture? John 4, Cultural Stereotypes of Women, and Public and Private Space." *Biblical Theology Bulletin* 24, no. 2 (1994): 77–91.

Nock, Arthur Darby. *Conversion: The Old and the New in Religion from Alexander the Great to Augustine of Hippo*. Oxford: Clarendon, 1933.

North, John A. "Religious Toleration in Republican Rome." *Proceedings of the Cambridge Philological Society* 205 (1979): 85–103.

Ollrog, Wolf-Henning. "Die Abfassungsverhältnisse von Röm 16." In *Kirche: Festschrift für Günther Bornkamm zum 75. Geburtstag*, edited by D. Lührmann and G. Strecker, 221–44. Tübingen: J. C. Mohr, 1980.

Origen. *Contra Celsum*. Translated into the French by Marcel Borret. *Sources chretiennes*, nos. 132, 136, 147, 150, 227. 5 vols. Paris: Editions du Cerf, 1967–1976.

Osiek, Carolyn. "The Family in Early Christianity: 'Family Values' Revisited." *CBQ* 58, no. 1 (1996): 1–24.

Osiek, Carolyn, and David Balch. *Families in the New Testament World: Households and Churches*. The Family, Religion, and Culture Series. Louisville, Ky.: Westminster/John Knox Press, 1997.

Pack, Roger A. *Greek and Latin Literary Texts from Greco-Roman Egypt*. 2d ed. Ann Arbor: University of Michigan Press, 1965.

Parsons, Mikeal C., and Richard I. Pervo. *Rethinking the Unity of Luke and Acts*. Minneapolis, Mn.: Fortress, 1993.

Perrin, Norman, and Dennis C. Duling. *The New Testament: An Introduction*. 2d ed. New York: Harcourt Brace Jovanovich, 1982.

Pervo, Richard I. "Social and Religious Aspects of the 'Western' Text." In *The Living Text: Essays in Honor of Ernest W. Saunders*, edited by Dennis E. Groh and Robert Jewett, 229–41. Lanham, Md.: University Press of America, 1985.

——. "Wisdom and Power." *Anglican Theological Review* 67 (1985): 307–25.

——. *Profit with Delight: The Literary Genre of the Acts of the Apostles*. Philadelphia, Pa.: Fortress, 1987.

——. *Luke's Story of Paul*. Minneapolis, Mn.: Fortress, 1990.

Peskowitz, Miriam. " 'Family/ies' in Antiquity: Evidence from Tannaitic Literature and Roman Galilean Architecture." In *The Jewish Family in Antiquity*, edited by Shaye J. D. Cohen, 9–36. Brown Judaic Studies 289. Atlanta, Ga.: Scholars Press, 1993.

Philo. *Works*. Translated by F. H. Colson et al. 12 vols. Loeb Classical Library. Cambridge, Mass.: Harvard University Press, 1929–1962.

Pleket, H. W. "Urban Elites and Business in the Greek Part of the Roman Empire." In *Trade in the Ancient Economy*, edited by P. Garnsey et al., 131–44. London: Chatto & Windus, 1983.

Plümacher, Eckhard. *Lukas als hellenistischer Schriftsteller: Studien zur Apostelgeschichte*. Studien zur Umwelt des Neuen Testaments 9. Göttingen: Vandenhoeck & Ruprecht, 1972.

Plutarch. *The Parallel Lives*. Vol. 9. Translated by B. Perrin. Loeb Classical Library. Cambridge, Mass.: Harvard University Press, 1920.

———. *Moralia*. Vol. 2. Translated by Frank C. Babbitt. Loeb Classical Library. Cambridge, Mass.: Harvard University Press, 1928.

———. *Moralia*. Vol. 8. Translated by P. A. Clement and H. B. Hoffleit. Loeb Classical Library. Cambridge, Mass.: Harvard University Press, 1969.

Pomeroy, Sarah B. "Reflections on Plutarch, *Advice to the Bride and Groom*," in *Plutarch's Advice to the Bride and Groom and A Consolation to His Wife*, edited by Sarah B. Pomeroy, 33–42. New York and Oxford: Oxford University Press, 1999.

Portefaix, Lilian. *Sisters Rejoice: Paul's Letter to the Philippians and Luke-Acts as Seen by First-Century Philippian Women*. Coniectanea biblica: New Testament Series 20. Stockholm: Almqvist & Wiksell, 1988.

Propertius. *Elegies*. Translated by G. P. Goold. Loeb Classical Library. Cambridge, Mass.: Harvard University Press, 1990.

Pseudo-Callisthenes. *Alexander Romance*. Translated by Ken Dowden. In *Collected Ancient Greek Novels*, edited by B. P. Reardon. Berkeley, Los Angeles, and London: University of California Press, 1989.

Purcell, Nicholas. "Livia and the Womanhood of Rome." *Proceedings of the Cambridge Philological Society* n.s. 32 (1986): 75–105.

Rabinowitz, Nancy Sorkin, and Amy Richlin, eds. *Feminist Theory and the Classics*. Thinking Gender Series. New York and London: Routledge, 1993.

Radin, Max. *The Jews Among the Greeks and Romans*. Philadelphia, Pa.: Jewish Publication Society, 1915.

Rajak, Tessa. "Moses in Ethiopia: Legend and Literature." *JJS* 29 (1978): 111–22.

———. *Josephus: The Historian and His Society*. Philadelphia, Pa.: Fortress, 1984.

———. "Was There a Roman Charter for the Jews?" *JRS* 74 (1984): 107–23.

———. "The Jewish Community and Its Boundaries." In *The Jews Among Pagans and Christians in the Roman Empire*, edited by Judith Lieu, John A. North, and Tessa Rajak, 9–28. London and New York: Routledge, 1992.

Redalié, Yann. "Conversion ou libération?" Notes sur Actes 16, 11–40. *Bulletin du centre protestant d'etudes* 26, no. 7 (1974): 6–17.

Reynolds, Joyce. *Aphrodisias and Rome*. London: Society for the Promotion of Roman Studies, 1982.

Reynolds, Joyce, and Robert Tannenbaum. *Jews and God-fearers at Aphrodisias: Greek Inscriptions with Commentary*. Cambridge Philological Society, Suppl. 12. Cambridge: Cambridge University Press, 1987.

Richlin, Amy. "Some Approaches to the Sources on Adultery at Rome." In *Reflections of Women in Antiquity*, edited by Helen P. Foley, 379–404. New York: Gordon & Breach, 1981.

——. *The Garden of Priapus: Sexuality and Aggression in Roman Humor*. New Haven, Conn., and London: Yale University Press, 1983.

——. "The Ethnographer's Dilemma and the Dream of a Lost Golden Age." In *Feminist Theory and the Classics*, edited by Nancy Sorkin Rabinowitz and Amy Richlin, 272–303. Thinking Gender Series. New York and London: Routledge, 1993.

Richter Reimer, Ivoni. *Women in the Acts of the Apostles: A Feminist Liberation Perspective*. Translated by Linda A. Maloney. Minneapolis, Mn.: Fortress, 1995.

Robert, L. *Etudes anatoliennes: recherches sur les inscriptions grecques de l'Asie Mineure*. Paris: Boccard, 1937.

Rogers, G. M. "The Constructions of Women at Ephesos." *Zeitschrift für Papyrologie und Epigraphik* 90 (1992): 215–23.

Rogers, Robert Samuel. "Fulvia Paulina C. Sentii Saturnini." *AJP* 53 (1932): 252–56.

Rohrbaugh, Richard L. "The Pre-Industrial City in Luke-Acts: Urban Social Relations." In *The Social World of Luke-Acts: Models for Interpretation*, edited by Jerome H. Neyrey, 125–49. Peabody, Mass.: Hendrickson, 1991.

Romaniuk, Kazimierz. "Die 'Gottesfürchtigen' im Neuen Testament." *Aegyptus* 44 (1964): 66–91.

Ruether, Rosemary Radford. "Misogynism and Virginal Feminism in the Fathers of the Church." In *Religion and Sexism: Images of Women in the Jewish and Christian Traditions*, edited by Rosemary Radford Ruether, 150–83. New York: Simon and Schuster, 1974.

Saller, Richard P. *Personal Patronage Under the Early Empire*. Cambridge and New York: Cambridge University Press, 1982.

Sanders, Jack T. *The Jews in Luke-Acts*. Philadelphia, Pa.: Fortress, 1987.

Sawyer, Deborah F. *Women and Religion in the First Christian Centuries*. London and New York: Routledge, 1996.

Scafuro, Adele. "Livy's Comic Narrative of the Bacchanalia." *Helios* 16, no. 2 (1989): 119–41.

Schiffman, Lawrence H. "The Conversion of the Royal House of Adiabene in Josephus and Rabbinic Sources." In *Josephus, Judaism, and Christianity*, edited by Louis H. Feldman and Gohei Hata, 293–312. Detroit, Mich.: Wayne State University Press, 1987.

Schille, Gottfried. *Die Apostelgeschichte des Lukas*. Theologischer Handkommentar zum Neuen Testament 5. Berlin: Evangelische Verlagsanstalt, 1983.

Schottroff, Luise. "Lydia: A New Quality of Power." In *Let the Oppressed Go Free: Feminist Perspectives on the New Testament*. Translated by Annemarie S. Kidder. Louisville, Ky.: Westminster/John Knox Press, 1993.

———. *Lydia's Impatient Sisters: A Feminist Social History of Early Christianity*. Translated by Barbara and Martin Rumscheidt. Louisville, Ky.: Westminster/ John Knox Press, 1995.

Schürer, Emil. *The History of the Jewish People in the Age of Jesus Christ*. Revised and edited by Geza Vermes et al. 3 vols. in 4. Edinburgh: T & T Clark, 1973– 1986.

Schüssler Fiorenza, Elisabeth. "Miracles, Mission, and Apologetics: An Introduction." In *Aspects of Religious Propaganda*, edited by Elizabeth Schüssler Fiorenza. University of Notre Dame Center for the Study of Judaism and Christianity in Antiquity 2. Notre Dame, Ind., and London: University of Notre Dame Press, 1976.

———. *In Memory of Her: A Feminist Theological Reconstruction of Christian Origins*. New York: Crossroad, 1983.

———. "A Feminist Critical Interpretation for Liberation: Martha and Mary (Luke 0:38–42)." *Religion and Intellectual Life* 3 (1986): 16–36.

———. "Missionaries, Apostles, Coworkers: Romans 16 and the Reconstruction of Women's Early Christian History." *Word and World* 6 (1986): 420–33.

———. "Text and Reality—Reality as Text: The Problem of a Feminist Historical and Social Reconstruction Based on Texts." *Studia theologica* 43 (1989): 19–34.

———. *Revelation: Vision of a Just World*. Proclamation Commentaries. Minneapolis, Mn.: Fortress, 1991.

———. *But She Said: Feminist Practices of Biblical Interpretation*. Boston: Beacon, 1992.

———. "The Rhetoricity of Historical Knowledge: Pauline Discourse and Its Contextualizations." In *Religious Propaganda and Missionary Competition in the New Testament World: Essays Honoring Dieter Georgi*, edited by Lukas Bormann, Kelly Del Tredici, and Angela Standhartinger, 443–69. Leiden and New York: Brill, 1994.

———. *Rhetoric and Ethic: The Politics of Biblical Studies*. Minneapolis, Mn.: Fortress, 1999.

Schüssler Fiorenza, Elisabeth, ed. *Aspects of Religious Propaganda in Judaism and Early Christianity*. University of Notre Dame Center for the Study of Judaism and Christianity in Antiquity 2. Notre Dame, Ind., and London: University of Notre Dame Press, 1976.

Schwartz, Daniel R. "ΚΑΤΑ ΤΟΥΤΟΝ ΤΟΝ ΚΑΙΡΟΝ: Josephus' Source on Agrippa II." *JQR* 72, no. 4 (1982): 241–68.

———. *Agrippa I: The Last King of Judaea*. Tübingen: Mohr/Siebeck, 1990.

Segal, Erich. *Roman Laughter*. Cambridge, Mass.: Harvard University Press, 1968.

Seim, Turid Karlsen. *The Double Message: Patterns of Gender in Luke-Acts*. Studies of the New Testament and Its World. Edinburgh: T & T Clark, 1994.

Siegert, Folkert. "Gottesfürchtige und Sympathisanten." *JSJ* 4, no. 2 (1973): 109–64.

Simon, Marcel. "Gottesfürchtiger." *Reallexikon für Antike und Christentum*, ed. T. Kluser et al. (Stuttgart, 1950–) 11 (1981): 1060–70.

———. *Verus Israel: A Study of the Relations Between Christians and Jews in the Roman Empire (135–425)*. Littman Library of Jewish Civilization. Oxford: Oxford University Press, 1986.

Sly, Dorothy. *Philo's Perception of Women*. Brown Judaic Studies 209. Atlanta, Ga.: Scholars Press, 1990.

Smallwood, E. Mary. "Domitian's Attitude Toward Jews and Judaism." *CP* 51 (1956): 1–13.

———. "Some Notes on the Jews under Tiberius." *Latomus* 15 (1956): 314–29.

———. "The Alleged Jewish Tendencies of Poppaea Sabina." *JTS* n.s. 10 (1959): 329–35.

———. *The Jews Under Roman Rule from Pompey to Diocletian*. Leiden: Brill, 1976.

Smith, Morton. "Prolegomena to a Discussion of Aretalogies," *JBL* 90 (1971): 174–98.

Spranger, Peter P. *Historische Untersuchungen zu den Sklavenfiguren des Plautus und Terenz*. Forschungen zur antiken Sklaverei 17. Stuttgart: Steiner-Verlag, 1984.

Stadter, Philip A. "*Philosophos kai Philandros*: Plutarch's View of Women in the Moralia and the Lives." In *Plutarch's Advice to the Bride and Groom and A Consolation to His Wife*, edited by Sarah B. Pomeroy, 173–82. New York and Oxford: Oxford University Press, 1999.

Staples, Ariadne. *From Good Goddess to Vestal Virgin: Sex and Category in Roman Religion*. London and New York: Routledge, 1998.

Stegemann, Wolfgang. *Zwischen Synagoge und Obrigkeit: Zur historischen Situation der lukanischen Christen*. Forschungen zur Religion und Literatur des Alten und Neuen Testaments 152. Göttingen: Vandenhoeck & Ruprecht, 1991.

Sterling, Gregory E. *Historiography and Self-Definition: Josephus, Luke-Acts and Apologetic Historiography*. Novum Testamentum Supplements 64. Leiden: Brill, 1992.

Stern, Menachem, *Greek and Latin Authors on Jews and Judaism*. 3 vols. Jerusalem: Academy of Sciences and Humanities, 1974–1984.

Stoops, Robert F. "Riot and Assembly: The Social Context of Acts 19:23–41." *JBL* 108, no. 1 (1989): 73–91.

Stowers, Stanley K. *A Rereading of Romans: Justice, Jews, and Gentiles*. New Haven, Conn., and London: Yale University Press, 1994.

Suetonius. *The Lives of the Caesars and the Lives of Illustrious Men*. Translated by

J. C. Rolfe. 2 vols. Loeb Classical Library. Cambridge, Mass.: Harvard University Press, 1913–1914.

Syme, Ronald. *Tacitus*. 2 vols. Oxford: Clarendon, 1958.

Tacitus. *The Histories and the Annals*. Translated by C. H. Moore and J. Jackson. 4 vols. Loeb Classical Library. Cambridge, Mass.: Harvard University Press, 1937.

Tannehill, Robert. *The Narrative Unity of Luke-Acts: A Literary Interpretation*. 2 vols. Philadelphia, Pa., and Minneapolis, Mn.: Fortress, 1986–1994.

Taylor, Miriam S. *Anti-Judaism and Early Christian Identity: A Critique of the Scholarly Consensus*. Studia Post-Biblica 46. Leiden, New York, Köln: E. J. Brill, 1995.

Tcherikover, Victor. "Jewish Apologetic Literature Reconsidered." *Eos* 48 (1956): 169–93.

Temporini, Hildegard. *Die Frauen am Hofe Trajans*. Berlin and New York: De Gruyter, 1978.

Theissen, Gerd. *The Social Setting of Pauline Christianity: Essays on Corinth*. Philadelphia, Pa.: Fortress, 1982.

Thompson, Leonard A. *The Book of Revelation: Apocalypse and Empire*. Oxford: Oxford University Press, 1990.

Torjesen, Karen Jo. *When Women Were Priests: Women's Leadership in the Early Church and the Scandal of Their Subordination in the Rise of Christianity*. San Francisco: HarperSanFrancisco, 1993.

Trebilco, Paul R. "Paul and Silas—'Servants of the Most High God' (Acts 16.16–18)." *JSNT* 36 (1989): 51–73.

——. *Jewish Communities in Asia Minor*. Society for New Testament Studies Monograph Series 69. Cambridge: Cambridge University Press, 1991.

Valerius Maximus. *Memorable Deeds and Saying*. Edited by Karl Friedrich Kempf. Bibliotheca scriptorum graecorum et romanorum Teubneriana. Leipzig: Teubner, 1888.

Versnel, H. S. *Inconsistencies in Greek and Roman Religion* 1. Studies in Greek and Roman Religion 6. Leiden: Brill, 1990.

Wallace-Hadrill, Andrew. "Elites and Trade in the Roman Town." In *City and Country in the Ancient World*, edited by John Rich and Andrew Wallace-Hadrill, 241–69. London and New York: Routledge, 1991.

Wan, Sze-Kar. "Charismatic Exegesis: Philo and Paul Compared." *Studia Philonica* 6 (1994): 54–82.

Wardman, Alan. *Religion and Statecraft Among the Romans*. Baltimore, Md.: Johns Hopkins University Press, 1982.

Weinreich, Otto. *Der Trug des Nektanebos: Wandlungen eines Novellenstoffs*. Leipzig and Berlin: Teubner, 1911.

——. "Gebet und Wunder." In *Genethliakon: Wilhelm Schmid zum siebzigstend*

Geburtstag, edited by Friedrich Focke et al., 200–462. Tübingen Beiträge zur Altertumswissenschaft 5. Stuttgart: Kohlhammer, 1929.

Wicker, Kathleen O'Brien. *"Mulierem Virtutes (Moralia 242E–263C),"* in *Plutarch's Ethical Writings and Early Christian Literatures*, edited by Hans D. Betz, 106–34. Leiden: Brill, 1978.

Wiesen, David S. "The Verbal Basis of Juvenal's Satiric Vision." *ANRW* 2, no. 33.1 (1989): 708–33.

Wilcox, Max. "The 'God-fearers' in Acts—A Reconsideration." *JSNT* 13 (1981): 102–22.

Wilken, Robert. *John Chrysostom and the Jews: Rhetoric and Reality in the Late 4th Century*. Berkeley, Los Angeles, and London: University of California Press, 1983.

——. *The Christians as the Romans Saw Them*. New Haven, Conn., and London: Yale University Press, 1984.

Will, Edouard, and Claude Orrieux. *"Prosélytisme Juif"? Histoire d'une erreur*. Paris: Belles Lettres, 1992.

Williams, Margaret H. "θεοσεβὴς γάρ ἦν—The Jewish Tendencies of Poppaea Sabina." *JTS* n.s. 39 (1988): 97–111.

——. "The Expulsion of the Jews from Rome in A.D. 19." *Latomus* 48 (1989): 765–84.

——. "Domitian, the Jews and the 'Judaizers,'—A Simple Matter of Cupiditas and Maiestas?" *Historia* 39, no. 2 (1990): 196–211.

Wills, Lawrence M. *The Jew in the Court of the Foreign King: Ancient Jewish Court Legends*. Harvard Dissertations in Religion 26. Minneapolis, Mn.: Fortress, 1990.

——. "The Depiction of the Jews in Acts." *JBL* 110, no. 4 (1991): 631–54.

——. *The Jewish Novel in the Ancient World*. Myth and Poetics. Ithaca, N.Y., and London: Cornell University Press, 1995.

——. "The Depiction of Slavery in the Ancient Novel." *Semeia* 83 (1998): 113–32.

Wire, Antoinette Clark. *The Corinthian Women Prophets: A Reconstruction Through Paul's Rhetoric*. Minneapolis, Mn.: Fortress, 1990.

Witherington, Ben. "The Anti-Feminist Tendencies of the 'Western' Text in Acts." *JBL* 103, no. 1 (1984): 82–84.

——. *Women in the Earliest Churches*. Society for New Testament Studies Monograph Series 58. Cambridge: Cambridge University Press, 1988.

Zanker, Paul. *The Power of Images in the Age of Augustus*. Jerome Lectures 16. Ann Arbor: University of Michigan Press, 1990.

Zeitlin, Froma I. "The Dynamics of Misogyny: Myth and Mythmaking in the Oresteia." *Arethusa* 11, no. 2 (1978): 149–83.

——. "Cultic Models of the Female: Rites of Dionysos and Demeter." *Arethsua* 15 (1982): 129–57.

INDEX

In this index an "f" after a number indicates a separate reference on the next page, and an "ff" indicates separate references on the next two pages. A continuous discussion over two or more pages is indicated by a span of page numbers, e.g., "57–59." *Passim* is used for a cluster of references in close but not consecutive sequence. Passages from ancient authors are referenced only where they are extensively treated.

Apologetics, religious, 3ff, 11, 17ff, 25, 47, 51–52, 62–66, 70, 80–87 *passim*

Appropriation: Flavian, of Isis cult, 18; Josephus, of Nektanebos legend, 19–20; Josephus, of Scylla legend, 38–39; Christian, of Judaism, 51–52; Christian, of Bacchic cult, 72–74; Jewish, of Dionysos cult, 80–82

Aretalogy, 74

Augustus, 21–22, 43, 48

Balch, David, 63, 97, 128n43, 142n2

Benefaction, elite women's, 30–40, 42f, 47–50, 64f, 67, 98–99

Berenice, 31, 48, 62

Beroea, 54–55, 60

Beturia Paulla, 26

Biblical prototypes, Joseph, 32

Binaries: ethics/ritual, 69; public/private, 84–85

Braun, Martin, 38

Bremen, Riet van, 43, 64

Caligula, Gaius, 17, 31f

Capitolina, 67, 99

Chariton, 92

Christian supersessionism, 52, 69ff

Christians, Judaizing, 68f, 71

Cicero, *De Legibus*, 25, 76, 78–79

Circumcision, 69–70

Class and status: anxieties about 23–25, 27f, 67, 94; of God-fearers, 69–70; in Acts, 85ff, 89f

Claudius, 31ff, 41, 45–46, 49–50

Cleopatra, 41, 45f

Codex D, 125n12

Cohen, Shaye, 2–3, 36, 141n1, 141n5

Conversion, and women, 4, 26–28, 34–35, 59–60, 69–75 *passim*, 98–99. *See also* Benefaction

Cooper, Kate, 6–7, 46–47

Cornelius, 55, 57, 59, 88

Corpus inscriptionum iudaicarum #462, 26

Corpus inscriptionum iudaicarum #256, 26

Delphic oracle, 90–92

Dio, *Histories* 57.18.5a, 13–14

Dionysos cult, women in, 21, 26–27, 75–82, 135n32. *See also* Euripides: *Bacchae*

Domitia, 36

Domitian, 11, 16–18, 23, 36

Ethics/ritual, 69

Euripides: *Bacchae*, 72–78, 132n7, 132n8; *Melanippe Captive*, 83

Exorcism, 89–90

Expulsion of Jews from Rome, *see under* Jews

Fiscus Judaicus, 16

Fischler, Suzanne, 44–45

Flavian Domitilla, 16

Flavian Isis veneration, 18–19

Flavius Clemens, 16

Foreign religions, *see* Dionysos cult; Jews; Isis cult; Roman religions; Sex as subversion; Women and foreign religions

Fulvia, 11–12, 37, 62, 67

Gaius Caligula, 17, 31–31

Georgi, Dieter, 1–2, 9

God-fearers, 34–35, 66–70; in Acts, 55–62, 88

Gold, Barbara, 8

Goodman, Martin, 2–3, 141n5

Greek Alexander Romance, 19–20, 114n33

Helena, Queen of Adiabene, 36–37, 61–62. *See also* Adiabene, royal family of

Heine, Susanne, 70

Henrichs, Albert, 26, 82

Herodias, 42

Heyob, Sharon Kelly, 26

Hillard, Tom, 42–43

Horace, *Odes* 3.6.1–4, 21–22

Horst, Pieter W. van der, 68–69, 130n67

Ida, 12, 28, 67

Imperial women, 40–50. *See also individual women by name*

Inscriptiones Latinae Selectae #8403, 43

Isis cult, 3, 12, 15, 18–19, 22–23, 26

Jews: expulsion from Rome, 12–14, 22–25,

28; Domitian's policy on, 16–18; legal standing of, 49f, 52, 70; in Acts, 52, 56–60

John Chrysostom: *Discourses Against Judaizing Christians*, 68, 71; *Homiliae in epistulam i ad Corinthios*, 91

Joshel, Sandra, 6–7

Judaism, as subversive, 15–15, 34–36, 120n19

Judaizing Christians, 68f, 71

Julia Severa, 64–65, 99

Justin Martyr: *Dialogue with Trypho*, 68

Juvenal *Satire 6*, 1–2, 4, 15, 21, 23, 27, 43, 100, 115n48; *Satire 14.*100–101, 15

Kittredge, Cynthia, 93

Kraabel, Alf Thomas, 2, 55f, 58, 66

Kraemer, Ross, 26, 83

Kuhn, Karl Georg, 69

Lake, Kirsopp, 55–56, 58f

Leon, Harry, 26

Lewy, Hans, 81

Livia, 30–31, 48, 65, 127n39

Livy, 20, 83; on the Bacchanalia, 21, 76, 98

Luke, preface, 51. *See also* Acts

Lydia, 59, 70, 73–74, 85–89, 93, 140n86

Lysias: *On the Murder of Eratosthenes*, 93

Martial, on Jews, 15, 18

Mason, Steve, 11

McKnight, Scot, 2–3

Messalina, 6–7, 40, 76–77

Mission, Jewish, 2–3, 11–16, 22–23, 96–98. *See also* Benefaction; Conversion; Apologetics; Propaganda

Moses, 15, 81; and Pharaoh's daughter, 37–38, 41, 62; and Ethiopian campaign, 38–39

Nektanebos, 19–20

Nero, 34–35

Nicolaus of Damascus, 121n39

Octavia, 47

Origen: *Against Celsus*, 92, 132n7

Orrieux, Claude, 2–3

Patronage, *see* Benefaction

Pentheus, 73, 77

Pervo, Richard, 74, 87

Philippi, 72–74, 93, 94

Philo: *On the Contemplative Life*, 79–81; *On the Special Laws*, 84–85

Pilate's wife, 61–62

Pliny's letter to Trajan, 94

Plotina, 61

Plutarch, *Conjugalia Praecepta*, 25, 62–63, 82; *Life of Anthony*, 46–47; *Mulierum virtutes*, 81–82; *Quaestionum convivialum*, 135n32

Pompeia Agrippinilla, 26

Poppaea Sabina, 33–36, 41, 45, 48, 66

Prisca, 53–54

Propaganda: religious and civic, 3ff, 72–75, 82–85, 87–88, 90–92, 137n52; Flavian, 18–19; Augustan, 21–22, 43; Egyptian, 20, 65–66

Psidian Antioch, 54–55, 59ff, 70

Public/private, 43, 64, 84–85

Pythia, 90

Revelation 2:20–23, 95

Rhetoric, 5–9

Richter Reimer, Ivoni, 86, 124n11

Roman religions, women in, 83

Romans 16, 25–26

Rome, and foreign religions, 11–19, 21–29, 76–77, 78

Salome Alexander, 41–42

Samos, 48

Schüssler Fiorenza, Elisabeth, 8, 53

Schwartz, Daniel, 32, 61

Seim, Turid Karlsen, 53

Senatus consultum de Bacchanalibus, 78

Sex as subversion, 12, 21–23, 27, 75–77, 92–93

St. Paul, 52, 87–88

Staples, Ariadne, 83, 92

Status, *see* Class and status

Stoops, Robert, 52, 70

Suetonius: *Tiberius*, 13–14, 23–24

Synagogue, 25, 55–60, 64–65, 68–71, 73

Tacitus: *Annales* 2.85.5, 13–14, 22–24; *Histories* 1.2, 22; *Histories* 5.5.2, 15

CONTRAVERSIONS

JEWS AND OTHER DIFFERENCES

Shelly Matthews, *First Converts: Rich Pagan Women and the Rhetoric of Mission in Early Judaism and Christianity*

Menachem Lorberbaum, *Politics and the Limits of Law: Secularizing the Political in Medieval Jewish Thought*

Gabriella Safran, *Rewriting the Jew: Assimilation Narratives in the Russian Empire*

Galit Hasan-Rokem, *Web of Life: Folklore in Rabbinic Literature*

Charlotte Fonrobert, *Menstrual Purity: Jewish and Christian Reconstructions of Biblical Gender*

James Matisoff, *Blessings, Curses, Hopes, and Fears: Psycho-Ostensive Expressions in Yiddish*, second edition

Benjamin Harshav, *The Meaning of Yiddish*

Benjamin Harshav, *Language in Time of Revolution*

Amir Sumaka'i Fink and Jacob Press, *Independence Park: The Lives of Gay Men in Israel*

Alon Goshen-Gottstein, *The Sinner and the Amnesiac: The Rabbinic Invention of Elisha ben Abuya and Eleazer ben Arach*

Bryan Cheyette and Laura Marcus, eds., *Modernity, Culture, and 'the Jew'*

Benjamin D. Sommer, *A Prophet Reads Scripture: Allusion in Isaiah 40–66*

Marilyn Reizbaum, *James Joyce's Judaic Other*